VOICES OF THE FUTURE

FUTURE

STORIES OF ADVENTURE & IMAGINATION

VOLUME 4

Cover design by Plethora Creative

Published by The Author Conservatory

TABLE OF CONTENTS

FOREWORD

G rowing up, I loved nothing more than to lose myself in books. In between the pages, I rode dragons and explored new worlds. I battled giant spiders and solved mysteries. I helped rope cattle in the Wild West and almost sank in the rowboat alongside Anne.

I lived adventure after adventure through the power of my own imagination transporting me into the world of books, and I cannot think of a more appropriate theme for this anthology than adventure and imagination.

Every adventure story has its ups and downs, its unexpected setbacks and hard-won victories. And I think if you ask any of the fourteen students who have contributed stories to this anthology about their experiences on their writing journey to publication, I think they'll agree that they've had their share of both challenges and victories.

This anthology is a collection of short stories from several up-and-coming young authors who have received training in writing and business through the Author Conservatory, a college-alternative author career training program co-founded by accomplished authors Brett Harris and Kara Swanson Matsumoto.

- Some have won awards for their writing.

- Some have founded and run successful businesses.

- Most have attended writing conferences and learned from industry professionals.

- Most have received interest from publishers and agents.

- All have completed multiple full-length novels and implemented multiple rounds of critique on multiple projects from professional editors.

- All have started growing their personal platforms after receiving extensive marketing training.

It's an honor to celebrate with these young writers, who will soon be taking the next step in the endless adventure of their author journey outside the Conservatory. It's been my pleasure to see them persevere through all the inevitable obstacles with courage and embrace their unique gifts, imagining what could be possible and then working so hard to bring those dreams to life. I have no doubt that many exciting adventures lie ahead for them, limited only by the scope of their imagination.

Upwards and onwards!

Katie Phillips

Editor & coach of multiple award-winning authors

Fiction Department Director

MIDDLE GRADE
FICTION

THE TEDDY HANDBOOK

MARIELLE HENNING

For Lena xx

T eddy rubbed his paw over the scribbled words, butterflies fluttering up and down in his stomach.

For the second—maybe tenth, actually—time, his gaze strayed to the picture propped up next to the bright *Toy Story* clock. He'd seen it as soon as the big girl had put him on the bed a few hours ago. Inside the wood frame, she was hugging a small girl with wild, messy curls, a thick red hoodie with floppy drawstrings, and a grin that made her nose crinkle. Teddy's heart beat hard against his stuffing as he tried a grin of his own.

It was a little stiff, but his snout crinkled, too. Just like hers.

Lena.

It suited her. Well, as much as a name could suit someone in a picture. Time would tell if it fit her in real life. Tightness tickled his throat and he cleared it with a growl, careful not to start coughing. Snapping a string was not a disaster he needed right now. Stay focused, stay in one piece. That was the plan. No big changes.

The clock flicked to the next minute.

7:01pm.

7:09.

7:19.

Would she notice if he got up and read one of her books? Probably.

No sense risking it.

7:39.

7:52.

By the time 8:06 rolled around, apprehension had made a comfy nest in the pit of Teddy's stomach.

The Teddy Handbook: Things Every Teddy Should Know Before They Meet Their Forever Child clearly stated that bedtimes were typically 7:00 sharp. But the sun was sinking now, lighting the top of the room with gold, and leaving a 7:00 bedtime in the dust.

"Pssst."

Teddy's startle left him face-first in Lena's unicorn blanket. How had she come in without him knowing? Why was she *talking* to him when he'd stayed perfectly still—

Something long, black, and wriggly slid under him and he scrambled back with a squeal at least two octaves too high for any respectable teddy. Especially a teddy who should have remembered that every room has a bed monster, and they don't always stay under the bed.

This one, for example, was laughing at him. It wasn't any particular shape, more like those splashes of oil you see drawn in children's books.

A smug splash of oil, dark and gloopy, with little bits of it shining in the light, and big eyes peering out of its centre.

"What are you doing out here?" Teddy smoothed his fur back over a bare patch, working on convincing his stomach to squirm with a little less enthusiasm. "It's not dark yet."

The eyes rolled. "It's sunset. Good enough."

Teddy's jaw slacked.

Good enough?

"I know, I know, have a heart attack later." The monster slid up onto the bed, settling on an embroidered rainbow peeking out of a cloud. "Lena is missing."

Well, he doesn't beat around the bush.

"I can see that." Teddy shifted back against the pillow, ignoring the twinge of pain in his chest. *This is always how it goes. Be calm.* "Bedtime is meant to be seven sharp. It's—" he checked the clock. "—quarter past *eight*."

Sun bounced off the door handle, transforming a black section of the monster into shimmery purple as it leaned in.

"Exactly. She's never late, something's wrong."

Of course. Teddy patted down a few muddled tufts of fur. "She's probably out dyeing her nails, or piercing her belly button, or something. Girls like that."

The monster fixed Teddy with a dark stare, knocking the pinpricks of pain dancing through his stuffing back a few paces.

"Not our girl."

Teddy pressed his mouth closed. Maybe this monster was new and didn't get how things worked in the real world. Emily's bedtime certainly hadn't stayed 7:00 for long.

"How do you know?" he tried, eventually.

"Because Lena isn't like that."

Ah yes. 'Logic'.

The monster shook his head, scoffing. "Piercing belly buttons? Please. She's missing, and you need to find her."

"I—" this monster was a few marbles short of a box. "*Me*?"

The monster nodded. "Who else? Bed monsters can't leave the house, and you're the only Real toy around. I need you to check the garden."

"Look out the window." Teddy tamped down a growing colony of butterflies. They were full-grown now, more active than Emily's footballer friends. The window was above the drawers, but not too hard to get to.

The monster's body rippled in a sigh.

"It couldn't be easy, could it?" he muttered under his breath.

Teddy opened his mouth to launch into an explanation that *easy* was not a word you could pair with something like going outside for a child who might not even care about his existence, but the monster spoke before he could.

"Lena likes the garden. I'd love to look, but we're on the wrong side of the house. All you need to do is go out the front door, poke around, and see if she's there. She won't mind you looking, before you burst a seam. After the first time we talked—"

"Ahh." The exclamation escaped Teddy sounding somewhat like a deflating balloon. "The first time you... what?" Talking to your child seemed to be a wonderful way to get thrown out on your fluffy behind. Not to mention it went directly against the Handbook.

"After the first time we talked," the monster repeated. "She's quite all right with it. Enjoys it, actually. She calls me Fred, and you should have seen her with good old Theo the Fourth."

"Theo the what?"

The look on the monster's face suggested he was questioning if factories even stuffed brains into teddies these days, but *really*. This whole situation was madness.

"Theodore the Fourth. As in, the fourth Theodore. Her sister's teddy. Anyway," Fred carried on as Teddy looked blankly at a prancing unicorn, hoping to find something with at least *some* sense. "Like I was saying, we need to go before it gets dark. She might be lost or in trouble. There are foxes around here, you know."

Of course. Of course there were foxes.

His stomach churned again, and Teddy rubbed his snout with his paw. This was not the plan. The plan was to find a child who would be around and wear a cuddly hoodie and give good hugs. One who would take him travelling and throw tea-parties and read books with him. Not leave him at bedtime or shove him under the bed to hold conversation with dust and plastic bags and prickly bed monsters.

He shook his head. "I don't think so."

"What do you mean 'I don't think so'?"

Teddy placed a paw firmly on his stomach. The butterflies ignored it. Obviously. "Maybe you bed monsters don't have handbooks, but I do. Going outside isn't allowed."

"Says who?"

"Says the Handbook," Teddy repeated. Speaking of teddies not getting brains, 'Fred' was obviously not too high in that department, either.

"Where?" Fred returned.

Teddy paused. "Well..."

The monster's head tipped to the side.

Insufferable.

"I don't know the *exact* page—"

"That's because it doesn't exist," Fred interjected, helpfully. Before Teddy could reply, the bed monster continued, looking way too pleased with himself for a little black blob that changed shape every two seconds. "You know what does exist? *The Teddy Handbook*, page one, line one: 'A teddy, first and foremost, is made for love. Any reasonable measure may be taken to serve/observe the teddy's primary goal of fostering relationship with their child.'" Teddy tried to interrupt, but Fred just cranked up the volume. "'The rules henceforth are merely to be used as guides for common practice. Each teddy must use his or her discretion as to how to love their child well, regardless of the 'typical' approach.'"

The clock flipped to 8:29 as Teddy tried to piece together a comeback. How did Fred know so much about this anyway?

"I can get the Handbook out if you want." Fred tilted his head to the side and slid closer. "She needs you." He paused. "Look, if you don't find her, or don't love her to pieces when you do, you can come back here and sulk, or... I'll find you a new home. They have a charity bag downstairs. You can get a whole new family."

That's what this is meant to be. The protest died on Teddy's lips as his gaze found the picture by the bed. Lena grinning at him with her wrinkled nose and crazy hair, arms wrapped around the big girl's neck.

8:30pm.

Teddy huffed a sigh, glaring at his faint reflection in the clock face.

This is the kind of thing that gets teddies broken and binned. You know that, right?

"Where is the garden?"

Apparently not.

"Just down the stairs." Fred poured off the bed. "I'll show you."

"Hold on, I didn't agree yet." Teddy shuffled to the edge of the bed, his legs dangling off the side. "Oh—no—oof." Teddy grunted as he let go, landing on his back on the carpet. Not even out of the room, and he was already getting the stuffing knocked out of him. It could have done him a solid and knocked his butterflies out instead, but no.

He stood, coming nose to nose with Fred. Well, nose to glob, anyway.

This is a bad idea.

"Just the garden?"

"Just the garden."

"And if she isn't there, you'll find me somewhere new?" Seams sagged and stretched at the mere thought of going back to the shop. Hot, loud, and stuffy were a far cry from a warm hug and a spacious bedtime. But... better than nothing. Right?

How long can I keep doing this?

"Sure." Fred spread himself into a shrug. "But I'll bet all my Christmas cookies that you'll fall in love with her the moment you bump into her. Which you will."

Who was he trying to convince here? Teddy sighed, closing his eyes.

"Fine."

"Perfect." Smooth skin slithered across the carpet, and Teddy opened one eye, watching Fred approach the door.

"What now?"

"Come over here." Fred motioned, and Teddy padded over to him, half-way through asking why when the bed-monster launched towards him, scrambling up to his shoulders. Fred felt how he looked: smooth and shiny, with just enough slick oiliness to make Teddy shiver.

"Excuse—"

The handle clicked open, and Teddy stumbled forwards, falling onto the floor in front of them as the door gaped open to a gigantic hallway. He looked up, neck craning to see the top of the picture-covered wall opposite him. The human world was *huge*.

Fred slipped to the top of the stairs, pausing to look back at Teddy. "Coming?"

"Ah." Teddy glanced back at the bed, pillows plumped up on the duvet with a Teddy-sized dip in them. "Um."

"You can get a whole new family."

He took a deep breath. "Yes. Yes, of course."

Closing his eyes again, he stepped over the metal threshold into the hallway, grimacing before daring to open his eyes and look around.

Nothing.

That's a start.

The door towered next to him, and stairs on his left led straight down to the front door where a can of loudly coloured umbrellas sat next to patterned glass. Maybe this wouldn't take as long as he'd thought it would.

Something—the door?—hit him hard in the side, and he staggered into Fred. The two of them fell in a furry-slimy tangle before Teddy could cry out. Stairs bashed into his head, legs, front paws, and then all of them all over again as the world rolled and spun—

"Ow!" Teddy landed on cold hard ground with a grunt, followed by a yelp from Fred.

"Dog!"

The fur on the back of Teddy's neck went stiff as he looked up. A large, cream, slobbering beast bounded down the stairs straight for them. Its curls might have been endearing if its mouth wasn't half open, showing off sharp, I-eat-teddies-for-breakfast teeth.

"Move!" Fred scrambled over him, wrapping a limb around Teddy's paw and dragging him towards the towering panes of glass blocking off the Outside.

Claws skittered on the floor behind them, and Teddy shot a panicked glance back, tripping over his paws. They wouldn't make it to the door before the dog caught them. No way.

Fred stopped with a jerk, pushing Teddy towards the wall on their left.

"Get in the can!"

"The *what*?" Teddy watched in horror as Fred darted to the other side of the hall, spreading himself out and flailing his liquid arms this way and that. The dog paused, ears pricking up.

"Oh no. Oh no, oh no, oh no." Teddy begged his stiff seams to behave as he ran to the can, reaching for the top. It wobbled, and a wild idea sparked.

Running behind the can, he rammed his shoulder into it as a bark shook the room. The can tipped, teetered, then fell back into place.

"Come *on*." He tried again, harder this time, pushing off the wall for extra leverage. This time it fell, umbrellas flying in all directions. Teddy ducked, cowering by the can as they scattered. Somewhere close, the dog yelped and skittered away with another few barks. Hearing muted thuds, Teddy dared to look up to see the back end of the dog disappearing up the stairs.

A squeak of relief escaped, and Teddy flopped back onto the floor.

"Fred?" he asked, blinking up at the ceiling.

No reply.

Wonderful.

If the monster had died of fright, he was going straight back upstairs to his soft pillow. If Lena didn't come, then...

"Nicely done!" Fred appeared from behind the fallen umbrella can, stretching out his gloopy limbs as if checking they were all there. They seemed to be, but Teddy was too busy being relieved he was alive to count.

"That's the closest he's got yet," Fred added with a laugh just too high to be as confident as he made out.

Teddy looked back up the stairs. "He might come again."

"Mm. I'll get the keys from the lounge. Stay here."

Teddy started to ask how he knew so much about the house and its dogs, but he gave up as Fred slipped under the door they'd passed at the bottom of the stairs, disappearing into the lounge. Letting out a long breath, he dared to look down at himself. His fur stuck this way and that, and the bald patch was bigger now. He winced, smoothing his fur down carefully. It covered the exposed seams. Just.

We're only going to the garden. Then straight back in.

Something bright by the umbrellas caught his eye, and his paws flew to his throat.

His label.

Running back to the can, he reached for the tag, letting his breath out in a puff. It was still in one piece, ribbon threaded through the hole in the top corner.

"Come back here," he muttered, scooping it up and turning it over to check the other side. Scrawled handwriting stared back at him.

Dear Lena,
Love you so much, little sis! Only four months till I'm back for Christmas <3 Get lots of hugs from this little guy until then, and have fun!
RayRay xx
P.S. Isn't he perfect? He's even got your hair :P

Perfect?

Teddy rubbed his eyes with his free paw, before smoothing down his tufty fur. Perfect was subjective. The seams of his arms, for example, strained as he worked to loop the ribbon around his neck.

"Come on, silly..." A thread in his bare patch shifted, and he stopped with a wince.

"It's a babysitter." Fred's voice came from behind him, and Teddy started, the ribbon floating to the floor.

"Don't sneak *up* on a person like that." When had he even come back in from the lounge?

"Sorry, sorry." Fred dropped a ring of keys, and they clattered against laminate flooring. Teddy shot a glance at the stairs. No dog. Yet.

Teddy clasped the tag between his paws to pick it up again. "What about a babysitter?" Then, "You just need to tie it on. It's not broken."

Fred reached out, and moments later the silk slid around Teddy's neck.

"In the lounge. On her phone." Teddy could practically hear the eye-roll in Fred's voice. "No wonder Lena is missing."

"Mm." Teddy peered back over his shoulder. Scores of babysitters came and went in homes, and from his experience they were somewhat hit or miss. "Can you tie it?"

Fred responded with a gentle tug on the ribbon as he finished the bow. "Of course. There."

Teddy checked it. Slightly uneven, but it would do.

"Thank you."

"Oh, no worries. Got to have you looking your best." Fred scooped up the keys again, sliding to the door. Teddy followed, eyeing the lock. He anticipated Fred's glance in his direction moments before it came, and sighed.

"Fine. But don't take too long. You weigh more than you'd think."

Fred's eyes twinkled as he climbed onto Teddy's shoulders again. "It's rude to talk about people weighing a lot."

"It's rude to stand on peoples' heads," Teddy retorted, wincing as one of Fred's limbs poked him in the eye.

"Stop grumbling. I won't be a minute." Fred wobbled, and Teddy looked through the glass door. It was swirly and clouded, a sea of green blobs on the other side. They didn't *look* like foxes, or Lena, but who knew? Maybe they were just outside, waiting for him.

He cleared his throat.

"How do you know so much, anyway?"

Fred chuckled. "About what?"

"You know, the Handbook, the keys, the charity bag... all of that."

"Oh, I've been here for months. Longer, actually, but they only moved in this year. You should have seen her when she first came." A fond laugh peeked through his voice. "I'm not the scariest bed monster, but let me just say we're not the most popular chaps out there. Anyway, when she came, neither of us were having a good night. So of course I poked my head out to see if there were any nightmares hanging around, and she saw me under the bed. I sort of... froze. And she froze. And then she goes, 'What's your name?'"

Teddy waited, his breath misting up the glass. He imagined Fred's eyes blinking out from the dark underbed at Lena, through the dust and cobwebs. Maybe she had been crying. Maybe he had, too.

I've been there.

"'What's your name?'" Fred repeated, his voice a funny mix of emotions and straining effort as he wrestled with the key. "No one asks a bed monster that."

"What happened?" Teddy managed eventually, swallowing down the rock in his throat.

"Well, we hit it off. There were no nightmares, she was just lonely. I'm sure you get it."

A small noise escaped Teddy. *You could say that.*

"Anyway—" Fred grunted, his weight shifting on Teddy's shoulders. "We've been best buddies ever since."

Scrape-thunk.

"There! Now we just need to turn the handle and pull."

Teddy shook himself out of the story, blinking until the glass in front of the green blobs came back into focus. "Yes, of course."

"Oof." Fred paused. "Harder than it looks. Give us a moment."

Teddy gave it, nose pressed against the glass as thoughts of the dark bedroom, and the girl with the crinkled smile flickered through his brain.

Fred's weight strained backwards, and the door popped open, sending them tumbling back onto the floor. A breeze rushed through, making the fur on Teddy's arms stick up. He patted it down again, sniffing. It smelt like the saltwater Emily had used when she got that eye infection one time, except fresher. Like spring instead of sickness.

He took a deep breath.

"Lovely, isn't it?" Fred picked himself up and stretched. Teddy copied him, peering through the crack between the door and the doorframe until Fred's silence made him look back. The bed monster was eyeing him, head tipped to the side. "She's never had her own teddy before, you know. She'll love you."

"Maybe." Doubt escaped before Teddy could smother it with stuffing.

Fred looked at him sharply. "Look, mate. It's always a risk. And yeah, maybe it hurts like a lobbed dictionary when it doesn't pay off. But boy, oh boy—" he shook himself. "—it's worth it. Teddy, bed-monster, girl. A match made in heaven, if you will. It works."

Teddy thought back to black plastic and dust mites pressed against his fur.

"And when it doesn't?"

Fred let out a small sigh. "Find yourself a good bruise cream, I suppose. And try again when it's less red."

Teddy shook his head and looked back to the cracked-open door, taking another slow breath. The green lumps were bushes, not Lenas or foxes, and they lined the edge of a garden full of scattered dandelions, buttercups, and daisies. The path to the gate was bright with pebbles and grass grew on either side, going bare in places like Teddy's loose seam. He patted it warily. This—all of this—was insane.

Fred pressed close to the doorframe, body glistening into a thousand rainbows as it caught the setting sun. "There are some wrong'uns out there, but she's not one of them, I can promise you that. One of her hugs is well worth a little garden stroll. Plus, you can hardly bounce from one person to the next without saying hello, right? Just a quick peek, then we'll go back upstairs."

Teddy put a tentative paw on the doorframe. "What about the foxes?"

"I was joking about the foxes. They won't be out," Fred said with more confidence than the butterflies in Teddy's stomach could muster.

Teddy nodded. Lifted a foot. Put it down again. "Are you sure?"

Fred rolled his eyes. "I'm sure. Go on before it actually does get dark. Teddies aren't the only ones who get scared, you know."

"Of course I know." Teddy nodded again, vigorously, like that would stop his legs from trembling. "In and out."

"Yep. Before it gets dark."

A bird called in the distance, and Teddy looked up. It sounded big enough to snack on him. Or what was left of him once the foxes were done.

Something nudged him from behind and he looked back with a squeak. Fred blinked sternly at him.

"Go on."

"Fine. I'm going." Teddy swallowed.

Out you go. One step at a time. One little st—

His paw hit gravel.

"*Ow.*"

Gingerly, Teddy heaved his other paw over the threshold. The ground was warmer than he'd expected. Sun-soaked rocks shifted under his feet as he picked his way across the path to the knee-joint length grass of the garden.

"If I die out here—" he called back, with only a slight wobble in his voice.

"—it's all your fault."

"Don't worry!" Fred's cheerful voice carried from the door to the tickly strands of grass and dandelion ahead of Teddy. "I'll give you a fitting funeral. Warrior's song, Viking ship, the lot."

A pained huff escaped Teddy. "Lovely."

Viking funerals—'the lot' or otherwise—had not been on the 'happy new home' list.

Hugs, yes. Games day and night, also yes. Honestly, Teddy wasn't even against visiting a Viking ship, if that's what it took, but the image of his lifeless, fluffless corpse floating out to sea in a big wooden monster was only mildly more off-putting than the insects flailing around his stomach. Somewhere between the doorway and the middle of the lawn, they had evolved from a butterfly colony to a full-on jungle population, tangled up in themselves as he made his way to the left hand side of the house. The garden wrapped around the corner, and on the other side... well, there could be anything.

She could be there.

Just around the corner, waiting.

Or not.

Teddy took a deep breath, braced himself, and tiptoed around the corner. He blinked at the long rectangular patch of grass and flowers, taking in his surroundings.

A hedge opposite him. A gate to the back garden. A few wheelie bins up against the left wall, even a little wooden playhouse that looked like it had been made way before his pattern had been designed. Down the right-hand side of the garden stretched a bank of colourful flowers, varying heights mixing with a few messy, too-long sprigs of bush.

No Lena.

Yet, Teddy reminded himself. She might be in the playhouse. Young children played hide-and-seek, right? He waded through the grass, pushing stray seed-heads out of the way as he reached the entrance of the playhouse and poked his head in.

"L-lena?" His voice came out gravelly as his eyes adjusted to the shadows inside. As steadily as the dark settled itself into shapes—the walls, the floor, a low bench—his heart sank.

Nothing.

Except—

A flash of white caught his eye, dull in the dim light, stuck into the slight gap between the wood slats of the bench. He walked over. If this was one of Emily's action novels, it would be a 'message in a bottle'. Lena somehow telling him where she was, and how sorry she was that she'd missed him.

Let him down again.

Keep your children straight, bear.

Teddy shook himself, and tugged the paper out of its crevice, unfolding it and taking in the picture before him.

Two crayon stick figures stood next to each other, with curly lines he took for hair scrawled over their backs. One was much bigger than the other, and blue scribbles took up the top half of the page, yellow covering the bottom. The lines for their arms overlapped, as though they were holding hands, and a boxy thing—a car?—sat to the side of the page. Two more scribbles that he took for parents stood by it.

"Why am I doing this?" Teddy sat down with a flop, his sigh shaking the edges of the paper in his paws.

After the whole heart attack with the dog, the broken label, Fred standing on his head—heck, after months of black bags, hot shops, and fancy teddies chosen ahead of him—all he was left with was two stick figures and a bed monster.

He pictured walking back to the house. Climbing back into another bag. Waiting, again. After all, he'd looked, and she wasn't here. Fred would have to keep his side of the deal, and he would have to reconcile himself to another shop shelf.

His label shifted under his chin, and he squinted down at it.

...Love you so much, little sis! Only four months till I'm back for Christmas
<3 Get lots of hugs from this little guy until then, and have fun!
RayRay xx
P.S. Isn't he perfect? He's even got your hair :P

"She's never had her own teddy before, you know. She'll love you."

"Insufferable bed monsters," Teddy muttered under his breath.

Teddy, bed-monster, girl, huh?

Except this was how it ended. Empty playhouses and scribbled drawings that didn't even include him. What good was putting yourself out there for a child who likely didn't know—or care—that you existed?

"A Teddy, first and foremost, is made for love."

Teddy huffed out a breath. Easily read, less easily done.

But she's lonely. Something in his heart stirred against his instinct to retreat. Which was madness, surely. She was lonely, but so was he. You didn't get shoved under a bed and forgotten, or left on the back shelf of a tired charity shop by your not-so-forever child without knowing what it felt like to be totally, utterly alone.

But something about the picture wouldn't let him stomp back to the bench to return it to its hiding place. Maybe it was the knowledge that the big stick figure was gone for months. Maybe it was Fred's insistence that 'their girl' was different.

Maybe it was the memory of a teddy, alone, and what he would have given to have someone search hard enough to find him when he was afraid to be found.

A groan escaped.

This is the kind of thing that gets teddies broken and binned. You know that, right?

He shoved the thought aside.

Because this was the risk a teddy took, wasn't it? Teddy, bed-monster, girl.

Even when it hurt.

He looked out to the sun-lit grass of the garden.

"At least a hello, old fellow." The picture fluttered in the breeze, a corner of the paper covering the big stick figure. He swallowed down the lump in his throat. "Just one hello."

Taking a trying-to-be-confident breath, he folded the picture and pressed it back into the crack, giving it a final pat for good luck.

Bracing himself, he turned to the outside.

"Lena?"

Nothing.

He checked behind the bins. Poked into the bushes. Learned the hard way that thorny bushes and fur don't mix. He even went to the back of the garden to look behind the house.

Nothing.

"Where are you hiding?" Teddy paused for breath at the edge of the hedge by the front gate. Fred was inevitably waiting, ready to poke him with one of his many limbs if he returned Lenaless. Lucky for Fred—and Teddy—he didn't plan to do that. She had to be *somewhere.*

Pressing his nose through the gaps in the gate, he studied the Great Unknown, on the off-chance she was sitting somewhere on the path outside.

A car rushed by in a streak of black metal, and Teddy flinched back.

Oh.

Oh, *great.*

He mentally bumped up "heart surgery to make sure I don't care so much" on his to-do list. Because there, across miles of glistening asphalt and up mountainous sand dunes, was a red hoodie. A red hoodie, moving and shifting, but not with the wind.

Lena.

"Did you find her?" Fred's voice drifted over to him from the doorway.

Teddy let out a slow breath, watching dunes.

The road.

The small figure, just out of reach.

"Yes."

"Where is she?"

Teddy shook his head at himself, stretching onto tiptoe to open the latch. "Outside," he called over his shoulder. Fred couldn't tell his knees were shaking, right? "I'm going to find her."

Fred's reply was lost to the wind as Teddy stepped out, stumbling as the gate closed behind him. He swallowed, looking out at the road.

Okay. "We'll just... walk quickly."

Another swallow as he took a step towards the road.

A second car rushed past, dark red, and something vaguely sick stirred in Teddy's stomach. He'd had bad ideas in his time—trying out pink toothpaste being one of them—but this? This was on another level.

"Just do it. Worth the risk, right?" He bounced on his paws, rocking backwards, forwards, then backwards again, before leaning forward and setting off at a trot, eyes firmly fixed on the ground beneath him. Lumps of tarmac passed by, stinging-hot. A white streak of paint followed them.

Almost there.

A faint roaring lifted his head.

Oh, no.

No, no, no.

Sun caught on the front of a car as it tore towards him.

He stood, unmoving, eyes fixed on the monster racing closer. Then his brains kicked in and he ran, tripping over himself, snout meeting ground once, then twice, before he flung himself onto the curb.

The world split into a roar so loud that Teddy wasn't sure if it was him yelling or the car shrieking as it thundered past. Heat washed down on him along with a flood of grit and tarmac. Even the dying light of the sun blacked out as Teddy's eyes squeezed shut.

One second.

Two.

Slowly, the thunder of the car faded, and silence fell again.

The call of a seagull drifted over his head, and Teddy let out what was meant to be a sigh of relief, but came out a whimper.

He cracked an eye open, blue sky smudged with pink and gold meeting him.

Looking over to his left, he tested out taking a breath.

Yep.

Moving a leg.

Yep.

Then a snout.

It hurt, but yep.

Teddy let out a shaky laugh, sitting up stiffly and looking around.

"Well... I'm alive," he announced to no one in particular.

A trickle of grit ran down through his fur onto the road as he stood, brushing himself off and climbing onto the curb. He glanced back at the road.

"Never doing *that* again." If Lena didn't want him, he'd just live with the seagulls and the sand dunes forever. It couldn't be that bad, right? Everyone said the sea was beautiful, and he could already hear a soft rush-roar only one sand dune away.

"Nothing wrong with living on a beach," he murmured to himself, checking himself over one more time before crossing the short path and stepping into the long grass. The sand gave under his paw, and he sucked in a deep breath of salt air.

"Just one paw after another."

Thankfully, the dune wasn't as steep as it looked. Aside from the sand being intent on trickling back down to the road at a moment's notice, the grass made it easy enough to pull himself up the mountain.

After the first few tries, he fell into a sort of rhythm.

Step, slip, grab—pull.

Step, slip, grab—pull.

Step, slip, grab...

Teddy's head broke through the last tuft of grass after an age of climbing, breath coming in quick puffs.

That's what comes of living the shelf life for too long.

He bent over, paws on his stomach as he caught his breath.

Quiet sobs coming from a few paces to his right nipped that in the bud, igniting the jungle in his stomach as he dared to look up and over.

She was right there.

A little bundle of red hoodie and curly hair, hunched up next to a patch of long grass. Sniffs accompanied every rise and fall of her shoulders, and Teddy's heart went out to her.

Go speak to her. Just one hello.

He opened his mouth. A small squeak fell out.

Really, Teddy? Get yourself together, bear.

Sand whispered as he took a step closer.

Here goes nothing.

He cleared his throat.

"Hi."

She looked up, scrubbing at her face with sandy hands, and Teddy couldn't help staring. She was just like the picture. Except better, because she was real and living and breathing and *there*.

"Who are you?"

Teddy took a deep breath, her curious gaze giving him just enough to offer a nervous laugh.

"Well. Um…"

A small, tearful giggle escaped her, and she pushed her curls off her face just enough for Teddy to see the slight crinkle of her nose and a watery smile.

A smile of his own snuck out in response. Wobbly, but there.

"I'm Teddy. I—" he stumbled to a stop. *What do you even do here?*

Gulping, he held out a paw—because that's what teddies do when they meet their forever child, obviously—but instead of her hand meeting his scuffed fur, it circled around him, replacing the cooling air with the thick, warm folds of her hoodie. Her cheek pressed to his head, stilling the flutters in his stomach.

Seagulls cried softly above as the words of introduction he'd planned faded away. His throat tightened, and he nestled closer, fitting as though the gap between her and her knees had been made just for him.

It's… Lena.

The realisation sank in, soft and steady and *right*.

Something warm trickled down his snout as he spoke again, just loud enough for him and his girl to hear.

Fred's going to be impossible about this.

"I think… I'm your bear."

MARIELLE HENNING

Marielle Henning has a deep passion for encouraging people to get back up and try again—no matter what life has dealt them. She writes stories of found family, laughter, and delinquents with shaky pasts learning to own their mistakes and face the future with hope. When not doing battle with her hard-headed characters, you can find her taking her favourite train route into London, cuddling as many dogs as possible, or trying to convince her friends and family that, despite appearances, she's *not* moving to America. Really.

Achievements

- Drafted seven novels and one short story.

- Completed three rounds of edits and received a professional developmental edit on her main work in progress.

- Runs an Instagram marketing business providing bespoke, ongoing services to authorpreneurs and small business owners.

- Designed promotional materials for Nova McBee, author of the Calculated series.

- Attended Blue Ridge Mountains Christian Writers Conference, Write-To-Publish, and Realm Makers.

Pitches

- *Letters to the Lost* meets *Fast & Furious* in a YA contemporary novel where a 16-year-old British boy turns to illegal motocross to keep a roof over his family's head, while avoiding the unflappable Scottish mentor the police assigned him after his last arrest.

- *Half-Moon Investigations* meets *Juniper Bean Resorts to Murder* in a white-collar crime comedy about an art student striving to prove her innocence after the hair she donated to charity turns up at a crime scene.

THE SISTERS OF STARFORD POINTE

HANNAH FOUTS

S ea salt sprayed my cheeks as I stared out at the gray waters.

A storm's blowing in.

My little sister, Norah, stood next to me, her shaggy blonde hair whipping furiously in the icy wind. Brushing her long bangs out of her chapped face with the back of her hand, she tried to scrape barnacles off the dock while holding her teddy bear with the little yellow raincoat in the other hand.

I wrapped my arm around her shoulders the way Mom used to.

She glanced up and yelled, "Here he comes, Olivia! I told you he'd be here, didn't I?"

Her grin spread wide enough to show the gap where her front teeth should be—large enough to insert a straw through it.

The outline of my dad's old fishing boat emerged through the mist.

I clutched the paper bag filled with a lunch made just for him. Norah ran to the end of the dock, waving the whole way.

I strained to see his catch inside of the boat. Today was the last day to bring in fish for the market tomorrow. If we couldn't sell a lot of them, we'd lose the boat. Dad never said what would happen if we lost the boat, but families of kids who lost it all moved away from our sleepy seaside town.

I frowned at the thought of leaving Maine and going to the big city, my stomach twisting in a pile of anxious knots. The past few days had been slow. We needed a good catch today.

Letting out a long sigh, I shook myself. The boat was nearly in reach now. This was only Norah's third time helping me bring it in. Dad said she was a natural, but she didn't tie her knots tight enough last time. When the boat had drifted from the dock, Dad nearly dropped a bucket of fish back into the water.

There was no room for error today.

A small swell broke against the dock as he slowed the boat to a crawl. He waved, smiling with his familiar bright grin his thick beard could never hide. "How are my favorite girls?"

Norah giggled, jumping up next to me. "Hi, Daddy!"

"Ready for orders, sir." I saluted, trying to remain lighthearted.

Beneath the roiling clouds, the familiar scent of dead fish wafted over us. It's the kind of smell that makes city kids hold their noses. But to me it smells more like Dad coming home after a long day.

I set my jaw, determined not to let anything go wrong. Marching to the opposite side of the dock, I caught the rope Dad tossed over the side, and since Norah kept missing it, I caught hers, too.

"Hey!" She scowled, snatching the rope from my hand.

"Sorry…" I grimaced, my fingers itching to tie the knot for her.

She hurried to the piling next to the boat. I clutched the rope tightly, my knuckles turning white. Her tongue worked from the left side of her lips to the right as she started tying. Watching closely, I resigned to keep my words to myself.

Until she crossed the rope under rather than over.

"Come on, you know how to tie a half hitch," I said. "Let me help you." I stooped next to her, blowing on my hands to warm them.

"Olivia, Teddy and I can do this! How else is he going to learn to be a fisherman?"

I let out a sigh. *What would Mom have done?*

I took the rope from her hands and tied the knot with ease. "I know you want to, but just let me show you first. Dad's counting on us and we can't—"

A light splash came from below us. I glanced around. My rope was nowhere to be seen.

Bang!

I whipped around just in time to see Dad half submerged and grabbing at the side of the dock. The bucketful of fish he'd been holding sank underneath the water.

"Dad! Hang on." With Norah close at my heels, I seized his coat.

"Hurry! His face is already going blue from the cold," Norah cried, holding onto my waist.

Norah and I pulled with all our might until Dad was able to climb onto the dock. I sat back and took in deep breaths, the frigid air stinging my lungs.

"Are you okay?" Norah asked, hugging him tightly.

I carefully leaned over the edge, scooped Dad's soaked hat out of the water, and set it down, next to him. That bucket and all those fish were long gone.

"I think so. I don't know what happened. I was walking off the boat when the plank fell out from under me."

Pulling at my coat sleeves, I waited for Dad to realize what I'd done.

To realize how I'd failed.

Dad surveyed the scene, and his eyes snapped to me. "Olivia, why didn't you tie down your rope?"

"I was just trying to show Norah how to tie her side! She wasn't doing it right."

He pursed his lips the way he always did before delivering a lecture, and began to stand. "Ah!"

"What's wrong?" Norah asked, her face pale.

He sank back to the puddle that had formed around him. "It's my ankle."

I worked quickly and carefully to pull off Dad's boot.

Dad never got hurt.

He was always there to wrap up our scraped knees and kiss our tear-stained cheeks.

I whipped my head around to look for anyone else who could help, but it was deserted.

Dad clutched at his leg, sucking in a sharp breath as I worked the boot off his swollen ankle. The small bit of skin visible between his sock and his pants was already turning a nasty shade of purple.

Norah gasped and clamped her eyes shut.

I shoved myself to my feet, wobbling slightly. "Norah. Stay here with Dad. I'll get help."

Blinking back the tears, Norah nodded and brushed away the hair from Dad's forehead.

My feet barely hit the planks on the dock as I ran.

Mom would never have let this happen. Some big sister I was. If I'd thought things through, I'd have shown Norah how to tie the knot long before Dad even got to the dock... or just done it on my own.

I sucked in deep cold breaths, wiped away the hot tears streaming down my cheeks, and slammed into the paint-peeled door of the marina to call for help.

The eerie sound of sirens cut through the sleepy fishing town. I waited, shifting from one foot to the next until the flashing lights of the ambulance came into view. I waved the paramedics in and practically dragged them towards my dad.

"This way. Hurry!"

We wove our way around the marina and onto the dock.

I sprinted the final stretch to him. Norah was as pale as a sheet. Mr. Nevey, the owner of the marina, was tying up our boat and unloading all the fish. Sweat dripped down Dad's face despite the nip in the air.

"I brought help," I cried, dropping to his side.

He nodded, his eyes darting from me to the abandoned boat. Reaching forward, he took my hand, guiding me closer. "Take the dinghy to the lighthouse and tell Uncle Silas to finish out the day on the boat. We can't miss the market tomorrow."

I stared at Dad. Was he serious? That was a long way to go on the dinghy.

Dad gently directed my chin back towards him. "I'm counting on you."

"Yes, sir." I studied his pain-etched face. "You'll be all right though?"

A light mist began to fall from the low clouds. It caught on my dad's beard and danced like little stars. He nodded as the ambulance crew surrounded and lifted him gingerly from the ground onto the stretcher. "I'll be fine. Keep Norah safe, okay?"

I nodded as Norah buried her face in my damp jacket. I wrapped my arms tightly around her, unsure if I was comforting myself or her.

As soon as the paramedics strapped him in, they wheeled him to the ambulance. I took a deep breath, trying to calm my nerves.

"Norah. We need to go. There's no time to waste." I gripped her hand and started for the other side of the place where Dad kept the dinghy.

"Wait!" Norah shrieked, ripping her hand out of mine and rushing to the edge. "I have to bring Teddy. He likes the lighthouse."

Once her Teddy had been securely tucked into Norah's jacket, we ran down the docks. Dad taught me how to drive the dinghy several years ago. Up until now, though, he'd always been with me.

That didn't matter now.

It *couldn't* matter now.

If we couldn't make it to Uncle Silas quickly...

Don't think like that, I huffed. *I won't let Dad down again.*

After a rough ten minute ride through the choppy waters, I could finally make out Starford Pointe Lighthouse jutting up from the small rocky island. I tried not to imagine what would happen to our boat if I lost control near its dock.

Sharp rocks lurked just beneath the surface at every turn.

The faint outline of Uncle Silas appeared from the thick treeline of firs.

He waved and headed towards the dock, arriving just as I pulled the dinghy up to the side. I only banged against the wooden planks twice, which I considered a win.

"Mornin' girls. What can I do for you? Did you run out of eggs already?" He nodded towards his small chicken coop.

Norah stretched her arms out, and Uncle Silas helped her onto the dock.

"No, it's about Dad!" I said, my voice cracking.

His smile dropped. "I thought he was fishing today."

I nodded, working to tie the boat as quickly as my shaking hands would let me. "There was an accident. I think his ankle is broken. He's going to the hospital now."

Uncle Silas ran a hand through his black, windblown whiskers. "Of course. Of all days something like that would happen today. Are you girls okay? Do you need me to find a ride to take you to the hospital?"

"No. He told us to come here. We have to sell our catch by tomorrow, or the bank will take the boat. Can you help?"

For a long moment, the crashing of the waves and the gentle knocking of the boat against the dock were the only sounds.

"I'll do it." Uncle Silas rested his hands on his hips and gazed thoughtfully at the lighthouse. "I won't be able to find someone to stand in for me on such short notice." He started toward the end of the dock. "Even if I could, by the time anyone got here, most of the daylight will be gone. Besides, I don't like the look of those clouds. I need to get on the other side of that storm quickly."

I scrambled off the dinghy to catch up. I didn't like the look on Uncle Silas's face.

"Olivia, Norah, I need you both to run the lighthouse while I'm gone."

He wanted us to do *what*?

What if I messed up again?

What if I couldn't get Norah to listen like mom could?

Someone could die out there at sea, and it would be my fault.

Dad's pale, drawn face flashed through my mind. "*I'm counting on you.*"

I locked eyes with Norah, who gave a small brave smile and a nod.

I took a deep breath while pulling my hair out of my face. I straightened my back, doing my best to look confident. "We'll do it."

Uncle Silas hurriedly put on his rain slickers as he told us what to do. He also reminded us that if for any reason the phone lines went out, there was a battery operated phone in the storage house. Once he asked about a hundred times if we'd be okay to run things, he took his boat and sped off toward the docks.

Leaving Norah and I waving at the shrinking ship in the bitter mist.

I shivered and glanced up at the gray clouds looming above us.

Taking Norah's hand, I guided her back towards the Starford Pointe Lighthouse. "Come on."

Norah clung to me with one hand and held up Teddy with the other. "Do you think Daddy is going to be okay?"

The feeling of her hand in mine made me more confident than I was before. "He's tough, Norah. You can't work on the seas all your life without getting tough. Besides, the doctors know what they're doing." I reached out for the door handle, doing my best to conceal my shaking hands.

The rusted hinges squealed as I shoved the door open with my shoulder. It swung free, hitting the stone wall with a bang. It echoed all the way to the top of the spiraling staircase.

"It never feels this creepy when Uncle Silas is here." Norah shuddered.

I rubbed her shoulders. "I'll go first, okay?"

Our wet boots squeaked on the metal stairs as our steps echoed off the circular stone walls. By the time we reached the top, my legs were burning. I pushed open the door to what almost felt like any old house. The warmth from the crackling fire on the other side of the room had us hurrying to strip off our damp jackets and shoes.

I shut the door behind us just as Norah sprawled in front of the fireplace. I did my best to stifle a giggle.

She shot me a look. "What? Teddy was cold."

I raised my hands in surrender. "I didn't say anything."

With Norah occupied, I turned my attention to the small window on the side of the lighthouse. It was the only window in Uncle Silas's bookshelf-covered living room. I took a deep breath of the salty air mixed with the scent of old books and ink. Standing on my tiptoes to see outside, I decided the storm hadn't gotten much worse... at least not yet.

"Norah, I'm going to head up to the lantern room. Uncle Silas said the lens needed to be polished before dark." I strode across the room to the ladder which led to the next set of stairs.

Norah scrambled to her feet, pulling her bear along with her. "We're coming too!"

I suppressed a groan. Norah thought we were just playing lighthouse keeper. She didn't understand the gravity of what Uncle Silas left us to do.

I would have to shoulder that burden alone.

We arrived at the watch room after several more rooms and more stairs. Even though we got to come up all the time, it was always my favorite. Windows wrapped all the way around to see the whole ocean and harbor.

When I was Norah's age, I'd thought I saw the whole world from up here.

We paused, taking in the choppy waves and graying skies. The mist had turned into a light drizzle.

"Look, Olivia! Way out there!"

I followed her finger to see the tiny pinprick of Dad's fishing boat. Somewhere on board, Uncle Silas was doing his best to get past the storm before it turned nasty.

I bit my lip. *Keep him safe,* I prayed silently.

Stroking Norah's hair, I repeated the phrase Uncle Silas told me countless times when I spotted a ship out at sea. "Good eye, Norah."

She beamed a toothless grin up at me. "It was Teddy who saw it first. He's going to make a great lighthouse keeper one day, right?"

"He sure will. How about you and Teddy keep a lookout down here? I'm going up to the lantern room to polish the lens."

Norah saluted, messing up her thin bangs. "Aye, aye, Captain!"

Scurrying up the ladder, I opened the small hatch into the lantern room.

There was no heat up here, and the cold air pushed its way between the cracks in the window panes. The only piece of furniture was a small wooden desk on the far side with a log journal and a jar of ink, apparently left open in Uncle Silas's hurry to leave.

On a normal day, I'd stop to enjoy the view. Maybe sit on a ledge and eat an apple or two. But not today.

I spotted the abandoned rag and polishing solution. The light continued to shine, spinning a quick circle around the lens while I carefully worked. As time passed, the smell of vinegar filled my nostrils, and my hands went numb from the cold.

Almost an hour later, Norah's head appeared through the hatch. "We came to help! It's boring down there."

I bit my lip, trying to come up with a fake job for Norah to do. "Perfect! Just in time. My hands are cramping from holding this bucket. Can you hold it for me while I work?"

Norah's shoulders slumped. "Come on, you always do stuff like that! Let me polish it."

I crossed my arms, giving her a no-nonsense look that I hoped resembled mom's. Norah had no idea what was at stake here. The job had to be done *right*. "No. You might miss a spot."

"Please! How else will Teddy learn to be a lighthouse keeper?"

I let the rag fall to my side as I took a deep breath. *How would mom handle this?*

"Norah. You're far too big to be acting like that. Dad left me in charge, and this is a big job. Please just let me handle this."

Norah snatched the other end of the rag. "I know it's a big job! That's why Uncle Silas asked us *both* to do it."

I shoved Norah out of the way. "I said no!"

She stumbled back, just managing to catch herself on the desk. The jar of ink toppled over on the log book and stained Teddy's bright-yellow coat with dark liquid.

Norah shrieked, jerking him out of the way, but it was too late. The ink blotch was already set into the pale fabric. Her eyes brimmed with tears as she tried to rub it away.

I swallowed, my anger gone. "It will be okay. I can go clean him up in the sink right now, and he'll be as good as new."

"No! He's ruined, and it's all your fault!" Norah blinked hard as if to keep the tears away. "Mom made him this coat."

I know. Sometimes I wished I had something to remember her by. "Come on. It will be okay. Let's both just take a deep breath and—"

"I don't want to take a deep breath. You ruined him," Norah bellowed before turning away, the stained bear clutched tightly to her heaving chest.

Tears stung my eyes. "I was just trying to be a help to Dad."

Head down, she muttered, "Teddy doesn't want to be a lighthouse keeper anymore. You can do it yourself." With that she slammed the trap door back in place, leaving me alone at the top of the lighthouse.

I threw the rag into the bucket on the floor and blinked hard against my stinging eyes. The only sound was the faint patter of the now steady rain on the glass panes.

Staring out at the gray horizon, I tried to remember how being held by Mom felt before she got sick. The early mornings we spent cuddled together in bed awaiting my dad's return from a fishing trip. The way she smelled and the details of her face photos could never capture.

But all my mind could conjure was Norah.

By the time I gave up trying to remember anything more, the sky was darkened from both the storm and the sinking sun.

I shifted my weight from one foot to the other.

Could it really hurt that much to let Norah do a bit of polishing?

Just as I moved toward the ladder, lightning flashed. Thunder boomed so loud the window panes rattled. I let out a small yelp.

I looked down at the rocky shores being bombarded by foamy wave after foamy wave, each growing taller than the last.

This storm was getting ugly.

The smallest mistake could be catastrophic.

When I turned to look out at the waters, a strange feeling came over me. Every hair on my body stood on end.

My fingers felt all tingly.

I stretched out my hand in front of my face when an ear splitting crack rushed through the air followed by a boom that drove me to my knees. I clamped my hands over my ears and clenched my eyes shut.

My ears rang so loudly, I couldn't make out the sounds of the storm surrounding me. My eyes fluttered open to find Norah clambering up the ladder, her face pale and eyes wide. Her mouth was moving, but I couldn't make out what she was saying.

Finally she pointed.

Then I saw it.

The light had gone out.

We were plunged into an early darkness that could only be brought about by the nastiest of storms.

Mind racing, I stood, waiting for the back up system to kick in. Waiting for the next bulb to be put in place.

Norah and I crowded around watching the light's mechanism pull the burnt out bulb out of the way and replace it with the back up bulb.

After what felt like an eternity, it clicked into place.

We stared.

Lightning flashed.

But the light didn't turn on.

I couldn't remember what Uncle Silas said to do if something like this happened. Every moment I stood thinking was a moment a boat could be heading into trouble.

As if on command, the ringing stopped, and the sounds of the storm tumbled back into my mind.

Norah shook my arm. "Are you okay?"

I took a deep breath and patted myself down. "I'm fine. Just a little rattled. Never mind that though! We have to figure out what to do."

I unscrewed the new bulb and looked closer. One of the filaments wasn't connected.

Useless.

"We have to go get the spare. Uncle Silas showed us where they were, remember?" Norah was already halfway down the ladder again.

I slapped my palm to my forehead. *Of course! Come on, Olivia, get a hold of yourself.*

Flying down the ladder and through the service room, I finally caught up with Norah in Uncle Silas's bedroom. I slipped on my shoes and rushed past her. "I need to hurry! You can come if you want, but I need to get this done as fast as possible."

She tried to say something, but the sound of her words were cut short by another crack of lightning. My footsteps echoed ominously against the metal stairs. A second pair of footsteps soon followed.

Once I reached the bottom, I slammed my shoulder into the storage room door, but it refused to budge.

"Come on. Come on!" I muttered.

Norah rushed up from behind and slammed into the door at the same time. The stubborn hinges gave way so abruptly, we landed in a heap on the damp floor.

She let out a laugh of victory. "Teddy saved the day!"

I brushed myself off. "No one's saved anything if we can't find those spare bulbs."

Norah jumped to her feet and switched on the light.

We searched for a few moments before she shrieked. "I found them! There's only two left." She held up one delicate bulb in her clumsy hands.

My breath hitched as I took it carefully from her. "These bulbs are very fragile. I'll carry it the rest of the way up. You're too young for this kind of responsibility."

She crossed her arms and yelled, "Stop trying to be my mom!"

I blinked stunned by the ferocity in her usually sweet voice. "Norah, I... Just let me do it, okay?"

The space between her brows creased.

I knew that look. She was about to let loose a torrent. Tucking the lightbulb inside my jacket, I held on tightly. I rushed past her up the stairs while trying to ignore the sudden guilt bubbling up inside my chest. I had to prove to Dad that I could do just as good as Mom would have.

By the time I reached the lantern room again, I had to pause. My chest heaved and my legs ached from all the stairs. I strained and carefully set the broken bulb on the desk next to the upset inkwell.

I took the new bulb out of my jacket just as Norah's face popped up from the hatch. "Teddy wants to do it! You owe him after ruining his coat."

I took a step back. Her Teddy was in a sorry state, but I couldn't let her do this. There was too much at risk.

"You can't, Norah. You'd break it." I needed to work quickly so there would be no more argument.

I took a quick step forward, and my foot landed in the bucket of polishing liquid.

I lost my balance.

The bucket tipped over.

The lightbulb slipped out of my fingers. Cartwheeled mid air. And shattered into a thousand pieces.

The world around us froze. Even the rain seemed to slow down.

Norah stared at the broken glass, her bear hanging limp at her side.

A single tear streaked down my cheek. This was my fault. Not hers.

If I hadn't been so focused on doing things the right way and filling Mom's shoes, none of this would have happened. Now there was only one lightbulb left in the storage closet. If I let the same thing happen to that one...

More lightning flashed, illuminating the pieces of glass like silver.

Norah screamed, making me jump. "Olivia! I just saw it!"

I rushed to her side, my shoes crunching on glass. "What are you talking about?"

"Out there." She pointed toward the open sea. "A boat coming toward the rocks!"

My mouth went dry as my eyes followed her finger to the rocking waves.

Lightning streaked across the sky after a few moments, just long enough for me to make out a small boat struggling against the wind and waves.

I had to call the coast guard. Fast.

I staggered forward to the phone hanging on the wall. I picked it up, but no dial tone. I tried once more and dialed the number frantically. The phone lines were down.

I can't replace the bulb and get to the emergency phone across the island at the same time!

I turned to Norah. Her eyes were wide, but she didn't look as terrified as I felt. As strange as it was, only then did I realize how much she'd grown this year. She wasn't "just" my little sister anymore. She was Norah. The one I needed to rely on now more than ever.

I pulled her into a hug, "I'm sorry I didn't let you help before. I was wrong and I've been all around awful to you lately. I have to go to the storage house to get the battery phone."

"I forgive you." She wrapped her arms around my shoulders. "Be careful, okay? Teddy doesn't want to make two hospital visits today. "

I let out a small laugh despite the tightness in my throat. "I'll do my best."

With that, I let her go. She gave me a small nod, clutching Teddy to her chest.

I planted a quick kiss on her forehead and shot down the ladder.

My legs pounded on my way down the lighthouse, the familiar ominous echoes all around me. When I reached the bottom, I pulled on my jacket. I ran through the route in my mind to the old house that Uncle Silas refused to live in because it was too far from the lighthouse.

I gripped the cold metal to yank the door open, when I saw the open storage room to my right. The other bulb was still safe and ready to use.

I shook myself. *Norah can do it.*

Pulling the door open, I fled out into the torrential rains. Doing my best to shield my eyes from the water already pouring down my face, I searched for the overgrown trail to the house.

Lightning cracked.

I didn't have time to search for it. If I was careful, I could skirt along the edge of the rocky shores, avoiding both the hungry waves and the thick confusing forest. I took off towards the beach, my boots squelching through puddles as the water seeped through to my socks.

When I broke over the hill, I caught my breath. The sea looked even angrier from down here. Wave after pounding wave hit the beach. I swallowed. The shore was narrower than I'd thought, and getting smaller.

I'd have to hurry.

Picking my way as fast as my legs would take me over the slippery rocks, I made good time until I came to the unfamiliar half of the island. Norah and I always turned around here unless Dad or Uncle Silas was with us.

I shook myself muttering, "How could I forget the flashlight?"

As I continued running, I glanced behind me. Everything was still dark.

Norah should have gotten the bulb back in the lighthouse by now.

Staring out at the inky sea, I fought back the lump of fear in my throat. Whoever was in that boat out there was counting on me... and Norah. I brushed my hair out of my face and pushed forward.

In a matter of minutes, I reached the old house. It sagged in the middle and appeared even more lonely in the raging storm.

The water sloshed in my boots as I sprinted through the clearing to the house. When I pulled the door handle, it wouldn't budge. *Locked!*

After a quick search under the doormat and above the frame, I found a fake rock next to the door where a key lay hidden inside.

Jamming it into the slot, I did my best to turn the key despite getting caught on itself several times. I slammed the door open and stepped out of the rain.

Water dripped from my soaked clothes onto the wooden floors. I flipped the light switch and hurried inside as the lights blinked on. The house didn't have a scrap of furniture inside. Just piles of boxes.

Rounding the corner into what was supposed to be the kitchen, I found the phone lying on the kitchen counter. I prayed silently that the batteries hadn't died long ago.

With trembling hands, I picked it up and switched it on. I nearly wept when I heard the familiar dial tone. I punched in the number to the coast guard.

It rang twice before someone finally picked up. I rushed over my words, and only managed to say where we were and that a boat was in trouble. The woman on the other end said they would send someone right away. I hung up the phone with a soft click.

The exhaustion and chill of the night finally sank into my bones.

I looked out the kitchen window toward the sea.

It was only then I noticed the familiar steady sweep of the lighthouse beam had returned. Despite the chaos of the night and the numbness of my body, I smiled.

I suppose Teddy would make a good lighthouse keeper after all.

My body ached all over. The cold crept through the walls of the house. Pretty soon I gave up on trying to get warm. At long last, the storm blew itself out. I locked up the house and put the key back under the fake rock. Everything but the lighthouse was still dark. The rising moon played peekaboo behind the thin clouds. As I started back toward Norah, the coast guard thundered past, towing a smaller boat in its wake.

I let out a long breath.

They made it.

Hurrying back to the lighthouse as quickly as my feet would take me, I dared not let my mind wander to what might have happened if Norah came out to look for me.

As I rounded the corner of the island, Starford Pointe Lighthouse came into view, shining as brightly as when Uncle Silas ran it. Tears sprung to my eyes as I broke into a run, not caring if the slippery rocks under my feet gave way.

The door opened and Norah ran out calling all the way in a mix of tears and laughter. "Olivia! Olivia! "

She jumped into my arms, trembling with sobs. "I—I didn't know if you were going to make it back."

I held the back of her head tightly and breathed in her warm sugar-cookie scent. "I'm so proud of you."

Norah pulled back just enough to see my face. "I think Teddy wants me to tell you that he forgives you... you know... for earlier."

A smile broke out on my weary face. "I tell you what. Let's go get dry, and we can work together to get Teddy cleaned up."

We turned to look toward the tossing sea. In the distance was a faint light bobbing along the horizon. I didn't need binoculars to recognize that boat.

Norah pointed, "Look! Here comes Uncle Silas!" She flashed her snaggle-toothed grin and slipped her small hand into mine.

I squeezed her tightly. "Good eye, Norah. Good eye."

Hannah Fouts

Hannah grew up with a knack for getting lost in her imagination . . . especially when she was supposed to do chores. Now, she writes stories for kids that spark imagination and protect innocence. Her favorite thing as a kid was to walk into the library, head straight to the children's section, and check out any book without having to worry about the content. That's hardly the case for kids today. To combat this issue, she writes novels that kids love and parents feel good about. When Hannah isn't daydreaming about her stories, she can be found stamping, doodling, and gluing new entries in her reading journal.

ACHIEVEMENTS

- Drafted five full length novels and eight short stories.

- Received and implemented an edit letter for one of her novels.

- Attended Write to Publish in 2024 and received interest from an agent on her novel.

- Successfully launched and marketed her own childcare business and booked all her available slots in one week.

- Works as a fiction writing instructor for Kids Write Novels to teach kids in her target audience to write and self publish novels.

- Has a growing email list with an open rate of 82.52% and an author Instagram account with over 3,000 followers.

PITCHES

- *Ramona and Her Father* meets *Wish* in a MG contemporary novel about a young girl who tries to matchmake her elderly great aunt and the grouchy next door neighbor.

- *The Secret Garden* meets *The Penderwicks on Gardam Street* in a MG contemporary novel about a boy who must repair the rift between two feuding towns with nothing but a trowel, some seeds, and an abandoned gardening clubhouse.

THE HUNGRY WOODS

VICTORIA SHANKS

I t is only fair to warn you up front. This story is about a wedding, and I am sorry for it. I will tell you of many more interesting things, such as a pie feud, trees with teeth, and a weeping moon-bright beetle, but there is a wedding in this story, and there is no escaping it. I can only attempt to clear the unpleasantries out of the way as quickly as possible.

The wedding business began years before the feud. A young Peter of the Whipplewild clan, the fifth of seven Peters then among their ranks, dropped a hairy spindle-spider on Miss Floraleen Limberlong. It was quite an accident, and once she bid the spider adieu, little miss Floraleen thought it all very funny and thought gangly Peter looked rather like a spider himself.

Peter, meanwhile, thought her blue eyes put the sky to shame, and her crooked smile was the nicest he'd ever seen, and perhaps—*perhaps*—meeting her was worth losing a perfect specimen of the rarest spider in the Hollow.

Of course, being Peter, it took him fifteen years to work up the courage to tell her so.

Under normal circumstances, the marriage of a Whipplewild and a Limberlong would be unthinkable. A Whipplewild jilted Great-Great-Great-Uncle Horace a hundred years earlier. But as Peter made a respectable salary studying insects, and Miss Floraleen's formidable height, freckles, and beakish nose had frightened off all other suitors, her father made no objection to the match. Mr. Limberlong even went so far as to hint that, if Peter stayed far from the Woods like a sensible chap, and remembered not to bring jars of thrumming cicadas to the supper table, he might in time grow to tolerate his son-in-law.

The wedding set the Hollow abuzz. A Whipplewild and a Limberlong! Now the families could speak to each other in public, their children wouldn't be obliged to fight after school every day; oh, it was marvelous!

Miss Floraleen's wedding-day dawned in a splendor of sunshine and bird-song. Cloven, the orphan girl who lived with her in the house inside a gimble-tree, helped the bride garland her hair with roses. Cloven's twin, Bramble, led guests to their seats on bales of hay. The ceremony took place in the glen where marriages had been performed as long as the Hollow could remember.

Every family brought a pie as a present.

At the altar, Miss Floraleen awaited the arrival of her groom...

... and she waited...

... and she waited...

... and she waited.

Clouds drew over the sun.

The roses in her hair began to wilt.

Miss Floraleen's father leaped up, suit straining at its buttons. "I knew it!" he cried. "Jilted again! You Whipplewilds are all the same!"

Peter's father hurled the nearest pie into Mr. Limberlong's face.

Every guest dashed for a pie. Each Limberlong aimed for a Whipplewild, and each Whipplewild aimed for a Limberlong. Somehow, in the confusion, Cloven found Miss Floraleen's hand and pulled her home to the cottage in the gimble-tree.

Miss Floraleen sat on her bed and stared at her hands as Cloven pulled the wilted roses from her long hair.

When Cloven left, Miss Floraleen curled into a knot of quilt and wedding dress and aching heart, and she wept.

Thus began the Great Hornswoggle Hollow Pie Feud.

One week later, Cloven Limberlong picked up her hairbrush and scowled at it. Then she scowled at her reflection in the mirror. Then she scowled at the reflection of her twin, Bramble, a mop-haired younker in the window seat behind her. He hunched over a sputtering candle and his dogeared copy of *A. Felonious's Adventure Tales, Volume XIV*.

The scowl was critical. It was Step One of her ritual.

Step Two began when she took a swipe at her tangled locks and whispered, slow and fierce, "Peter Whipplewild, I hate you!"

Between brush-strokes, she whispered it seven times—once for each night since the almost-wedding. If she put enough hate into the words, Peter would feel it, wherever he was.

It wasn't right to hate, Miss Floraleen said... but anyone who hurt her deserved it. And *Peter* deserved to shrivel into a husk, blow away on the wind until he caught in a treetop, and hang there until he starved.

Bramble set his book aside and hugged his knees to his chest. "Clo? D'you think Peter misses us?"

Cloven thumped her brush down on the nightstand. "I think you had better keep working out ways to cheer up Miss Floraleen, or else I will box your ears." She clambered into her bunk, her cast clomping against the ladder.

In the moonlight, the cast encasing her right foot looked more than ever like a great white grub. It itched horribly, and even sticking a knitting needle down it couldn't quite scratch it. Stupid itch. Stupid cast. Stupid fragile ankle.

Bramble stared at the moon-silver roses brushing the outside of his window. "I wonder where he is."

Run off to marry some other lady, according to Mrs. Snicklewart.

Before Cloven could open her mouth, the bedroom door creaked open.

Miss Floraleen stepped in, spectacles teetering off the tip of her nose, inkpot and quill in hand. Eyes red-rimmed.

Cloven smoothed her frown away. Not in front of Miss Floraleen.

Miss Floraleen scaled the ladder to Cloven's bunk, smiling weakly. One corner of her mouth still quivered downward.

Cloven vowed to bake Peter into a mincemeat pie.

Bramble scrambled onto the bunk on Miss Floraleen's other side. "Tell us a story! One about Zedwin the Ranger!"

The other corner of Miss Floraleen's mouth quirked up as she ruffled his hair. "Well, back when the Hollow was young, Zedwin patrolled the edge of the Hungry Woods..."

Zedwin the Ranger. Cloven rolled her eyes. Why did Bramble care? It was just a fairy story. Not real. Not like Miss Floraleen.

As Miss Floraleen spoke, she took the quill in her bony fingers and began to draw on the plaster of Cloven's cast. Something rounded... a flick of her wrist, and it had a tail... couldn't be the cat, she drew him two weeks ago...

The teapot! The chipped black teapot Cloven had pulled from a rubbish heap when she was five. Cloven remembered holding it out to Miss Floraleen, lisping through missing front teeth, "I stoled it, but it was lonely, and you're the best at loving lonely things!"

Miss Floraleen finished the inky teapot with a handle-shaped flourish of her quill. "... so Zedwin snipped off the mole's nose with his scissors, and nobody else has been gobbled by it to this day. The end."

"I want to be a ranger when I grow up." Bramble nestled closer to Miss Floraleen. "I'll have a giant axe, and I'll chop the Hungry Woods up whenever it tries to creep into the Hollow."

"You—" Miss Floraleen kissed the top of his head, then Cloven's— "will be the greatest ranger who's ever lived."

When the door closed behind Miss Floraleen, Bramble turned to Cloven. "I know how to make her happy again!"

Cloven sat up straighter. "How?"

"Find Peter! We'll bring him home, and they can get married after all, and the feud will be over—"

Cloven's chest felt oven-hot, and she gritted her teeth. "Shut up."

Did she have enough yarn? Miss Floraleen pulled her rocking chair closer to the window and riffled through her knitting basket. Three skeins of Peter's blue... it would have to be enough.

One more trail. She'd leave just one more trail for him. He'd gotten lost a thousand times before, like when he chased that butterfly through the meadows and spent two days wandering before he found her yarn trails.

But that was two days.

Not a week.

Never a week.

He must be hurt. Or... no, she wouldn't allow herself to think that. Peter was all right. He would come home.

Something thudded against the window. Floraleen dropped her yarn.

A beetle.

An ice-white beetle big as a dinner plate, glowing wanly, its sobs shaking the windowpane as it clung to the glass and stared wild-eyed at Floraleen. Her breath caught. What—?

In its mandibles, it held a snippet of Peter-blue yarn.

"Bzzt!" said the beetle, beckoning with three of its legs and wiping its tears with a fourth. "Bzzt bzzzz!"

Come.

She emptied her knitting basket, keeping only the blue skeins and her needles, and whisked on her shawl on the way out the door. She paused to knot the yarn around the doorknob, and she dashed after the beetle, leaving a trail of blue behind.

The beetle whirred through the knobblenut orchard just ahead of her, glowing brighter with every second. Its tears splatted on the grass, leaving crisp patches of frost. Then it veered right, toward the rim of the Hollows.

The Hungry Woods.

Peter was in the Hungry Woods.

Vines that latch onto you and suck you dry, trees with gaping mouths and branchy hands ready to grab any man or beast within reach... could Peter have truly gone in the Woods?

The forest loomed nightmare-black above Floraleen. Wind rattled the boughs like chattering teeth.

Her feet felt like stones. *Can't go in there, not even the rangers go in the Woods... but if Peter...?*

She took a step forward.

A tendril of vine curled out to her.

The beetle glanced back at Floraleen with a reassuring nod, and its antennae brushed the vine.

The vine went stiff, sparkling icy in the beetle's moon-bright glow.

Floraleen drew up all five-foot-eleven-and-three-quarters inches of herself.

"Peter," she said, "I'm coming."

Cloven squeezed her eyes shut tight as the hall clock chimed midnight.

If *she* couldn't sleep, how much worse off was Miss Floraleen?

And how could Peter do this to them? He'd seemed like the papa Cloven and Bramble always wanted.

Her lower lip quivered, and she bit it to make it stop. She was wrong. Peter only came to hurt them, and they let him. She should've known he didn't love them. She should've known the day of the picnic.

Oh, she remembered every detail of that day. Peter took her and Bramble to Looking-Glass Lake. Cloven climbed that snapapple tree and the branch broke...

Trying not to cry and unable to walk, all she wanted to do was scream. She'd never hurt so badly.

And Peter didn't notice.

He was too busy writing about that stupid glowing beetle.

Cloven's ankle itched worse than ever. She rolled onto her back, staring at the raftered ceiling. Maybe if she stared hard enough, she could burn holes in it.

Then she could burn holes in Peter next time she saw him.

Smiling thinly, she kept staring until she fell asleep.

Greenish-gold morning light filtered through the rose bushes into Cloven's room. She pulled her quilt over her face to block out the brightness.

Wait.

Too bright.

Why did Miss Floraleen let her oversleep?

She sprang from her bunk, remembered her cast in midair, and twisted so her side bore the brunt of the impact with the floor. She'd have a cast on her ribs, too, if she kept that up.

Rubbing her side, she hobbled to the hallway door. "Miss Floraleen?"

"Clo!" Bramble barreled around the corner. "Clo, she's gone!"

Cloven pushed past Bramble into the kitchen. No fire in the woodstove, no porridge simmering on the hob. The chipped black teapot sat empty atop the breadbox.

She limped to Miss Floraleen's room. Bed still neat as a pin, save Mouse the cat sprawled over the mountain of cushions. As if Miss Floraleen had never slept there.

Out in the parlor, half-knitted socks were strewn over the floor, and the basket and Peter-blue yarn were missing.

Miss Floraleen used that yarn for only one thing.

Hands curled into trembling fists, Cloven marched to the cottage door and shoved it open.

Knotted to the knob was a thick wool thread.

Cloven's throat felt tight. Anger-hot. "Go find her. I'll catch up once I'm dressed." She spun on her heel for the bedroom.

She yanked on her pinafore with the patched skirt and tugged a shoe over her good foot. Socks—sock, at the moment—were a luxury she didn't have time for.

After looping through a bumbleberry orchard and past the millpond, Cloven caught up to Bramble at the one place the blue path never led before.

The edge of the Hungry Woods.

Through the leering trees, snapping things rose toward the sun and shrank down again. Flowers with petals like tongues, covered in bumps that could scrape somebody's skin right off. The howl of a skunkwolf echoed out from the dim depths.

Bramble kicked at the grass. Probably pretending not to cry. Just like a boy. "Why'd she go...?"

"Peter." Cloven spat the name, staring at the yarn trail. "Because of Peter."

Gone for a week, and he still found ways to hurt them.

Her jaw set. "We've got to find help." And she limped for the village as fast as her bad leg would take her.

The false-front mercantile dripped berries from hurled pies, so thick Cloven couldn't even see the door. She felt through the jam until she found the latch.

"Friend or foe?" bellowed Miss Floraleen's father from behind the counter, brandishing a piecrust oozing cornmeal mush and pickled hog feet.

"Mr. Limberlong, Miss Floraleen's in trouble!" Cloven cried.

"Ah." He lowered the pie and readjusted his spectacles. "Not now, child. I've got to deal with those rotten Whipplewilds."

What? "But Miss Floraleen—"

"I said, not now! Off with you, unless you want a pie to that nice clean dress!"

Cloven stomped out. He cared more about that stupid feud than his own daughter. All fathers were like that. Peter would've been just the same.

Everywhere she looked in Hornswoggle Hollow, villagers made pies, threw pies, and cleaned pies off themselves, their children, or their livestock. Great-Great-Great Aunt Malinda wailed about her antique lace curtains, now bruised purple from scratchberry juice. Mr. Hinkleton's prize rooster had been murdered by an appleshot projectile pie to the head. Little Sam Limberlong was bedridden after a hot pepper jam pie—spicy enough to raise the dead—set his clothes afire.

Everyone was still angry about that stupid wedding, but nobody cared about sweet Miss Floraleen, who'd been hurt more than any of them that day.

At last Cloven and Bramble found a ranger. The brave soldier stood at attention at the edge of the Woods nearest the Hollow, his cuirass battered from battling the forest, his razor-sharp hoe at the ready.

To get his attention, Cloven lobbed a green apple at the man's head. It connected with a satisfying thwack. He stumbled backward onto his haunch.

Cloven stood over him, arms folded. "Your job is to protect us from the Woods, right, sir?"

The man looked from her to Bramble to Cloven again, rubbing his head. "What hit me?"

"Never mind that." She took a step closer. "We need you to protect some-one."

Bramble stepped up, too. "Miss Floraleen went into the Woods! She left a trail so we can follow her, but she went in alone, and—"

"Slow down, son." The ranger held up his hands. "You want me to go into the Woods after a lady who's probably already dead, so I can *maybe* find her bones, and *certainly* get eaten myself?"

"You're a ranger!" Cloven burst out. "It's your job!"

"Missy, my job's to keep the Woods out of the Hollow, not to keep the Hollow out of the Woods." The man rubbed his temple again. "If your... Florabelle? Flora Jean?... went into the Woods, that's her business. Far be it from me to interfere."

Cloven snatched up her apple and sent it into his nose before darting away.

Once she was certain the ranger hadn't followed, Cloven collapsed at the foot of a storm oak and stared at her hands.

Bramble sniffled. "What're we gonna do?"

"I don't know." Cloven's voice sounded flat as paper. Miss Floraleen—the only person who'd ever loved her—alone in the Woods.

I can't lose her.

I can't.

"Bramble," she said, "we're going after her."

He blinked at her. "Going... into... the Woods?"

"Yes!" Cloven grabbed his hands and dragged him to his feet. "And we can't waste another minute! Run back to the Hollow and fetch us a hot pepper jam pie!"

"But—"

"Listen to me, and you listen close." Cloven pushed her face very near his. "Miss Floraleen needs us. Are you going to be a great big coward like that ranger? Or will you finally do something heroic like in your stupid adventure books?"

A tear dripped off Bramble's nose. "But what if..."

"If Miss Floraleen dies, who's going to take care of us and make us tea and tell us stories before bed?" Tears burned in her own eyes. "We've got to save her, Bramble!"

Bramble pushed Cloven away. "We need hot pepper jam pie, and... anything else?"

A spark of pride for her twin lit in Cloven's chest. "A hatchet. I'll get Miss Floraleen's hedge clippers."

Bramble nodded and, with a wobbly smile, sprinted away.

At the edge of the Woods, the twins hesitated. Cloven's palms felt clammy, the handles of her clippers slick with sweat.

The thorny forest loomed over them. Was it really haunted by the ghosts of the people it ate?

"Clo," Bramble whispered, "d'you think she's still alive?"

Her throat tightened. "She'd better be."

And she stepped into the Woods.

Instantly a vine lashed out for her cast. Cloven dispatched it with a snip of her clippers. It recoiled, squealing.

Bramble fell into step behind her, clutching his hatchet. "Are you... sure?"

Cloven pointed her clippers at the blue trail and kept walking.

With every step, Cloven's shoe rubbed against her sockless foot, and her bad ankle ached, and the knapsack with the hot pepper jam pie thumped against her back. The trees grew farther apart now, but that didn't keep branches from reaching for her, or roots from snaking out to trip her, or thorns from lunging for her legs. She kept her eyes on the blue yarn, their guide to Miss Floraleen and home.

"What—" Bramble paused mid-question to hack at the moss trapping his feet— "What's with all the ice?"

Cloven paused and scanned the forest. Sure enough, here and there a frozen leaf sparkled in the sun. "It looks like it's following Miss Floraleen."

"What if it's an ice monster?"

"I've never heard of those here." She scanned the ground for footprints. Nothing she could see, which didn't mean it wasn't a monster. Just that it flew or wasn't heavy enough to leave prints.

"In *A. Felonious's Adventure Tales* volume fifty-eight, there was an ice monster with big tusks and breath that turned people to ice!"

"But that wasn't in the Hollow." Cloven snipped at a vine. "All we have are man-eating moles—" And she froze.

At her feet, tangled in roots, lay a sun-bleached human skeleton.

Miss Floraleen?

Then she saw the yarn trail stretch past the skeleton. She dropped to the forest floor in a trembly puddle of relief.

Bramble poked something with his hatchet. A rusted hoe.

"He was a ranger," he whispered.

If a ranger couldn't survive the Woods, how could they?

She let out a shaky breath. Would Miss Floraleen want them to die looking for her?

Already they were braver than anyone else in the Hollow. They at least *tried*.

Miss Floraleen was probably already eaten. Probably before Cloven and Bramble even found her yarn.

"Clo," Bramble said, his voice very small, "d'you think Zedwin was scared? When he fought the man-eating mole?"

Cloven spun to glare at him. Bramble and his stupid stories. Then a picture formed in her mind: Miss Floraleen, drawing on Cloven's cast as she told that same stupid story.

With a savage shake of her head, Cloven stared into the Woods, at the drifting tentacles of vine ready for the next time she turned her back.

Miss Floraleen was out there.

Because of Peter.

If Miss Floraleen loved that horrible, horrible man enough to keep looking for him, surely they loved Miss Floraleen enough to keep looking for *her*.

So there it was. Run like rabbits? Or keep looking?

Cloven straightened her pinafore.

"Bramble," she said, "if you say one more thing about being scared, I shall feed you to the Woods myself."

The sinking sun cast long shadows through the woods by the time Floraleen ran out of yarn, but the moon-bright beetle buzzed on. A whisper of wind stirred the air, carrying a spicy-sweet scent. Gingerbread?

She scanned the Woods. No life save the chattering trees.

Then a thread of red earth peeked through the leaf mold at her feet. A path.

Surely the only paths in the Woods were made by monsters. Yet it was the most obvious way to go. Perhaps Peter had taken it.

"This way," she said to the beetle.

Its antennae bobbled as it shook its head.

Floraleen swallowed down the lump in her throat. "Please."

With a reluctant hum, the beetle turned down the path.

The gingerbread scent grew stronger. Then white dazzled her eyes through a break in the trees.

She ducked under an icy branch, and her mouth fell open.

A cottage with shingles made of gingerbread, the walls decorated with swirls of red candies. The doorposts and window lintels were immense striped sugarsticks.

Who could live in the Hungry Woods? In a house of candy?

The cottage door drifted open, and a tiny woman with wooly white hair peeped out.

Perhaps she'd seen Peter. Perhaps he was inside!

Floraleen gave her widest smile as she loped toward the house. "Hello!"

The old woman waved without looking. Her dress was odd, papery.

"Excuse me, ma'am." Surely her skin wasn't greenish. It must just be the forest light. "Has a man been this way?"

The woman only waved again.

Floraleen took one more step forward, and the house erupted into the gaping maw of a flower.

It dove straight for her—she shielded her head with her basket.

Then the flower screeched an ear-piercing hiss.

Floraleen stumbled back, gasping. The flower loomed higher than a barn above her, drooling gingerbread-scented nectar.

Ice crawled over its petals.

"Bzzzzzt!" said the beetle, its mouth as scowly as a beetle's could possibly be. "Bzzz!"

"Oh," Floraleen whispered, pulse thumping in her chest and the palms of her hands. "*Oh.*"

The old woman must have been at the end of one of the flower's stamens. A lure for travelers.

Could the flower have eaten Peter?

No. No, Floraleen mustn't let herself think that. The beetle would lead her to him.

She cleared her head with a shake and looked back at the beetle. "Thank you for saving me."

"Bzzzt!" Every one of its legs pointed back toward the path.

"Peter," she whispered. "We'll find him. We *must*."

Cloven's cast weighed more with each step. Far-off she was sure she heard a cricket chirp. Her stomach growled.

Then her stomach turned a flip and dove into her toes.

The yarn trail ended.

Cloven staring into the gloom. Still as a grave, if graves were swarms of writhing green. Everywhere she looked, trees snapped with teeth that had no business existing.

Her ankle throbbed, and the pit of her stomach felt stone-heavy. Like it did after she fell from that stupid snapapple tree and broke her stupid ankle. That was probably Peter's fault, too. If he'd warned her the branch was dead, she wouldn't be in this awful cast. She and Bramble could've run after Miss Floraleen instead of limping. Maybe they would have found her by now.

How were they to find her without the trail?

Bramble stared at her. "Are you crying?"

"No!" she snapped as a tear dripped off her chin.

Bramble pointed at her. "Yes, you are!"

"My eyes are leaky, that's all!" Cloven's cast dragged in the rotting leaves as she limped another step.

"Liar!"

She wheeled. Left a red handprint on his cheek before she even knew she'd slapped him. "Miss Floraleen is lost, Bramble! And it's all Peter's fault!"

Bramble gaped.

"Everything is Peter's fault!" Her voice cracked. "The wedding, Miss Floraleen, my stupid ankle—"

"Your ankle? What're you talking about?"

Her knees wobbled and she crumpled to the ground. "Peter didn't notice I was hurt for ages and ages, and—"

"Clo, you're an idiot." Bramble plopped down beside her, apparently unfazed by her cocked-and-ready slapping hand. "Of course it took him ages and ages. You hid it! What was he supposed to do, magically know you got a broken ankle?"

Cloven swiped at her eyes with the back of her hand. It still stung from hitting him. "He *left*! It's his fault we're in this mess!"

"We're here because Miss Floraleen loves him." He swatted away an exploratory vine. "Just like she loves us. Would you be mad if she went out here looking for me?"

Her gaze fastened on her cast. On that little ink teapot. "No, but Peter—"

"Peter got lost, Clo." *How is Bramble so patient?* "He wouldn't just leave. D'you think Miss Floraleen's stupid enough to love somebody as nasty as you say Peter is?"

If he was right... then the problem wasn't Peter.

It was Cloven.

She closed her eyes tight, then pushed herself to her feet. "The ice," she said. "If we can't follow the yarn, maybe we can follow the ice."

Bramble immediately set off to the left. "Miss Floraleen!" he called. "Can you hear us?"

With a snick at an overly ambitious branch, Cloven marched after him.

They'd hardly gone a hundred steps when Cloven heard a footstep thud behind her.

Then another.

Bramble stopped. "Clo...?"

"It'll be fine." Couldn't have him panicking. Very slowly she turned 'round to look.

A black thing reared tall as a house, long ears twitching above sharp antlers and two gleaming front teeth. A jackalope.

It would *not* be fine.

"Run!" she screamed, grabbing Bramble's hand and bolting.

The jackalope's reeking breath huffed on the back of her neck, and the earth shook each time it leaped. She could almost hear the wiggle of its rabbity nose.

"Faster, Bramble!"

He ran ahead of her, the distance between them growing. If the jackalope ate anyone it'd be her. Maybe that'd give him time to escape.

A vine coiled around Bramble's ankle. He crashed to the ground, hatchet flying out of his hand.

What can I do?

Cloven whipped the hot pepper jam pie from her pack and spun to face the monster.

It loomed on its haunches, mouth open to chomp, and then—

It turned to ice.

A great glowing beetle buzzed off its head and hovered over Cloven and Bramble.

The beetle from the picnic. The one Peter had never seen before. He wanted to write a book about it, didn't he?

Miss Floraleen stepped out from behind the jackalope. "What in the Hollows are you doing here?"

Cloven choked back a sob and sprang to her, hiding her face in Miss Floraleen's shirtwaist. "You're alive!"

"We came to rescue you." Bramble said, sounding sheepish.

"Oh, children..." Miss Floraleen planted a kiss atop Cloven's head and led her over to Bramble, cutting the vine biting his ankle with a snick-snick of her sewing shears. "Oh, my sweet children!"

Cloven pulled back to study Miss Floraleen's face. Ghost-pale in the glow of the beetle, and behind her spectacles tears sparkled as she knelt and bandaged Bramble's ankle with her handkerchief. "Imagine what could have happened to you," she whispered.

"We thought you were in trouble," Cloven offered feebly.

"No." Miss Floraleen's lips trembled, and she nodded at the icy beetle. "He had a piece of Peter's yarn. I thought he could lead me to him."

"Bzz!" The weeping beetle cut her off, pointing with three of its arms off into the Woods. "Bzz! Bzzzt!"

Cloven and Bramble looked at each other, then at Miss Floraleen.

She sighed. "He wants us to follow him." Her hand tightened around Cloven's. "We'll have to hurry to reach the Hollows before dark."

Go home?

Miss Floraleen came all this way hunting Peter, and now... she'd give up to bring them home?

Cloven looked at Bramble, and Bramble looked back at her.

She pulled her hand free. "We need to discuss this," she said and limped behind the frozen jackalope.

"Why do we need..." Bramble trailed behind. "Wait. You want to follow the Weepy Moonbug Thing?"

Did she?

Cloven scuffed her cast in the dirt. What if she *was* wrong about Peter?

"It would make Miss Floraleen happy," she said at last.

Bramble gave a firm nod. "It would make all of us happy."

"Maybe." Cloven picked up the hot pepper jam pie once more. Steam swirled from it and sent drips of water melting off the jackalope. "Miss Floraleen," she said, "Bramble and I have decided to follow the Weepy Moonbug Thing."

"Peter's our family, too." Bramble found his hatchet and tucked it into his belt. "We ought to help look for him."

Miss Floraleen's lips quivered into a smile, and she took Cloven's hand in one of hers and Bramble's hand in the other. "Together."

And they set out after the weeping beetle.

Cloven kept a firm grip on Miss Floraleen as they trekked deeper into the gloaming forest. If Bramble and Miss Floraleen were right about Peter... well, it was worth finding out.

A spider as tall as Cloven's waist shuffled by, just outside the beetle's aureole of light. Its collection of eyes were beady and black and baleful. She looked away, staring at the embroidered blue flowers on Miss Floraleen's apron until the spider was well past.

On Miss Floraleen's other side, Bramble limped along with his head held high, scanning the Woods. He didn't seem bothered by the bats fluttering through the treetops. Cloven had heard the bats in the Woods would swarm you and stick their fangs into your throat. If it weren't for the beetle, Cloven had no doubt they all would have been gobbled up.

Tears still dripped from the beetle's eyes, but resolve gleamed in them too. With each step they took its crystalline light glowed brighter against the black leaves. Whatever it wanted, whatever was wrong, the Weepy Moonbug Thing was sure they could fix it. The thought made Cloven straighten up a bit.

Suddenly the beetle stopped, tears gushing like a fountain to form an icicle spike on the ground. "Bzzzz! *Bzzzzzzzzzzz!*"

In a clearing ahead, moonlight filtered through a break in the trees, shimmering off a giant lump of ice.

A lump that, the longer Cloven looked at it, began to look an awful lot like a man.

Miss Floraleen's hands flew to her mouth. "Peter!"

Cloven hobbled to the ice and crouched before it.

It was Peter. Face frozen in an expression of wonder, hand outstretched as if to touch—

Peter must not have known what the Weepy Moonbug Thing could do.

And he'd touched it.

Dear Peter. He didn't abandon them after all. He'd just seen a bug, the thing Cloven knew he loved in the Hollow above all else, and followed it. He didn't know it would kill.... No, Cloven refused to think he was dead.

Miss Floraleen hugged Frozen Peter tight as the Moonbug sobbed overhead. This was all his fault, but surely he hadn't meant to do it. That was why he brought them here.

But what could they do?

Then Cloven remembered.

Swiping at her eyes and giving a determined sniffle, she shrugged off her knapsack and produced the hot pepper jam pie. If anything could save Peter...

She stabbed a stick into the pie. The wood burst into flames, and she daubed the bubbling jam onto Peter's shoulder.

The ice trickled away, leaving a perfectly dry, thawed spot on Peter's shirt.

Miss Floraleen, hiding her face against Frozen Peter's neck, didn't seem to notice. But Bramble stared, a grin creeping from ear to ear.

Please let it work!

In less than a minute, the last bit of ice melted, and Peter fell limp to the ground.

Miss Floraleen leaned over him, cradling his face in her bony hands. "Peter," she whispered, "wake up."

After an achingly long moment, his eyes fluttered open.

"Floraleen," he murmured, a smile spreading across his face. "I was dreaming about you."

Cloven and Bramble deemed it prudent to turn their backs and cover their ears, for a tone like that meant only one thing. They did not care to witness kissing, no matter how much adults insisted it was "sweet," and they "would like it when they're older."

Soon a hand touched Cloven's shoulder. She turned to see Peter and Miss Floraleen, smiling so wide it must have hurt their faces.

Something in Cloven's heart seemed to crack. She hugged them both tight, a sob rising in her throat. "Don't ever leave us again!"

"I won't," said Peter's warm voice as he ruffled her hair. "Let's go home."

Cloven released her grip on Peter and Miss Floraleen long enough to scan the air for the Weepy Moonbug Thing. There it hovered, smiling the buggiest smile Cloven had ever seen.

"Thank you, Mr. Bug." Cloven blew it a kiss. The beetle turned from crystal blue to a deep rose-pink. She giggled.

Miss Floraleen stood, one arm around Peter. "Mr. Bug, would you lead us home?"

The Bug gave an eager buzz, its blush dimming a little, and started off into the Woods.

Peter scooped up Cloven with his free arm, and Miss Floraleen's hand held Bramble's tight. "How long have I been gone?"

"A week," Bramble said. "And boy, has the Hollow changed! Everyone's throwing pies at each other, and all the Limberlongs are mad at the Whipplewilds, and all the Whipplewilds are mad at the Limberlongs..."

Peter blanched, glancing at Miss Floraleen. "I... missed our wedding?"

Miss Floraleen's cheeks flushed. "No, just postponed it by accident."

"I'm sorry," Peter murmured. "I'm so, so sorry. To all of you."

Cloven laid her head on his shoulder. "It's all right." She closed her eyes, smiling just a little. "After all this time waiting for a papa, what's a few extra days?"

"You, little sapling—" she could hear the smile in his voice— "raise a very good point."

I am pleased to inform you that the family, led by the glow of the Weepy Moonbug Thing, which no longer wept, straggled out of the Woods just in time to see the first rosy rays of sunlight kiss the sky.

I am less pleased to inform you that they saw a good many more kisses that day, all less metaphorical than the first.

The moment the villagers laid eyes on Miss Floraleen and Peter, every Whipplewild and Limberlong among them decided there was nothing for it but to hold the wedding at once.

The whole troop, dripping jam, marched straight to the marriage glen; it was all Cloven could do to pick a bridal bouquet of pinkweed en route. Peter, held fast between a barn-broad cousin and Miss Floraleen's equally burly third-cousin twice-removed, hardly had time to straighten his jacket before the parson asked for vows.

Cloven and Bramble decided, to avoid as many unpleasantries as possible, they had better close their eyes for the entire ceremony.

Afterward the family returned to the cottage in the gimble-tree. If you were to look for them, you would find them happy there still.

And if you were to ask how I know for certain, I would tell you that I, long ago, was a little girl named Cloven.

VICTORIA SHANKS

Victoria Shanks is the oldest of five siblings raised on the Bible, Bigfoot stories, and creek mud. She writes vibrant fantasy and science fiction about faith and family, found and blood—stories to remind her readers they are never alone.

Between midnight writing sessions, you can find Victoria deep in bluegrass country, hiking the woods, cooking with too much garlic, or consuming caffeine while muttering to her black cat Fish.

Achievements

- Has written four novels and multiple short stories.

- Received and implemented multiple professional edits on her projects, including from science fiction author Daniel Schwabauer.

- Published short stories "Resurgam" in the 2019 One Spark anthology, "Memory Knife" with Story Embers in 2023, and "What Happens at the Lake" with Havok Publishing in 2024.

- Honorable mention in the 2020 Writers of the Future contest.

- One Year Adventure Novel student contest winner in 2018 (2nd Place) and 2019 (1st Place).

- Runner-up in the 2022 Story Embers short story contest.

- Attended the 2024 RealmMakers writing conference.

- Received extensive training in platform-building, focusing on email marketing.

- Taught middle school and high school students literature and creative writing for three years.

Pitches

- An adult space western in the vein of *The Mandalorian*, centering on a bounty hunter hired to save a crystal-mining town from the outlaw who killed his family.

- *Winter, White and Wicked* meets *The Line Between* in a YA fantasy following a con artist and his estranged father's journey to deliver a cure for the plague ravaging their nation.

- *Sky's End* meets *Pirates of the Caribbean* in a YA fantasy trilogy about a scientist-turned-sky-whaler's quest to cure the ailing behemoth beneath her planet's gas sea.

THE FIRST ADVENTURE

LEXI JO HEUSER

"Peanut Butter, no!"

But twelve-year-old Harley's cry came too late. The chunky pug with the curly tail vanished. His empty harness thunked down on the cracked sidewalk.

A second later the puppy reappeared a few feet away, next to an empty Doritos bag. He promptly shoved his face inside of it.

"You would think I didn't feed you," Harley grumbled as she quickened her step, the now-empty harness dangling from the blue leash. "And what have I told you about teleporting out of your harness?"

"But you don't... Mmmffff. Grmmfff... feed me Doritos." Peanut Butter shook the bag off his head and allowed Harley to put his harness back on his round body.

"That's because they're bad for you."

"You eat them."

Harley couldn't deny his logic, nor could she hide the smile that came over her face as she studied her new sidekick puppy. He was a bribe from her father, an effort to convince her not to throw a fit because he was leaving Albuquerque, NM on yet another work trip come summer.

Harley's heart lurched at the thought. His work was dangerous. It wasn't like the movies. Superheroes could die. Her mother was the proof. Why couldn't her father see that she needed him, too? If she lost both parents....

No. She refused to think about it. He would be safe and come join her at her uncle's ranch like he had promised.

Her father's bribe wasn't going to work the way he wanted, because she wasn't about to stop asking him to stay home. Still, she would hug Peanut Butter close. It was impossible not to love the little guy.

"We have to get home." She picked up the empty chip bag and started off down the sidewalk, her shadow tall in the evening light.

Once they reached a trash can, illuminated by a light post, she chucked the bag inside. Harley glanced up at the post, noting the wind-battered flyer taped to it.

"Missing: Sidekick Beagle Puppy. Use caution, power includes ability to deafen those in a twenty foot radius with his bark. $100 reward for any information that leads to Marvin's recovery."

Harley pursed her lips and shook her head. Those poor people. She knew firsthand how quickly people grew attached to a new puppy.

Who would steal one anyway? Granted, sidekick pets could be powerful, but stealing them was illegal, not to mention just wrong on so many levels. Plus, non-supers had a difficult time containing and training them. So, whoever stole him had to be a super.

The real question was *why*. Harley's criminal investigating dad always talked about how important determining motive was to solving a crime. Knowing why someone might steal sidekick animals would make finding the culprit much easier.

Harley shook her head and focused on the chilly fall air. She didn't want to care about the stolen dog. Solving crime was dangerous. Her mother's absence was all the proof she needed.

She quickened her step towards home.

"Wait up!" She glanced back to see PB running to keep up with her.

"Oh, sorry bud." She slowed down until he caught up.

"Thanks! Can I have dinner when we get home?" He wagged his curly tail so hard Harley thought he was going to fall over.

"We can both have dinner when we get home."

"Ooooo, can I try some of yours? I love human food!"

Harley laughed. "You can have a bite. But only one."

"All right." He turned his pouty brown eyes on her, but then a little dust devil rose up in the park, full of swirling leaves, and caught her attention. PB shimmered for a split second before teleporting.

Harley glanced around, but all she saw was the empty street, the trees dancing in the breeze, and the small park.

"PB? Peanut Butter?" she hollered. Her eyes stung with threatening tears. She couldn't lose him.

A small, startled yip caught her attention, and she wheeled towards the park.

A boy with curly brown hair who looked to be a couple years older than her held Peanut Butter in his arms. He looked vaguely familiar, but she was too relieved to care.

"Oh thank you!" Harley said, running across the street towards the boy. "He gets distracted by—"

The boy took off, clutching Peanut Butter tight.

Harley activated her power and chased after them.

To his eyes, she would be invisible. He would still be able to hear her, though, so she sprinted through the grass where her footsteps would be quieter.

Harley quickly gained on the curly-haired boy. Zipping in front of him, she plucked Peanut Butter out of his arms, dropped to the ground, and kicked one leg out to trip him.

He hit the ground with a grunt, and his backpack fell off his shoulder. A green notebook spilled onto the ground, his name, "Richard Greven," was written on the front in bold, black print. She had seen him at lunch, sitting alone at a table while doing his homework.

He dove for the notebook. Harley stifled a yelp as she grabbed Peanut butter and ran from Richard.

She slowed to glance over her shoulder. He wasn't chasing after her, but instead running in the opposite direction.

"Are you okay, boy?" Her voice wobbled.

She hugged Peanut Butter tightly to her chest, feeling her muscles relax as he burrowed in closer, his small frame trembling. Her own hands were still shaking and she looked around make sure Richard wasn't coming back.

"I-I-I tried to teleport back to you, but I was too scared."

Harley parroted the words her father had told her at least a hundred times. "It's not your fault. It takes a lot of training to use your powers in stressful situations." A stick cracked under her foot, and she flinched. With another wary glance around, she jogged for home.

"Am I invisible right now? Or does it look like a floating pug is going down the street?" Peanut Butter asked.

Harley let out a faint chuckle. "You're invisible with me. Even if you were on a leash and I was invisible while touching it, you would turn invisible." *Thankfully.*

Harley turned left at the stop sign and beelined for the white house with the red trim.

The one her father had promised would start to feel like home soon.

She yanked the key out of her jeans pocket, supporting Peanut Butter with the other hand, and burst into the house. The door banged against the wall.

"Dad!" The word came out in a wail.

"Harley! Where are you? What's wrong?" His presence immediately eased the tension in her shoulders. His searching gaze confused her for a moment before realizing she was still invisible. Harley quickly flipped the internal switch so her father could see her.

"Somebody tried to steal Peanut Butter." Her voice broke, and she launched herself at her father's chest.

He pulled her close, smooshing Peanut Butter between them.

What if she hadn't been fast enough? The very thought made tears come into her eyes.

"Tell me what happened." His calm voice helped her to push back the tears.

"His name was Richard Grevin. He's about fourteen years old, five feet eight inches tall, wearing a dark Abercrombie hoodie. No visible weapons, and I didn't see him use any powers."

Peanut Butter wiggled his way free and bounded towards his water dish as Harley recounted the rest of the tale.

"He has math for first period," she continued. "I pass him in the hall every morning. Do you think he could be behind the other stolen sidekick pets?"

"I don't know. Maybe. I'll report this, love, but we're all focused on the string of store robberies. An eleventh happened just two days ago. Finding stolen pets—even sidekicks—won't be their main priority. If you think he's behind the other disappearances, you might have to do a little bit of legwork of your own."

Harley tensed. She wanted nothing to do with superhero work. But then she thought back to the stolen beagle puppy. Sure, it wasn't as big a deal as the robberies, but crime was crime. It mattered. Especially to the people who had lost their puppy.

"He can't just get away with it. Dad, surely you can get them to at least interrogate him."

"I'll do my best, love." He squeezed her shoulders, something he always did when trying to let her down gently. While he was in high demand as a superhero who could tell lies from truth, he traveled far too much for anyone to truly *know* him or to have any clout with the department, yet. Harley could never lie to him and get away with it, either.

A piercing beep interrupted her thoughts.

"Now, why don't you feed your pooch and I'll get our dinner out of the oven?"

Her dad smiled at her, his strong jaw and wide forehead softening. He ruffled her brown hair, an exact match to his own.

"Dad!" she squawked, but did as she was told.

"PB, time for dinner." She opened the plastic food container and poured half a cup into his bowl.

"Food, food, food, food! I love you!" PB teleported from the next room and paused to lick Harley's hand before diving headfirst into his food bowl.

Harley sighed. Everything in her life seemed to revolve around solving crimes no matter how much she yearned for a safe, peaceful life. What would having a parent who worked an office job be like? Who wasn't always moving around solving unsolvable crimes like her father? Who never had to face anyone or anything that wanted to kill them?

She still needed to refine her argument about why they should move to

Colorado and join her uncle on his ranch permanently. But even if she wasn't going to admit it, she already knew her father would never give up his job. Not even for her. He cared too much about other people.

Once they finished dinner, Harley walked to the living room and sat on the couch. PB jumped up next to her and laid his head on her thigh. The stolen beagle puppy was probably about his age.

Perhaps she could do some digging. Just a little. Then she would take her evidence to the police and let them handle it.

As she followed the river of other kids to the lunch room, Haley's phone pinged. She removed it from her bag to see a text from her Dad:

> *Another side kick was stolen last night, a cat this time.*

Harley texted back:

> *Do you know what powers it has? Can you look into it?*

Dad:

> *It can shoot low-powered lasers from its eyes. Not enough to harm a person though, so the robberies are still our focus. I'll be questioning a suspect today, so I can't kiddo, sorry.*

Harley:

> *I'm going to keep an eye on Richard today. Maybe I'll find something you can use.*

Harley slid her phone back into her pocket and stepped into the lunch line.

Three sidekicks had been stolen from the area over the last two months. Apparently Richard was smart enough to steal sidekicks that couldn't harm people. Not like the fire-breathing sidekicks.

She shuddered at the thought.

Harley thanked the lunch lady for her food and looked for an empty seat. Since she'd only been here for a week, she didn't have a set table, nor had she found many friends.

Her eyes landed on Richard Grevin, once again sitting at a table by himself. She looked away before he could notice her, and her eyes caught on brown-haired Katie. She was perky and talkative and had told her all about how she was going to be a cheerleader in their gym class that morning. When she noticed Harley, she waved.

Harley took her tray topped with lumpy mashed potatoes and limp green beans and walked towards her. She made sure that she passed by Richard and noted animal fur on one of the sleeves of his hoodie. It looked much like Peanut Butter's, which she was forever pulling off her own clothing.

Why would he steal sidekick animals?

All Harley had been able to dig up on social media so far was that Richard had an older brother, liked video games, and his father worked in the safe-making business.

She arrived at the red square table and sat in the old, plastic chair.

"Hey Harley! How's it going?" Katie had mentioned that she was practicing her enthusiasm in order to be a cheerleader. Harley didn't think she needed to practice anymore.

"It's good. How about you?" Harley forced down the first bite of over-salted mashed potatoes.

Katie's lips turned down into a pout. "I hate math. It's, like, so confusing. At least it's Friday, and I have the whole weekend to figure out the homework."

"I can help you this weekend if you want to do it together." Harley liked the friendly seventh grader. She had been the first one to try and talk to her. It would be nice to finally have a friend. Plus Harley was good at math, so she really could help the girl out.

"That would so totally rock!" Katie pumped her fist.

"Hey, what do you know about Richard?" Harley tilted her head toward his table.

Katie's eyes turned towards him. "He's a total nerd." Katie said it the same way she would announce that the sky was blue. "He's probably the smartest person in school, and he always makes straight As. He keeps to himself though. I know he was bullied at the beginning of the year, but those guys got in so much trouble that it hasn't happened again. Principal Briggs like, almost expelled them."

"Wow."

"Yeah. It's funny, too, because his older brother is one of the best football players in the high school." Katie poked at a green bean with her fork. "But Richard is nothing like him. Hey, maybe I should ask Richard to tutor me in math?"

Harley pursed her lips. She didn't want to feel pity for him after he nearly stole Peanut Butter, but she couldn't help feeling kind of sorry for him. His life sounded lonely. A bit like her own.

Harley and Katie ate as they chatted, although neither touched their green beans. They finished their food and Harley dumped her tray, listening as Katie described the latest drama about who was going with who.

She dropped her fork into the bowl of sudsy water and turned to follow Katie.

Richard was right in front of her. Her eyes strayed to his sleeve, and she tried to decide if it was cat or dog fur.

What was he doing with the sidekicks?

The mystery consumed Harley's thoughts for the rest of the school day. Not even the normally fascinating history of the American Revolution could distract her.

When the final bell rang, she hurried to her locker and pulled her phone out. She pressed send on her dad's number and spun the combination lock as it rang.

"Hey kiddo. I'm already outside with Peanut Butter. How did your digging go?"

She explained what she'd learned as she put her history book in the locker and pulled out her homework assignments for the weekend.

"Hmmm. So nothing concrete."

"Could we keep an eye on him? Just see if he goes home or somewhere else?" Harley asked. If her dad saw him with the animals, Richard was done for.

"I'm sorry Harley, but I can't. I have to go back to the station after I take you home. You, however, could follow him and see where he goes. He'll never know you're there. And, if you need me, I'm only a phone call away."

"Dad, I don't want to be a superhero. I don't even want *you* to be a super-hero." Being a superhero got people killed, and because of that, she had to grow up without her mother.

Even as the words left her mouth, her gaze latched onto Richard.

His bulging gray backpack was slung over his shoulder, and he wove his way through the hallway with fast, yet deliberate steps.

What was he doing with those puppies? Was he feeding them? Peanut Butter could be one of the missing right now, and she wouldn't have rested until she found him. Could she really do less for these animals and their no-doubt frantic owners?

If she stayed invisible the whole time, she would be safe. Then she could take any evidence to the police.

"You can do this, Harley. Don't let fear stop you from helping people."

"All right. But I'm going to take Peanut Butter if that's okay."

"Good. He won't stop chatting my ear off. Somehow he talked me into sharing my burrito with him."

"Da-ad, he's gonna get fat!"

Her dad laughed as he hung up.

As she headed toward the parking lot, she stayed far enough behind Richard to be unnoticeable, yet close enough to keep him in her sight. She hoped he didn't get into a car, otherwise her stakeout would end before it began.

He kept on the sidewalk like he was going into the city.

"Harley, Harley, Harley, Harley, I missed you!" Harley jumped as the curly-tailed, smushed faced pup appeared at her feet. This time he had teleported his harness and leash with him.

"I missed you too." She glanced over and saw her father giving her a wave as he pulled away from the curb.

She stiffened her spine as she continued to watch Richard. *There's no turning back now.* She stooped to pick Peanut Butter's leash up, then eased around the corner of the middle school until she was out of sight.

Harley flipped her internal switch and turned invisible.

"Okay, Harley. You can do this."

"You can do anything! But can we get a snack on the way?" Peanut Butter asked as he wriggled in circles.

"Probably not, bud. You'll have to wait until dinner."

He let out a long-suffering sigh, but settled beside her. She was careful to keep her steps quiet, but as they entered the city, she stayed closer to Richard, afraid of losing him in the downtown foot traffic.

Hours passed in which Harley learned very little. Richard would stop in front of various stores and just stare at them for awhile. Then he would go inside and walk around like he was inspecting the place for mold before leaving again. Harley followed him inside, but she couldn't figure out what he was up to. He never bought anything and the stores seemed very random. One was a joke shop, another was a candy shop, and one was a phone store.

Dinnertime came and went. Her feet hurt from all the walking. Her stomach let out a gurgle to match the ones coming from Peanut Butter's belly. She had hoped Richard would lead her straight to the pets, but as he paused at the back of the local mall, her hopes were dashed again.

"Can we get frozen yogurt?" Peanut Butter asked.

Harley looked through the side mall doors. A frozen yogurt place was front and center.

"No, the mall closed about an hour ago."

Only a few cars remained in the parking lot, perhaps belonging to the janitors.

Why was Richard here?

She sent a quick text update to her father as she crouched behind a shrub at the edge of the parking lot.

"Hey, could that be one of the missing puppies?" PB asked.

Harley looked up and inhaled sharply. A husky puppy walked up to Richard, but its movements were stilted. Like a puppet's.

"There's more," she whispered as a cat and a beagle puppy approached Richard in the same manner. His face was screwed in concentration, but he seemed to relax slightly as the animals drew closer.

Harley counted. All the missing pets were accounted for. But what was Richard doing to them? They all sat at his feet, completely motionless.

He stood away from the doors, and pulled his hood up. Was he going to—

The beagle stepped to the doors, threw back its little head, and bayed.

Harley cried out and clutched at her ears, crouching down to cover Peanut Butter's with her elbows.

Harley dropped her hands, but she could no longer hear birds chirping, PB breathing, and the beagle puppy's bay. She wanted to speak or even yell to see if she could hear herself, but she stopped herself.

She put a finger to her lips and smiled when PB nodded and shut his mouth.

Maybe Richard's power was controlling sidekicks somehow. Harley had heard of people who could control animals, but she never heard of someone controlling *sidekick* animals.

The husky stepped forward next. He threw his head back like he was howling. And he must have been, because the mall windows shattered and fell in a soundless waterfall.

Of course a husky would have a supersonic cry.

Harley shook her head in the hope her hearing would return faster. She doubted anyone within hearing distance of the mall would have heard the windows shatter because of the beagle's deafening bark.

Richard had really thought this through.

The husky pawed at its ears in the most normal motion Harley had seen from it yet. Richard glared at the dog, and its paw dropped like a stone.

Bright green beams shot out of the cat's eyes, hitting the cameras inside the mall lobby. Harley was certain either the beagle's bark or the husky's cry took out the rest of the security system.

Richard was going to rob the mall. He was probably the one behind all the robberies. Those stops at the stores, had those been him determining the best ways to rob them?

Harley forced her mind back to the present.

What could she do? What *should* she do?

Sweat formed on the back of her neck as she watched the cat finish shooting out the cameras.

Her breaths came faster and the world seemed to grow dim. Blackness threatened her vision.

"Harley?"

Peanut Butter's voice helped her focus. Harley's vision cleared.

The cat returned to the line, but the beagle puppy was sniffing the ground. Richard turned and kicked at him.

The beagle cowered back into line. Richard apparently couldn't control all the animals at once.

"Stay where I put you, stupid mutt." Richard half-yelled.

The beagle's deafening bark had worn off.

Harley took a deep breath and whipped out her phone. She texted her father with shaking fingers, but he would never get here in time to stop Richard. She didn't even know where the closest police station was.

She was the only person close enough to do anything.

Tears threatened as she thought about her mother, the only one close enough to help when a bank was robbed over a year ago. They had taken hostages. Her mother apparently figured walking through solid objects was the perfect solution. Bullets would go right through her.

Yet when the robbers fired his gun at a hostage, she purposefully didn't use her powers. She was a superhero and trained to save lives. Even if it meant sacrificing her own.

Because of that sacrifice, Harley would never again feel her mother's arms around her, never get to ask her for advice, never hear her laugh, or a million other things.

Harley decided that day she would *never* use her powers to become a superhero. She would never be taken from her family and devastate them the way losing her superhero mother had devastated her.

But now Richard was robbing the mall, and Harley was the only one here. She could try to stop him. Try to save the hard work and property of the store owners, and most importantly, rescue those poor sidekicks.

Or she could continue watching and keep herself and PB safe. She would be a good witness, and the police would be able to catch him later. That was the perfect solution.

"What's the plan, Harley?" Peanut Butter whispered, his little face crinkled in concentration. He was trembling, probably as afraid as she was, but he also seemed determined to help.

Shame washed over Harley. She had the power to make a difference here, to do the right thing and stop Richard from hurting people and those poor animals.

She was letting fear stop her.

Her parents had raised her to be better. She wanted to be brave, like them, and like Peanut Butter.

She took another deep breath.

"Do you think you can teleport us into the building if I grab Richard?" she asked.

Peanut Butter nodded. She smiled at him. His sidekick bloodlines were strong. He might be a small dog, but his power was not.

"I think controlling multiple animals at a time is difficult for him. If we distract him, I bet they can run away. Let's drop him in the frozen yogurt store, then teleport out. He'll be locked in there for the police. Then we can get those other animals out of here."

As she spoke, her fingers flew over her phone screen, giving her dad a brief explanation and begging him to hurry.

Still invisible, she picked up Peanut Butter and crept towards Richard, her feet as silent as possible. She clutched Peanut Butter tightly in her left arm as she threw herself forward and wrapped her right arm around Richard's throat.

"Now!" she yelled to Peanut Butter.

Within a blink they appeared in the frozen yogurt shop, locked inside.

Harley's invisibility flipped off as Richard jerked out of her hold.

Any second now Peanut Butter would get them out of here...

Suddenly Peanut Butter stiffened like his limbs were made of wood. He twisted his neck and tried to bite her arm.

"Peanut Butter! Stop, what are you—"

Richard was controlling him!

Harley set the still-fighting pug down and went invisible.

"Let him go!" she yelled, kicking Richard in the shins.

He let out a yelp and hopped on one foot.

"Harley?" Peanut Butter said as he shook his head, his legs wobbly.

As she hoped, the pain broke Richard's concentration.

He wouldn't be able to get them both out in the state he seemed to be in, and Richard could take control of him again in seconds.

"Get out!"

PB vanished.

"Who are you?" Richard looked around, still massaging his shin.

She stayed invisible, but decided to answer as she stepped behind a table.

"I'm the girl whose pug you tried to steal yesterday." She clenched her fists and tried to keep her voice from trembling.

"You're ruining everything!" he yelled, a hand slicing through the air.

"Why are you doing this, Richard?" She glanced back, making sure the gate was still shut. She wasn't going to take any chances of him escaping and taking control of the animals again.

"Everybody underestimates me," he said, his gaze near where Harley stood. "My own father is ashamed of me and my 'fake power.'"

"So you decided robbing stores was the way to prove him wrong?" She tsked like her father always did at a crook who did something unintelligent.

This seemed to be a cry for attention, and a part of her felt bad for him. But not bad enough to let him get away with it.

With a wordless roar, he charged in her direction. She dodged, then dropped into a crouch the same way she had yesterday. As he tripped over her, he threw his arms out in front of him. Instead of catching himself on the floor, his grasping hands caught her arm.

He staggered to his feet, yanking her up with him. Once he was steady, he wrenched her around until her back was towards him.

Pain stabbed through her arm, but her father's training kicked in.

She slammed her heel down on his instep at the same time she jabbed her free elbow into his stomach. He grunted, and his grip loosened enough for her to wheel and kick him right in the same shin.

She ignored her throbbing toes and backed up.

"Albuquerque PD, freeze!"

A cop cut the lock on the door while others, including her father, brandished their guns on a pale Richard. After they cuffed him, she let her invisibility go and stood with her hands raised high.

"This your kid?" an officer with a thick mustache asked, looking Harley over. Her father moved out of the shadows towards her.

"She's mine," he said, hugging her tight. She hugged him back, the adrenaline beginning to fade.

"We did it, we did it, we did it!" Peanut Butter appeared and ran from one end of the frozen yogurt shop to the other, pausing once to chase his own tail.

"And you did so good!" Harley knelt. She flipped him over and rubbed his belly.

"Does that mean I get an extra snack tonight?" he asked as he sat up, tongue lolling out to the side.

She laughed and shook her head as she stood and followed her father outside. "Maybe we can come back and get some yogurt when the store is open tomorrow."

"Can mine be peanut butter flavored?"

Harley laughed again.

One of the police officers took her statement, and asked how she got inside the mall and why. He then walked over to her father, and they spoke in low tones that she couldn't make out. Eventually, they told her she was free to go.

"What about the other pups, and the kitty?" she asked her father as he walked towards her.

"I thought we could return them, if you're up for it."

Harley nodded like a bobble-head and followed her father towards the animals.

"Honestly, do I look like the kind of cat that should be *caged*?" The gray cat licked her paw while an officer stared. Harley sensed interviewing talking sidekicks was not a regular part of his job.

"You, invisible girl." The cat looked up at Harley. "Thank you."

"You saved us!" Two rambunctious puppies ran up to her. The beagle wagged his tail until he smelled something on her shoe.

"I'm glad I could help." Harley dropped to her knees and scratched the husky's ears.

"Oh yes, right there. That's it," he said.

Harley and her father laughed as the husky thumped his back leg.

"Are you guys ready to go home?" Harley's dad asked.

"Yes please!" The beagle bounded to his feet. Once they reached the SUV, Harley opened the back door and helped the three puppies get in.

"Would you rather come up front with me?" she asked the cat.

"Indeed." She swished her tail as she waited. They climbed in the front seat and Harley's father punched the first address into the GPS.

A few minutes later, she deposited the cat into a blonde woman's arms.

The grateful tears pulled at Harley as she listened to her dad explain how Harley saved the animals. She blushed at the woman's thanks.

At the next stop, a boy a few years younger than Harley ran out of his house and yelled "Marvin!" The beagle wiggled in the boy's arms and licked his face.

At the last house, the husky leaped into a huge man's arms. He shed a tear, and something clicked into place. *This.* This was why her parents protected and served others. Why her father still did it.

Her father wrapped his arm around her shoulders as they walked back to their car. She slid hers around his waist and laid her head against his arm for a beat.

"Your mother would be so proud of you, kiddo."

"I hope so."

"I know so."

She laughed, even though it was cringey. He let go as they reached the car and she walked to the passenger side.

"I'm sorry I tried to get you to quit your job." Harley clicked the seatbelt into place.

"It's alright, Harley barley."

"Guys, come on! I'm starving!" Peanut Butter jumped onto her lap and licked her face.

"Gross, PB!" She pushed him down as her father laughed.

"Let's go home."

Home, Harley thought. She liked the sound of that.

LEXI JO HEUSER

Lexi Jo Heuser was raised on a ranch in a tiny cow town in Colorado. She fell in love with reading in second grade, and now crafts adventurous young adult and middle grade fantasy novels with western flair and plenty of animal sidekicks. When she's not working as a vet tech, you'll find her astride a horse, performing or teaching trick riding. Her favorite way to spend an afternoon is chasing cows or hanging off her horse upside down.

ACHIEVEMENTS

- Finished seven full length projects and one short story.

- Received and implemented a professional developmental edit letter.

- Started a successful business performing and teaching trick riding.

- Graduated from CSU Pueblo with an English BA- creative writing emphasis.

- Worked as a writing tutor through college.

- Self-published a ranch-style *Pride and Prejudice* retelling as her college thesis.

- Has a lifetime of ranching and animal experience that makes for realistic details.

- Is attending the Author Conservatory to hone her writing craft and learn business skills.

PITCHES

- A pegasus pony-express meets Louis L'Amour adventure novel where a girl and her trusty steeds must take on dangerous winged-courier work in order to save their pegasus ranch.

- An *Annie*-inspired tale of a young pixie who will do anything to find her real family—even work as a hand on a cattle drive.

- A Joan of Arc meets Greek mythology novel where a peasant girl and her loyal hog are sacrificed to monsters by her village—but nothing is what it seems.

WHAT LIVES BENEATH THE SKIN

JOSEPH BRINK

R *iiing!*

"Come on, Mum! Pick up!"

Cradling the phone to my ear, I double-check the number for the restaurant Mum and Dad are at for the evening.

I'm babysitting. So far, it's going great.

Quirk Number One of our new house: all the doors have at least three deadbolts. All the lights are on, the dinner dishes are stacked in the sink, and I've only had to call Mum and Dad four times with questions. Thus far, a smashing success, I'd say!

Riiing!

Through the huge living room windows, a distant flash of lightning illuminates the gnarled peach trees out back. Our house is dead center in a rambling, wild orchard, full of ripe, sticky fruit.

Since moving in three days ago, my little sister Milo and I have eaten so many peaches, we'd happily never see the fruit again. Unfortunately, the whole house reeks of them—Quirk Number Two, I guess—and the sickeningly sweet smell seems to get stronger every day.

Riiing!

What's taking them so long to answer?

Through the kitchen doorway, I notice the tub of cookie dough ice cream melting on the counter from dessert. *Shoot.*

"Milo! Can you put the ice cream in the freezer?"

At the same moment, a man speaks over the phone. "You've reached the Lake Monster Inn, Montgomery's top fine dining experience."

Milo darts out of the front hall wearing her yellow rubber boots. She sticks the tub of ice cream in the freezer, then hurries to the back door. "I'm looking out in the yard, Timmy!"

"Oh no, you're not!" I shout to Milo, before turning my attention to the phone. "Hi! Sorry about that."

Three deadbolts click, and the sliding back door scrapes open.

"Milo!"

I switch back to the phone. "Sorry, I need to talk to my Mum or Dad—Mr. and Mrs. Bancroft? They're at your restaurant right now."

I hurry into the kitchen as I talk.

The man laughs. "You must be Timmy! Your mom mentioned you may call. Said you'd already called several times. First time babysitting, eh?"

"Um... No."

I'm almost thirteen, and I've babysat Milo several times. The last time was two days ago, while Mum and Dad went out to buy cleaning supplies. They only left me babysitting for an hour, but that was long enough for everything to go wrong.

"Please, Sir, my parents?" I would have just called them directly, but last time I did, Mum said their cell phone was about to die and gave me the restaurant's number.

"Give me a moment." The line goes quiet.

Milo—who's seven—stands in the open doorway, staring into the dark back-yard. I grab her shoulder.

"No going out yet, okay, Milo? I'm about to ask Mum."

Veins of white lightning flicker on the black horizon, silhouetting the ancient trees. A warm, August breeze tickles my cheeks and rustles the sagging wallpaper around the doorway.

Quirk Number Three: The walls are all *way* thicker than normal walls and are clad in wrinkly, stained green wallpaper, with a dreadful, endlessly-looping pattern.

Oh, and they're gouged here and there as if slashed with a kitchen knife.

Guess that's what you get when you move into a house last owned by an old eccentric who abandoned it for several months. The place needs a *lot* of work. Mum and Dad plan on gutting the house, but we're stuck living here for a bit first.

Milo squirms out of my grip. "I'm just going to call." Face flushed under her blonde curls, she leans out the doorway. "Mr. Birdie! Where are you? Come to Auntie Milo!"

The darkness outside is thick, tangible. It coils around the house, drawing ever nearer. Trapping us inside.

Shivering, I pull Milo in and shut the door.

She presses her chubby face against the glass. "What if Bad-Squash gets him?"

I raise my eyebrows. "Bad-Squash?"

"Yeah! They talked about him in the newspaper!" Milo runs into the living room and returns with a rumpled news clipping. "It says a castaway escaped from that petting zoo, and that the zoo is best known for its Bad-Squash! Maybe it escaped too!"

Milo's at that age where she reads everything—and assumes it's all true.

I laugh. "You mean *Batsquatch*."

I'd seen the mascot on the petting zoo's sign—a Sasquatch with wings.

"You can't believe everything you read, Milo. Especially not in a town like this. Mum says the townspeople try to draw tourism by making up monster stories. It's probably just a guy in a suit."

"Maybe." Milo puts her hands on her hips. "But what about the castaway that escaped? What if he gets Mr. Birdie?"

"Castaways don't live in zoos, Milo."

She frowns. "Why? What is a castaway?"

I scratch my head. That wasn't something I'd ever thought about. "Someone who—um—is cast away, I guess?"

"Hey Timmy, what's up?" Dad's voice over the phone startles me. "Everything going okay back home?"

"Hi, Dad! Sorry for calling again. I had another question."

"Let me guess. The dishwasher?"

"No... well, I *was* wondering if I should run the dishwasher. But mainly I was wondering about Mr. Birdie. You know, Milo's stuffed flamingo? We can't find him anywhere, and Milo won't go to bed without him. She thinks he might be outside, but it's dark."

Dad sighs. "What do *you* think you should do?"

"I don't know. That's why I called you.'"

"Timmy, I know you'll be careful either way, so I don't really mind if you step out into the backyard. It's up to you. We love that you want our advice, but you've always been a great babysitter, and we trust you."

The scene from two days ago flashes through my mind: a broken lamp, shattered glass everywhere, Milo crying, all my fault.

I grip the phone tighter. "Everything always goes wrong—"

"No, not *always*. It went wrong once, but Milo's okay now, and we can all move on. You'll be more careful; I know you will. And if any emergencies do arise, call us immediately, okay? I want to help, but your mom and I think it's important that you make some decisions for yourself now that you're almost a teenager."

I swallow, mind flitting through everything that could go awry in an evening. "Okay, Dad. Sorry for calling—"

"Don't be, Tim-Tom. Hey, I need to go now. We love you, and will see you in a couple of hours, okay? Tell Milo Daddy says, 'Be good for Timmy.'"

"Okay. Bye, Dad."

"Bye, Timmy." The phone clicks as Dad hangs up.

Milo darts over and grabs the receiver. "Bye Daddy!" She plops it down again. "*Now* can we go find Mr. Birdie?"

Thunder rumbles. A breeze sends branches laden with golden fruit thudding against the window. A huge glossy feather, barely visible in the dark grass, drifts in the breeze outside.

Does Batsquatch have feathered wings or bat-like wings?

I tear my gaze away. *There's no such thing as Batsquatch.*

"Sorry, Milo, you're going to have to go to bed without him. I'd rather not have you going out there right now, and Daddy says you've got to listen to me."

Pouting, Milo lets me lead her down the hall.

She halts. "Mr. Birdie!"

A stuffed flamingo sits at the foot of the stairs, staring at me with beady black eyes, his leash—an old skipping rope—piled around him. Directly behind him is a three-foot gash in the sagging wallpaper. Next to it, the locked cellar door.

Milo sweeps the stuffie into a passionate embrace. "You naughty boy! Auntie Milo was worried sick about you!"

I frown at him. "We walked through this hall! Where were you, silly bird?"

Mr. Birdie's glass eyes glitter at me as if suppressing laughter.

Milo grabs my hand. *"Now* it's bedtime."

"All aboard! *The Bedtime Express!*"

With Milo and Mr. Birdie on my back, I march up the stairs.

"Choo! Choo!" Milo shrieks.

Fixing my gaze on the door at the end of the upstairs hall, I break into a run.

Milo laughs. "Chugga-chugga-chugga—"

"Choo! Choo!" we scream in unison as we duck through the doorway, cut into the much-too-thick wall, and crash-land on her bed. Milo squeals with laughter.

She scrambles across the bed and retrieves *The Magician's Nephew* from her shelf. "Read to me?"

"Not tonight. It's late enough as it is."

"Mommy would let me!"

Would she? I half-consider calling her, but I already know the answer.

"No, Milo. Sorry. Another night, okay?"

We'd already finished the teeth-brushing and pajama-putting-on before discovering Mr. Birdie's untimely absence, so it doesn't take long to pray together and kiss her—and Mr. Birdie—goodnight.

I pause in the doorway. Dad never answered about using the dishwasher, and

I'm hesitant to call him a sixth time.

"Milo, do *you* think I should run the dishwasher?"

Milo sits up. "No way."

"Oh?"

"You'll break it, like you broke that lamp! Then *you'll* have to go to the hospital."

I shove my hands into my pockets. "I'm sorry. Are you still mad? I was just trying to fix it."

She flops onto her pillow. *"Milo* isn't mad, but Milo's foot is a bit mad. It's still a bit owies from the glass."

My gaze drops to Milo's feet, twin lumps under her quilt. I'd just been trying to change a lightbulb. Who knew glass broke so easily?

"Sorry, foot. Sorry, Milo."

She giggles. "Foot wants a goodnight kiss too!"

I make a gagging face. "*You* can give 'Foot' her goodnight kiss. Goodnight, Milo. Sleep tight. Don't let the monsters bite!"

Wincing at my own words, I turn off the light. I step into the hall, closing the door against the darkness within.

I wash the dishes by hand, carefully, not wanting to shatter anything again. I'm wrestling hardened-on pasta off a pan when footsteps pad down the hall.

Milo peeks around the corner, dressed in her fuzzy pink PJs. Mr. Birdie's leash stretches behind her. "Timmy, there are noises in my room."

I stop scrubbing. "What sort of noises?"

"Growly noises, coming from the walls." She inches closer.

I begin washing again, unable to meet her eyes. "It's an old house, Milo."

Milo pulls Mr. Birdie closer. "What's that mean?"

I stare into the sink. "It's what Dad told me when I mentioned hearing some noises in the house. He said he'd look into it, but it was probably just the house settling, because it's old. Whatever that means."

Milo darts forward. "You've heard them, too?"

"Yeah, but they can't hurt us. It's probably just mice or bugs or something."

"Bugs? Eww!" A huge grin spreads across her face. She's one of those girls who finds bugs both repulsive and wonderful. "It's not bugs, though. It sounds *way* bigger. Unless they're *people-sized* bugs!" Her eyes light up. "Or maybe it's Bad-Squash or the castaway!"

I glance at the adjacent wall. I wouldn't be surprised if a person-sized creature *could* move inside that much-too-wide wall.

What would Mum do?

That one's easy.

Drying my hands, I head down the hall. I avoid looking at the three-foot gash in the wallpaper at the foot of the stairs.

"Let's get you back to bed, Milo. Mr. Birdie will keep you safe from any giant bugs."

Milo scoops up her stuffie and follows me up the stairs. "Very funny. Mr. Birdie's superdy-duperdy scared of bugs. I keep *him* safe. I'll eat the bugs before they can eat him."

I laugh. "You're so weird!"

She darts past me, cackling.

I freeze in her bedroom doorway. "Milo! You took my light?"

My lighthouse night-light sticks out of a wall plug, casting strange shadows against the opposite side.

Milo flops onto her bed. "Mr. Birdie needed it! There were noises in the wall! Mummy says you're too big for a night-light anyway."

"*You* don't need it; you're not scared of the dark! You're not scared of anything." The words come out higher and louder than intended.

Milo crosses her arms. "The dark never had scrapy, whispering walls before. Mr. Birdie's tewwified!"

I bend down to unplug the lighthouse.

Milo darts in front of me. "Timmy, please? Pretty please? Mr. Birdie will *die* of nightmares otherwise!" She holds up Mr. Birdie in my face and wiggles his stubby, stuffed wings. "Think of the poor wittle flamingo! See how scared he is? Besides, you just said monsters aren't real!"

I frown. I'm supposed to be the mature babysitter here, and I don't want her to be scared. Monsters aren't real, right?

I'll be safe without it. Maybe.

"Fine. But just this once."

"Yay! You da best, Mr. Timmy!" Milo growls in Mr. Birdie's voice. She pushes Mr. Birdie's plush beak into my face.

"All right, back to bed, Milo!"

I set *A Monster Calls* on my bedside dresser. I can't focus on reading.

Switching off my reading light, I pull my covers higher. Without my night-light, the darkness crowds in, suffocating me.

My mouth tastes dry and papery. A clock ticks, punctuating the stillness.

Something rustles.

Just the loose wallpaper. *Probably.*

A quiet hiss.

Click—click.

Like someone repeatedly pressing the button of a pen.

I reach for my reading light. Something rustles as I move—

Just my starched sheets against my clammy skin.

I flick the light on, and the noises stop. The room is unchanged. After three nights here, it still feels unfamiliar and alien. My old dresser and bookshelf look out of place against the green wallpaper.

I flick the light off.

Click. Click.

It still sounds like a pen. Or perhaps two sharp objects clacking together.

I freeze as a deep, throaty growl rumbles through the darkness. Thunder? My imagination?

I switch the light on.

Silence.

Shivering, I slide under my covers.

I lie there for a long time, joints stiff, eyes wide. Sweat makes my sheets cling to me. The smell of peaches saturates the room.

Then the lights go out, plunging me into suffocating darkness.

Not just my reading lamp.

The front hall light I'd left on no longer shines up the stairs. Nor does the light in the bathroom.

I lie there, petrified. The rumbling growl returns. So low it's barely audible. So quiet I can't be sure it's real. The hissing and clicking begin anew.

I clutch my blankets closer. My pillow is icy under my cheek, and yet a bead of sweat trickles down my forehead.

It's just bugs. Just big bugs crawling through the wall. Human-sized bugs.

Not reassuring at all.

The noises seem to pass through the walls, down the hall, down the stairs, fading...

What could it be? Batsquatch?

Monsters aren't real! Right?

A new sound comes from the other direction, like something being dragged along the floor.

I sit up.

Milo?

The moonlight paints a stripe across the hardwood floor outside my open door. My breath catches in my throat.

Something *is* being dragged outside my door.

A pink lump, pulled by a skipping rope.

I slip out of bed. I peer through the doorway. Mr. Birdie glides down the hall and out of sight around the corner. He *thump-thump-thumps* down the stairs.

I tiptoe down the dark hallway, staying in the center, away from the gouged walls. I try the light switch. Still not working.

At the top of the stairs, I stop. Mr. Birdie lies on the fourth step from the bottom. Below him, something crouches beside the cellar door, details impossible to make out. It looks too small to be Batsquatch...

Now that I think about it, though, I don't know how big Batsquatch really is.

Batsquatch doesn't exist, silly!

"Milo?" My voice comes out as a whisper.

The small figure is pulling back the flaps of wallpaper, next to where we'd found Mr. Birdie. It straightens at my voice.

I let out a breath I didn't know I was holding.

"Timmy! I'm *sure* there's something in the wall!" Milo gives the wallpaper a tug. It rips wider.

Goosebumps prickle down my bare arms. Hurrying to Milo, I pull her gently away.

"Let's not touch that. We should get back to bed."

Milo tugs on my hand. "I don't want to go to bed! Your nightlight broke, and Mr. Birdie's trau—trauta-mized."

"Traumatized," I say instinctively.

"Trauz-matized?" She frowns. "Anyways he's that, whatever that is. Can you fix the light, Timmy?"

"The hydro's out, Milo. Sorry."

"Then can I have a flashlight?"

"I don't know where they are. Except the one down in the cellar with all the unpacked boxes." In the dark.

Milo squeezes my hand. "In the dungeon? Can you get it, Timmy?"

I don't want to think about the darkness lurking in that windowless concrete room beneath our house. But I also don't want to think about Milo lying awake all night, eyes peeled for motion in the shadows. I've endured too many nights like that and can't let my sweet sister suffer that way.

Batsquatch won't be in our cellar. Of course not.

I fish the key off the hook beside the door and unlock the cellar. "Fine. Can you hold the door open?"

Milo nods and pulls open the thick door, grunting under its weight. I hesitate in the pitch-black opening, heart thud-thud-thudding a staccato rhythm in my chest.

Don't let Milo know you're scared, Timmy. Be brave for her.

I count the steps as I tiptoe down. The hallway above casts a faint light, but not enough to see much.

I remember Dad had set the flashlight on top of the box nearest the door. I feel around for it.

"Milo?"

"What is it, Timmy?" she calls back.

"Nothing." My hand closes around the flashlight.

I just wanted to hear your voice.

Milo gives a sudden cry.

The heavy cellar door slams shut. Sealing me in darkness.

I flick on the flashlight, dismayed at how little light it gives. Charging up the stairs, I wrestle the door open.

The hall is empty.

No Milo.

No Mr. Birdie.

No nothing.

The gash in the wallpaper is slightly wider now. For the first time, I realize there's no drywall behind the wallpaper here. Just a gaping, black hole. Big enough for Milo to fit through.

Steeling myself, I lift the flap and look inside. Immediately, I'm hit by the strong stench of peaches. So, *this* is where the smell was coming from.

"Milo?"

No answer.

Pointing my flashlight inside, I see dark, hollow emptiness stretching out in either direction. A fresh bout of shivers passes through me.

I guess this is Quirk Number Four: Creepy passages in the walls.

Milo can't be in there.

She's upstairs. She must be.

I charge up the steps. "Milo? *Milo!*"

In her room, the bedsheets lay tangled together, still warm.

My room's also empty. Same with Mum and Dad's. I avoid the deepest shadows. My skin prickles with the horrible sensation of being watched.

Where could she be?

I call her name as I run downstairs and scour the kitchen, dining room, and living room. The ticking of a clock, a faint rustling, and my pulse thudding in my skull are the only answers.

Why would she crawl into the wall?

Unless she didn't have a choice.

An icy dread seeps through me.

What if my imagination isn't playing with me? What if something's in there, living beneath the skin of our new house?

The picture from the petting zoo's logo flashes through my mind. A huge ape-man, fangs bared, muscles bulging, wings outstretched.

Multiple gashes scar the living room walls, the largest over in the far corner.

What if the slashes came from inside the walls? Batsquatch had pretty sharp claws in the picture.

Calm down, Timmy, I tell myself as I pace the living room, gaze gliding across the ugly wallpaper.

But I don't know what to do! Tears sting my eyes. Despite my best efforts to keep Milo safe, everything's gone wrong!

Do what you always do. Ask an adult. Mum and Dad will know what to do.

I can barely make out the living room furniture in the trace glow of moon-light through the curtains. My eyes settle on the tall floor lamp I broke, splintered glass shade still hanging on it. I wish Mum and Dad would get rid of it. I wish they'd learned not to trust me with Milo. Every time I babysit her in this house, I end up landing her in the hospital or getting her abducted or something.

My fingers tremble as I attempt to dial the number for the restaurant. The buttons on the landline don't beep like they usually do. I hold the phone to my ear. No ringing. Not even a dial tone.

My fingers go white around the phone.

No.

It must have died when the hydro went out.

I set it down with a dull thud.

I'm completely alone.

I grab the receiver again and stare at it, but it's useless. Slamming it back into its holder, I choke back a sob. My mouth feels dry as sandpaper, despite the water welling in my eyes.

What do I do?

An inhuman low growl reverberates in the wall next to me. I flinch.

What is in there with my sister?

"I'm going to save you, Milo," I murmur.

But how? What would Mum or Dad do?

"We trust you," Dad had said. *"It's important that you make some decisions for yourself."*

The growl swells.

Click. Click.

Could that be Batsquatch's teeth clacking together?

I have no clue what Mum or Dad would do. I have to figure this one out for myself, and I don't have much time.

After taking several deep breaths and saying a quick prayer, I hurry to the hole in the front hall. I hesitate, reviewing my half-formed plan.

Climb into the secret passage, find Milo, and get out—while hopefully avoiding the monster.

I can't stop thinking about what could go wrong, but I also can't stop thinking of my little sister. Her messy curls, her infectious smile, and her motherly love for poor trauz-matized Mr. Birdie.

Trying to banish thoughts of sharp claws and sharper teeth, I plunge my hands into the ripped wallpaper and pull it open.

I'm coming, Milo.

Letting the paper fall around me, I climb inside, into deeper darkness. Drywall fragments crunch underfoot. The air reeks of peaches.

I point my flashlight's weak beam down the narrow passageway. Another large black feather lies next to my shoe.

Did Batsquatch have feathers? I can't remember.

Several wires cross overhead, but otherwise, the path is clear.

Gritting my teeth, I pick a direction and set off. Dust motes spin in my flashlight beam. Rotting peaches litter the floor alongside lumpy black droppings. Something's living in here, all right.

The corridor quickly reaches a "T," forcing me to choose a new direction. I go right. Wooden steps ascend to a dark hole in the ceiling.

Behind me, a deep rumbling echoes through the walls, seeming to come from all directions.

What if there is more than one monster in here?

I need to keep moving. I need to find Milo.

I scramble up the steps and enter an identical narrow corridor.

"Milo?" I whisper.

Something hisses in the darkness.

I hope it doesn't see my light, because I can't bear to walk the path in total darkness.

Around another corner, fluffy pink insulation clings to one side. I must be walking through an exterior wall. The floor opens with another set of steps descending.

As I go down, I nearly gag on the smell of rotting peaches. Underneath it, though, I detect a faint scent of fresh night air. The floor is carpeted with shredded insulation, sticky peach pits, animal droppings, and more black feathers.

The singing of cicadas wafts in on a warm summer breeze. Strange that I can hear them in here.

There! Along the floor, a large gap in the brick wall opens out into the night. This must be how the Batsquatch comes and goes.

Ahead, the path branches. I have three options: forward, to the left, or back the way I came.

Actually, make that four options. I could duck through the hole in the exterior wall and into the peach-scented night. *Escape.*

The fresh air tugs at me.

I shake my head.

I'm not leaving without Milo.

I don't have time to dawdle. Who knows what that monster is doing with my sister?

But if I keep picking passages at random, how will I ever find her?

I crouch, looking for footprints.

And find something better.

Running along the floor, half-buried by piles of insulation lies a skipping rope. Mr. Birdie's leash!

I follow the cord around two corners, moving deeper into the huge house.

Until I reach the end of the rope.

No Mr. Birdie, no Milo.

In the dark corridor ahead, I can just make out another turn.

A lump rises in my throat.

"Milo?" My voice is weak.

"Timmy!"

My breath catches.

Her voice! It sounds nearby!

Tears of relief well up in my eyes. I break into a run.

"Milo, I'm coming!"

Her small figure appears in my flashlight beam, squinting up at me. "Timmy—"

The shadows behind me shift.

Click. Click—

I spin.

Milo screams.

My body turns to ice.

A spindly appendage stretches over me, shimmering blue and blood-red in the light of my flashlight. Something long and sharp glints on the end of it. In a blink, it stabs down at me.

I dive toward Milo. Claws swipe through the air next to me. They slash easily through the drywall beside me, barely missing me.

Grabbing Milo, I run.

The creature charges, far too fast.

Ahead the passage splits. Huge scissor-like blades snap just beside my head.

Flicking off my light, I plunge to the left. I drop to the floor. Curled into a ball, I clutch Milo. She doesn't make a peep. Good girl.

The monster skids to a stop. A low hiss rattles through the corridor.

I squeeze Milo, tears flooding my eyes. The dark, my old nemesis, has saved us. For now.

Behind us, the throaty rumbling and *click-clicking* echoes through the walls, fading.

What was that thing? The blades, the flashes of blue and red, the tall spindly shape... None of it matched the picture of Batsquatch.

"I'm so sorry for going into the wall, Timmy!" Milo whispers into my ear. "It took Mr. Birdie! It grabbed his leash and pulled him into the wall while I was holding open the dungeon door, so I climbed in after Mr. Birdie but got lost in here! I thought I heard you calling, but I was scared it would hear me if I answered."

I keep my voice low. "I guess I was wrong about no monsters wanting stuffed animals."

We need to get out of here, but where? I can't remember the way back to the exterior exit I'd found.

The clicking stops. I hold my breath, listening.

There it is again, but muted. Different. Like the tapping of claws on polished hardwood floor.

The sound vanishes again.

The monster's out of the walls, in our house. There must be a way out of the walls nearby.

I wait for as long as I can stand before switching on the flashlight. The beam catches a curl of ripped wallpaper hanging through a large gash in the drywall farther down the corridor.

Crawling to the gash, I peer out. Moonlight shines through white curtains, silhouetting the living room couch and high-backed armchair. No sign of the monster.

Milo sidles up beside me. "Is it gone?"

I put my mouth to her ear. "Milo, I'm going to crawl out the wall and look for the monster. If it's there I'll distract it. You need run to the nearest piece of furniture and slip behind it. Try sneak to the front door while I distract it. Okay?"

Milo nods.

I climb through the hole, lifting her out behind me.

Taking a step into the dark room, I knock into something tall. I grab it before it hits the floor, the metal shaft cool in my hands. A floor lamp. The floor lamp *I* broke.

I'm in the corner of the living room. I've crawled out of the enlarged crack I saw earlier.

Something rumbles in the shadows beside me. Two shining eyes blink at me. A bladed head coils out of the darkness on a shimmering blue and red neck.

Mr. Birdie dangles from one of the blades.

Behind me, soft footsteps patter across the floor. Milo.

The creature drops Mr. Birdie and lunges.

Instinctively I bring the lamp up to block the blow. Breath hot on my face, its sharp, blade-like jaws snap an inch from my eyes.

I pull back, pressed into the corner against the couch.

In the moonlight, I see Milo, halfway along the far wall, crouching by the high-backed armchair. She starts to slide along the wall, toward me. Away from the hall.

I quickly shake my head at her. *Not this way!*

"Run!" I hiss.

She darts toward Mr. Birdie, lying splayed in the middle of the living room.

The creature's bladed head swivels. Clutching her stuffie, Milo ducks behind the coffee table just in time.

I tighten my grip on the floor lamp. The mistake that hurt my sister is now my weapon to save her. "Come get me."

Blindingly fast, the creature knocks me off balance. I crash backward, striking wildly with the metal shaft of the lamp. The broken glass shade comes off, shattering at the creature's feet.

A sharp claw swipes the air next to my face, ripping deep into the couch cushion. Breathless, I jab it with the lamp. Behind it, Milo disappears into the hall.

Hissing, the beast rears up, taller than Dad, fast, and vicious. A huge horn crowns its head. Dark feathers ruffle along its body.

Growling, it slams against the lamp, knocking it aside.

I dodge, bolting into the hall. Frozen in the far junction where the hall splits, Milo stares at my pursuer.

Claws clatter on the hardwood floor, gaining fast.

Grabbing Milo, I dive left toward the stairs and cellar. I yank open the cellar door. Shoving Milo into the gash in the wallpaper, I duck behind the door.

Simultaneously, the beast charges around the corner. It careens through the open cellar door. It halts halfway down the creaking steps and lets out a series of deep, rumbling hisses.

"Looking for me?"

Okay, that line sounded cooler in my head.

As the monster lurches towards me, I slam the heavy door.

A guttural cry erupts from the other side. Steps clatter under its feet. The creature hurls its weight against the door.

Ducking past me, Milo grabs the key off the hook and inserts it. The bolt slides into place with a thud.

I stagger back. Drenched in sweat, panting for breath, I flash a grin at Milo. Dirt streaks her fuzzy pink pajamas, and her curls stick out in all directions.

"We did it, Milo!"

Milo tries to smile, but bursts into tears.

"Oh, Milo." I wrap her in a tight hug.

The creature slams into the door again, hissing.

Milo shudders in my arms. Unlocking the front door, I pull her onto the porch, away from the "dungeon" and its occupant.

I gasp.

The wind has swept the clouds from the sky, setting it alight with fiery constellations. Below the domed cathedral of the night, tiny flickering yellow lights dance in the gnarled branches of the peach trees.

"Look, Milo! Fireflies! Have you ever seen fireflies?"

I've never seen fireflies or how bright the stars could be in a clear night sky. I've always been too afraid of the dark to go out this late.

Milo rubs her eyes, sniffing. "There's so many!"

She lunges at a firefly as it darts just above our heads. She misses, but laughs through her tears.

Who knew the night could hold such beauty?

What is this strange world, containing nights full of such terror and courage? Full of stars and fireflies and sweet sisters and creatures as strange and deadly as the one we have trapped in our cellar?

Now what? What should I do with Milo? And the monster?

But these thoughts no longer worry me. I'll figure it out.

I sit on the steps.

Milo scoots next to me, her warm body pressed against mine. "We beat him?"

I nod, holding her small, soft hand. "I'm so proud of you, Milo. You stayed calm and helped me catch the monster. You don't have to be scared anymore." I kick a pebble off the steps and listen to it skitter away into the dark. "I wonder what that thing was. It clearly wasn't Batsquatch."

Milo raises her eyebrows. "It was a castaway! *Obviously.*"

"What?" I laugh.

"There was a picture in the newspaper!" Milo pulls a rumpled piece of paper from her pajama's pocket. "See? I bet it came here for the peaches while the house was empty and moved in."

I take the newspaper clipping. The picture displays a funny-looking creature: black with two spindly clawed legs, and a horned, beaked head on a blue and red neck.

I scan the article.

"You're right! As soon as we get the telephone working, we'll have to call the zookeeper."

A huge grin spreads across Milo's face. "See? Told you so!"

I squeeze Mr. Birdie. His glass eyes catch a little starlight and twinkles. "I bet it thought Mr. Birdie was one of its babies, or one of its species, at any rate."

Milo squints at Mr. Birdie. "But Mr. Birdie's not—"

"A castaway?" I laugh. "It's pronounced Cassowary, Milo. It's not a monster. Just a big exotic bird."

"A bird?" Milo takes the picture back. "Aww, it's so cute!"

"It did still try to kill us, Milo."

Down the driveway, headlights come into sight. Our parents!

I stand. "Come on. We have quite a story to tell!"

Hand-in-hand, we step off the porch, into the night and into a sea of fireflies.

She smiles up at me. "You're the bestest brother in the whole wide world, Timmy."

That dimpled smile, those sparkling eyes. Those are worth all the fear, all the danger, all the pain. She's worth it all.

I laugh. "Love you too, Milo."

JOSEPH BRINK

Growing up, Joseph Brink steered clear of scary stories. Now he writes delightfully scary stories that give kids courage to face the frightening things in their own lives, intentionally weaving in threads of light, beauty, and hope. When he's not writing, brainstorming a new story, or reading 100-year-old horror novels and books about cryptids, Joseph loves spending time with his kid siblings, reading aloud to them, and sharing his favourite books.

ACHIEVEMENTS

- Drafted ten full-length novels and several novellas and short stories.

- Received and implemented a professional edit letter.

- Has drafted a 90K word novel in less than a month . . . twice.

- Attended the Write to Publish writers conference in 2023 where he received two full manuscript requests.

- Started a landscaping business with over 30 regular clients where he practices marketing skills.

- Has been published with Havok Publishing and Keys for Kids Ministries.

- Built an email list to more than 200 subscribers in the first month.

PITCHES

- *The Mothman Prophecies* meets "Gravity Falls" in a Middle-Grade Mystery about a 13-year-old skeptic, who, to save her family's small town radio station, must investigate local cryptid sightings connected to her father's death.

- Jonathan Auxier's *The Night Gardener* meets Katherine Arden's *Small Spaces* in a dream-like Middle-Grade thriller about a boy in foster care who must choose between his new family and his old when he and his twin brother become the targets of a sentient nightmare.

- *The Magician's Nephew* meets *Coraline* in a quietly unnerving Middle-Grade novel about a girl who sets out to save her only friend from the new girl on the block—a girl who *collects* friends.

SAPLING OF THE SEA

SEA

A.A. ROLLINS

A cool water current brushes against my shoulders. I pat the sand around a tiny seaweed plant and smile at Mr. Weedle. "I love doing this."

Mr. Weedle's gray beard twitches. "You're a natural, Malcolm. Ready for the next one?"

I gaze at the plants lining my sandy driveway. Their leaves dance as the water ripples over them. I sway, too, imagining a gentle tune.

I whisper to the new plant. "You've got this. You're gonna grow big and tall, just like your friends." I rub the soft, rubbery leaves between my fingers and let out a breath. A bubble forms before floating away in the current.

In the distance stands the Great Tree, the dancing of its seaweed leaves visible from here. I smile as I think of how its roots sustain Lanori.

How cool would it be if I got to play a part in fostering plants that help our community thrive?

I shake my head to clear the thought away. I can't do that if I'm a Handyman.

"Hey, Mom!" I glide into the living room where she's resting on the cushy couch.

"Malcolm! How was your gardening session?" Mom places her leaflet on the driftwood table and kisses my cheek. The scent of roses drifts to my nose.

"Good! I laid three plants and told each of them my saying." I blush at the last words.

Why am I always embarrassed about talking to plants?

Mom ruffles my hair, which she always says is the same color as sand. "That's swell."

"What is?" My brother Preston swishes into the room, a wrench in hand. His electric blue tailfin flicks back and forth.

I gulp. "Nothing."

He shrugs. "Do you want to help me and Dad with a welding project? We're gonna start soon." His voice cracks and his face flushes pink.

I unsuccessfully try to suppress a grin. They want *me* to help?

"Sure!" I launch after Preston toward the wooden workshop door.

The emerald green in my tailfin catches the light as it flutters with excitement. Tools hang from the wall opposite me, and Dad hovers by a large wheel.

Dad blows out a breath. "Welcome, boys! Ready for a rad project?"

I push stones and metal scraps aside and plop down on the counter. "What is it?"

"We're making a wagon. A customer had a run-in with a turtle and needs a new one."

"Don't want that to happen again, right?" I chuckle, but the room around me stays silent.

I swim forward and take the wrench from Dad. He puts a hood over the scrap pile, and Preston pumps a lever. Water flows out from under the hood, the current yanking a tiny sprout back and forth.

I don't notice I'm swaying with the tiny sprout until it stops. It shrivels up and falls over, its life source gone.

Why am I suddenly out of breath?

Dad leans forward and gestures to Preston. "Hand me the torch, Son."

Fire ignites inside of the water-free zone, and Dad sticks his gloved hand under the hood. He bends a piece of metal, his tongue sticking out in concentration. He gestures for the wrench, and I jump, quickly passing it over. Dad bends the metal until it's like an elbow, then waits until the fire turns it blue.

Dad hands the torch to me, the movement so fast I fling my hands out to catch it.

It slips from my fingers at the same time Dad yells, "No!"

The torch falls, smacking Preston's hand.

Preston sucks in a breath and grips his red-hot fingers. Blisters bubble up along his knuckles.

"I'm sorry!" I rush toward him only to be shooed away.

"Get some ice, Malcolm," Dad says.

I look around frantically.

"Not here. In the kitchen." Preston's gaze is hard.

I rush to the door, retrieve some ice, and rush back to the workshop only to have Preston yank the ice from my grasp.

"You're never gonna be like Dad at this rate! He was working for the king by the time he was thirteen. You can't make that much progress in two years. But hey, that makes sense based on how stupid Gardeners are."

An image of dark caves fills my mind. I remember when a Gardener passed by and every mermaid in the vicinity snickered and pointed.

I ball my fists, but Dad's hand on my shoulder eases my tension.

"Preston, please don't be rude." Dad turns to me. "Thanks for your help, Malcolm. How about you go see if Mr. Weedle needs anything?"

My heart sinks like a pebble to the ocean floor. Even Dad doesn't want me here now.

How can I possibly help Dad if I can't hold a torch?

I flip my tailfin and watch sand clouds float up. The current overtakes me, and I sway back and forth.

In the distance, the seaweed leaves of the Great Tree sway in the water.

A smile touches my lips, but it's gone when the memory of dropping the torch flashes through my mind.

I toss my lucky stone upward, and cup my hands to catch it as it sinks.

A rattling pulls me from my trance, and I turn to see two vibrant yellow sea-horses pulling a chariot. I almost topple from the waves but regain my balance. All I can see through the dust are gold wheels shimmering in the sunlight.

"Wow. That thing goes fast." Dad must've made it. Will I ever make something that cool?

A movement catches my gaze. In front of me, a drooping piece of seaweed shivers.

An inner tug pulls me toward it, and I flop onto the ground. I pat sand around it and lift its leaves. It can't die!

"There you go." I give a leaf a kiss. "You'll be all right."

The seaweed plant stops shivering and begins dancing with the current again. Warmth floods through me.

"Hey, Malcolm. How goes it?" Alex, my best friend, gazes at the chariot. "Did your dad make that?"

I hope he didn't see me kiss the plant.

I force a chuckle as I place myself between Alex and the plant. "He must've. Isn't it amazing? I want to be just like him one day." I punch the sand. "Probably won't be, though."

"How come?"

I explain how I tried to help with a project and ended up hurting Preston. "I just wanted to help, but I just mess everything up."

"You sure do!"

I whirl around at my accuser.

Preston floats there, holding up his bandaged hand. "But hey, I guess that makes sense. Gardeners don't do much anyway."

"Just because you don't know what we do doesn't mean we don't do anything."

Wait. Did I say *we*?

"Keep telling yourself that."

I glance at the seaweed, and a sudden calm fills my veins. The feeling vanishes when I turn back to Preston, who smirks.

He rushes away, tail snagging on the plant I just saved. The sand around it crumbles, exposing the roots. Sharp pain jolts through my chest.

"Stop!" I race to untangle Preston before he can rip the plant out completely. My focus and the pain in my chest drown out his protests.

I push the plant into the ground and pat sand around it. "There you go. You'll be okay." The pang in my chest weakens to a slight throb, then vanishes. A couple of leaves curl up against my skin like they're hugging me.

When I go to glare at Preston, he's gone.

Meanie.

I turn to Alex, trying to think of what to say. "When do you go for your test?"

"In a few days. Dad's convinced I'm going to be a Builder. Wouldn't that be cool?" His eyes light up.

I chuckle. "Yeah! You've always been fascinated with how stuff works around here."

"Mhmm. What about you?"

"I don't know yet. Hopefully soon—I'm tired of worrying I'll be a Gardener."

A merman passes by. "Let's hope not," he whispers.

I, the son of the king's Handyman, can't afford to be a Gardener. I'd lose everything.

Hopefully I can figure out what to do. Soon.

Alex pats my shoulder. "For what it's worth, Malcolm, I think this ocean could use more merpeople like you."

"Thanks. I think I need to go home."

Alex gives me a high-five, and I sprint away before he can see my first tear fall.

Knowing my way home, I don't care that I can barely see through my tears.

Crack.

Electricity shoots through my arm, and I blink to clear my vision. Bubbles of blood float to the surface of my skin. Lying on the ground is a thick, dark brown branch.

Don't let it be.

I look around. There, on the side of the town's Great Tree, is a splintered edge where the broken branch used to be.

I broke the Tree. I broke the Tree.

The tips of the broken branch curl up and wither.

What have I done?

I dash home, hoping no one saw what I did to the Tree. By the time I reach the front yard, my tears are being pulled into the ocean's current. I blink so it doesn't look like I've been crying, then twist the wood-slatted door's seashell knob.

"You okay, Malcolm?"

I ignore Mr. Weedle's concern and throw the door open. As I tumble inside, only a broken whisper as a cry for help comes out.

"What's wrong?" Mom asks.

"I broke the..." I swallow the lump in my throat. "I broke the Tree." A cry that sounds like a wheeze escapes me.

Why can't I hold a sob in?

"Shh. It's all right." Mom pats my back. "What happened?"

"I was with Alex, and then swam home." I suck in a breath. "The next thing I knew I had busted a limb off the tree!" My arms shake despite my begging them to stop.

Mom squeezes me tight before pulling away with her hands on my shoulders. "Listen to me. You're okay. We'll figure this out."

"It w-withered." A searing pain in my chest pulsates.

"It withered?" Mom takes a deep breath then lets me go. "We'll figure out what to do. Okay?"

"Figure out what?" A deep voice booms through the water.

I slowly turn to Dad. "I broke a branch off the Tree."

Dad frowns, then his eyebrows shoot up. "The Great Tree? That can't happen. It's the town's power source!"

"I know." My steady voice doesn't match my nerves.

"What's going on?" Preston huffs as he swims into the room. "Oh. Did Malcolm do something again?"

I ball my fists. "Don't. You're not perfect, either!"

Preston laughs. "Maybe not, but I'm on my way to far greater things than you, Gardener."

I try to shove the pain in my chest away. If I broke the Tree and can't make things, Preston may be right.

But I won't let him win this time.

"Ready to go?" Dad slings his chain-link pack over his shoulder.

I suppress a groan and steel myself. "Ready as I'll ever be." My insides sink more than a trident in the water.

Dad grins. "Great!"

As we exit the house, the sun's bright light makes me squint. We swim across the sand-packed road towards a dark stone cave nestled in a strip of shops. Its exterior stretches far above the roofs of a bejeweled tail salon and a seashell-decorated restaurant.

The water's temperature drops as we enter the dark stone cave, and I shiver.

A few tail flaps later, we enter an unexpectedly bright pink room with an unnecessary plush carpet. Large teardrop-shaped jewels hang from a chandelier bigger than my entire body, and my nose burns from the thick, musty smell.

"Malcolm Murphy?" A mermaid with stringy black hair looks over her thick-framed glasses at me.

Is she staring into my soul?

"That's me." I raise my head and follow her through a curtain of beads.

The lights are so bright I can't see where I'm going. Suddenly they disappear, making my head spin.

Is this all meant to feel like a dream?

A dark cove sucks me in as I swim over the threshold. I blink and look around. The dark room is lit up by fluorescent green lights hanging from the high ceiling.

A rush of warmth flows through my chest, and the knots in my stomach unravel. I sigh. Maybe this isn't so bad after all.

"Hello there, young mermaid!" A sing-song voice drifts through the water and pulls me gently from my trance. "My name is Rosemarine."

A mermaid with a glittery pink tail swims toward me. Her curly white hair hangs in a braid over her right shoulder, partly obscuring the pearl chain clinging to her red-rimmed glasses.

"How are you today, young man?" She pats me on the shoulder.

"I'm okay. Just nervous."

Rosemarine lets out a bubbly giggle. "No need to worry about that! You'll do just fine." She places her glasses on a desk and picks up a pair of green rectangular ones.

She beckons me closer and smiles gently. "I'm going to put my spectacles on and whatever color I see coming from you will tell me what you are meant to be! Sound good?"

I gulp. "Sure."

I close my eyes and ball my hands into fists, waiting for the moment that'll determine the rest of my life.

Silence follows.

I open my eyes to see Rosemarine frowning, flipping through an ancient book on her desk.

"Hmm." She looks at me, then at the pages. "Weird."

I tense. *Does it usually take this long?*

She takes off her glasses, closes her eyes, then puts a different set of frames on. She blinks twice, and her frown slowly turns upwards.

"Ooh, I don't see many like you!" She giggles. "You're a Gardener, young man!"

I stare open-mouthed at a grinning Rosemarine. "A Gardener?"

"Indeed. You're a magnificent Gardener!"

I swear I hear the sound of a record scratching. "Magnificent?"

Rosemarine blinks. "Yes. Gardeners are wonderful. Don't you know?"

I shake my head. "Everyone makes fun of them."

"Everyone who does so is as ignorant as they think Gardeners are." A rough laugh escapes her. "You're more important than you know, dear boy."

I uncurl my fists. Maybe Preston is wrong.

The swim home seems to take an eternity. I feel like everyone is staring at me. *Do they know?*

Dad says nothing when I swim through the door, so I flick my tailfin in silence as I chew my cheek.

What will my training involve?

I stop in my currents. Will I have to leave home and live with the Gardeners? Most apprentices live at home, but I don't know about Gardeners.

An image of a dark, cold cave fills my mind, and I shudder. I'd like to live at home.

"Well, hello!" Mom's voice drifts in from the living room.

I swim to the couch and lean over it.

Mom grins at me. "So, what was your result?"

I bite my lip. "I'm a Gardener."

Clapping ensues. "I knew it! My boy, a Gardener. What a pleasure to have something new in this house."

Did I hear her right? "It's a good thing?"

"Yes! We could use someone who likes plants around here."

"What about Mr. Weedle?" I wring my hands.

Mom's eyebrows rise. "That's perfect! He can teach you."

"You're not embarrassed?" I ask.

Mom frowns. "Why would I be?"

"Dad is the king's Handyman, and you design clothes for royalty. I didn't want to be a disappointment."

Dad grunts at my last words and swishes out of the room.

"I want to be normal. Like you two."

Mom pats my arm. "Normal is overrated."

Maybe. But at least it's not frowned upon.

I think of the broken branch, and the pain in my chest returns, but I ignore it. Maybe Rosemarine was wrong. Maybe I *can* be normal. I just need to try.

"Thanks, Mom." I swim to my room, smiling, but as soon as I see my kelp plant my resolve falters.

Will I have to give up loving plants? Who will take care of the Tree if I'm not a Gardener? I broke it after all. I need to be the one to fix it.

I decide to talk to Alex. He's normal.

I swim out the front door and am met by an array of multi-colored plants on the driveway.

"Hey, Malcolm!" Mr. Weedle calls as I rush past him. "Wanna see a cool new plant real quick?"

"Maybe later." I wave, but I can't resist the pulling in my gut. I *have* to see that plant.

I shake my head, willing the sensation to go away.

Why am I short of breath all of a sudden? I pull the pebble from my pocket and rub it. Maybe it wouldn't hurt to go check it out...

I take a deep breath and speed toward Mr. Weedle. The water current is so strong I nearly crash into him. I skid to a stop.

"Hey! Can I see the new plant?"

Mr. Weedle chuckles. "Changed your mind?"

I let out a nervous laugh. "Yeah, I just had to see it. Also, why am I out of breath? I swim fast all the time."

Mr. Weedle shakes his head, a tiny grin touching his lips. "You'll find out soon enough."

I tilt my head. *What?*

"Here it is." He lifts up a plant in the palms of his hands. Its leaves dance in the water, looking bluish this way and greenish that.

My mouth drops open. "It's different colors!" The plant's leaves stretch toward me. "And it's coming to me!"

"Indeed."

I reach out and touch a leaf. It wraps around my finger, tickling my skin.

"Is it hugging me?" Warmth erupts inside me like an underwater volcano.

Mr. Weedle winks. "It likes you."

I smile. It *likes* me.

"I'll plant it under your window, so you can watch it grow." Mr. Weedle sets it in a pot.

"Okay!" My grin practically touches each ear. "I'll come back to see it later. Thanks!" I wave, this time swimming away with a happy heart and lungs full of oxygen.

I swim to Alex's house as fast as my tail can push me.

Alex answers my knock almost instantly, and we head up to his room. I plop onto Alex's bed and sigh. "How do I become normal?"

Alex raises a finger. "You'll need to start by avoiding gardening."

"I can't do that if I want the Great Tree to live!"

Alex rolls his eyes. "There are other people who can fix it, Malcolm."

"But I told my family I would fix it." *They'll be upset if I don't. Right?*

Alex shrugs. "I don't know what to tell you. Maybe you could try to fix the Tree and *then* forget about plants?"

That could work. "Let's do that."

As we flow through the town center to get to the Great Tree, I rub my lucky stone. Despite Alex and me carrying a giant piece of wood, nobody stares. I doubt it would be the same way if we were carrying a giant plant, though.

I catch a glimpse of a Handyman working on a storefront. As he hammers nails into a sign, I can't help but wonder if that's really the kind of work I want to do.

As we near the Great Tree, my doubts deepen like a blue hole. Can I really give up caring for plants?

"You sure you want to do this?" Alex asks as we set down the wood.

No.

"It'll help fix the Tree. My contraption will hold up the sick branch while I stick the broken piece on. Then it'll act as a support while the Tree heals."

Alex blows out a breath and props his weight against the large board.

I lift Dad's hammer and roll the nails around in my palm.

Let's do this.

I place a nail on the giant board. I lift the hammer to hit it and miss.

"Ow!" I drop the nail and suck my fingers. "That hurt."

Alex snorts.

I frown. "Don't laugh at me."

He only shrugs, bending to pick up the nail. "Take two!"

When we're done, we both study our handiwork. The broken branch is now stuck to its host, and the plywood is supporting it.

I rub my hands together. "There we go!"

Something creaks, and the plywood crashes to the sand. A cloud of fine sand erupts in my face.

"I'm not sure I'm a Handyman."

Alex rolls his eyes. "That's because you're a *Gardener*." He claps my shoulder. "Come on. Let's go do something else."

I watch as my little plant, Hedgie, sways back and forth. The water current pushes against it, but it just takes it as it comes. I begin to sway with it.

Should I just accept what comes my way, too? What if it's terrible? What if I'm never accepted again?

I focus on fluttering with Hedgie. *Take it as it comes. Take it as it comes.*

"You ready?" A chipper voice asks.

Is it time already? I turn to see Mom peeking around the door. She's smiling, her eyes bright as if my future isn't about to be placed into the hands of cave people.

I wave goodbye to Hedgie, and Dad gives me a tight smile.

The swim to the caves is so silent, I can hear my blood pounding in my ears.

We pass the Great Tree, its broken branch convicting me. Parts of other branches have started to wither, even turning gray.

I wince.

Mom puts an arm around my shoulder. "It's okay, Malcolm. Everything will be okay."

Stay strong.

I look up at her and nod, but I can't help thinking I broke a tree, and I'm a Gardener? I can't build, and I'm certainly not a Fashion Designer. So who am I?

Can Gardeners teach me what to do like Handymen do for their apprentices? Or do I have to have a knack for it already?

We head down a sandy slope, the waters getting darker, colder, and quieter. Many of the caves are taller than my house, and I try not to think of pitch-black rooms and crazy mermaids.

I rub my lucky stone. *Calm down, Malcolm.*

"Well, hello there!" A merman waves. His smile could light up every single dark corner of a cave.

I can't help but smile back.

"Hi." My voice is shaky, but my fears have lessened. He doesn't seem as scary as I imagined.

"I hear you're our newest addition." The man sticks out a hand, and I shake it. "I'm Mart."

"Yes. I'm M-Malcolm."

"Malcolm!" His grin widens. "What a wonderful name! You're going to love it here."

I follow Mart into the nearest cave. I clench my teeth, readying myself for darkness.

What greets me is a large room brightly lit by a massive hole overhead. I look up with wide eyes. The hole is a tunnel leading up into the open sea, and the sun winks at me.

Around me mermaids carry containers of green-leaved plants and pots of purple and pink flowers. The water shimmers like sparkles suspended in the air. The sand beneath my tail is soft and thick, perfect for burying even the most delicate of plants.

"Welcome to the Sea Tunnel." Mart extends his arms. "This is our center of activity. It's a meeting area that connects to other rooms. Everyone loves it here because the light is brightest. But don't worry! Everywhere else is bright, too."

We tour the rest of the Gardeners' headquarters, which consists of three floors, each with a dozen different rooms. Each are filled with plants of all varieties. Some I've never seen before. In planters on the walls, on shelves, growing out of chests, sitting in windowsills.

This place is alive.

And I've never felt better.

We end up back in the Sea Tunnel, and Mart blows bubbles, creating a *hmmmmm* noise. Everyone turns to him.

"Our new addition has arrived! Malcolm, our next Gardener, will be joining us soon to take on the noble art of Gardening. Please welcome him with the best bubbles!"

Hmmmm. The sound swims around me from all directions. When the bubbles cease, crinkles fill the corners of each Gardener's eyes.

They're not just happy I'm here.

They're happy to *be* here.

As I flick the latch of my window, push the circular pane outward, and breathe deeply, I wonder what I'm going to do about the Great Tree.

The salty scent mingled with soil and seaweed relaxes my muscles. The sea is bright today, but not enough to make me squint. The city spires gleam in the distance.

Taking one last look at my room, I pocket my stone, and swim through the window.

Straight toward the Gardener's caves.

A little shaded area greets me as I near the caves. The water is cool, and the constant buzzing in my ears is gone. I don't ever want to leave.

I peer into the opening of the Sea Tunnel and smile. Among the busy Gardeners, a merboy a little older than me pauses, his white-blond hair swishing to a stop.

"Hey, you're the new Gardener, right? Let me show you around." He swims deeper into the room without waiting for a response.

I shake my head and follow him, veering off my path when my tail twitches excitedly.

"I bet Mart has shown you everything," he says as he turns a corner.

I stop short and my eyes go wide at the sight of tall, thick columns in every corner. Fluorescent green liquid floats inside each one, lighting up the purple walls.

"What do you guys do in here?" I whisper almost reverently.

"This is my favorite room. It's where we play games when we're not studying." The boy moves to a table on the left wall and pulls out a chair. "Let me show you what I'm working on!"

I sit beside him. "What's your name?"

"Theor. I've been a Gardener since...how old are you?"

"Eleven."

"Since I was twelve," Theor finishes. "Man, you must have a lot of potential! I don't know any Gardener who was discovered at eleven."

I frown. "What do you mean? I thought a bunch of kids got tested at my age."

"Yeah, but Gardeners don't always show at that age. Something in their DNA makes it hard for Rosemarine to tell." Theor shrugs. "Like I said, you're one-of-a-kind!"

I rub my lucky stone. Is that a good thing?

"Who's your mentor?" Theor leans back in his chair.

"I don't know yet, but I'm hoping Mr. Weedle. Do you know him?"

"Yeah! He's like a legend here. Always disappearing to do mysterious stuff." Theor's eyes glaze over as if he's dreaming.

"Cool. So, what's being an apprentice like? Do you live here?"

"Yes. My family are Gardeners, too. I know plenty of mers who go home at night." He tilts his head. "Don't worry about your family. You can live at home!"

I blow out a breath so hard it makes a rush of bubbles. "Okay. Thank you."

"Mhmm. As for being an apprentice, your mentor will teach you what you need to know, plus his specialty. Hands-on training is the way we do things here, so you'll be a shadow and helper. Sometimes mentors will bring their apprentices on a field trip."

I smile. I never liked sitting still in class.

"Here's my current project!" Theor scoots a glass container with six sections over to me.

Green seedlings sit in water instead of soil, their roots different colors and sizes. Their leaves flutter in the current, and I'm reminded of the little plant who danced with me.

"Why are they in water?" I stick my face in front of one, studying the roots. They pulsate, just like a beating heart.

Theor grins. "I thought you'd never ask. I'm experimenting with water growing conditions. If we can see what the roots are doing, maybe we can encourage growth and limit disease." Theor takes a deep breath. "No one knew plant roots beat like a heart, at least not in water! I'm trying to figure out if they do it in soil too."

"Interesting! Do you think they'll move in soil?"

Theor shakes his head. "I'm inclined to think they only pulsate in water because they have room to move around." He frowns. "But how else would plants grow in soil if they couldn't move?"

An idea forms. "What if you made some sort of device that helped you know what's going on underneath soil? Maybe something that can detect movement."

I start bouncing in my chair. "Maybe like a beluga's echo-whatever."

Theor's mouth drops open. "That's brilliant! I told you you were one-of-a-kind."

Next, Theor takes me to the library. We flutter down a hall to a door at the end.

I freeze when I enter the room, and I can't help but stare, unable to breathe. The ceiling is higher than anything I've seen before.

Bookshelves made of shimmering agate, iridescent opal, and shiny marble tower over me. Books sorted by color shimmer in the light from the domed ceiling, and oak tables with books piled ten high on their surfaces line the center of the room. The sand beneath my tail is tightly packed with crystal bits, and they sparkle when the light hits them just right.

I rotate, trying to see every angle. But it's too much to take in, and my vision starts to spot with color. I rub my eyes.

"It's amazing," I breathe.

Theor clears his throat. "I love the light."

"I think I'll spend forever in here." I grin, but my smile quickly fades. *Am I ready to be a Gardener?* It sure seems like it.

I look to Theor. "I think I should get home."

"Bye!" Theor waves.

I flip my stone into the open water and watch as it slowly sinks into my palm.

The pain in my chest flares when the Tree comes into view. Its leaves sag, its branches a little more gray than the last time I saw them. It looks like the Tree is frowning.

This is something I need to fix. I flick my tail, and a sand cloud bursts at my fin.

I suck in a breath. Why can I not breathe suddenly?

Making a silent promise to the Great Tree to fix it, I rush away, lucky stone pressed into my palm so hard it hurts. It doesn't feel so lucky now.

I swim to the outskirts of the city where the houses become few, and the plants run wild. I stop in the middle of a patch of plants. From blush pink petals to emerald leaves to spiky stems, they all dance to their own song. Before I know it, I'm humming as my body sways to the rhythm of the plants.

My lungs fill with oxygen, lighting up my mind and healing my aching head.

I stop swaying. Can I breathe better here? I shake the question away and kneel by a plant. I touch its velvety purple flowers, and a grin spreads across my face.

The air here is a symphony of each plant's song, and I'm lucky enough to breathe it in.

I rush back to the Gardening library.

Minutes go by as I scan each bookshelf. Every book here relates to Gardening, so finding one specifically about the Tree is uber difficult.

I clench my fists. I won't give up. I spin around, taking in the vast array of shelves, books, and plants fluttering in the water.

A hunter green book flashes in the corner of my eye, tugging me toward it.

I swim to the second highest shelf of the amethyst bookcase.

The air is easier to breathe up here where the seaweed is—just like the field I visited earlier. I take a slow breath, closing my eyes as I imagine the oxygen filling my lungs.

When I open them again, I run my finger down the green book's spine. *Healing: A Beginner's Guide* stares back at me.

I check the book out and rush home.

The airy feeling I have vanishes when I reach the Tree. In the few minutes I've been gone, it's drooped even more. The green leaves are falling off, floating in the water. The bark is peeling away, leaving the Tree looking more like a skeleton than a brilliant coral.

I swallow the lump in my throat.

I need to get home.

When I reach my house, I climb through the window, lock it, and toss the book on my bed.

Lanori's golden, moss-covered city roofs and seaweed-blanketed building walls catch my gaze. I sigh as I turn away.

I hope I can grow beautiful plants like those one day. I just need to fix the Tree first.

A thought slams into me. Could I be a Gardener because my skills are needed? If I fix the Tree, maybe I'm useful after all.

The book is heavy yet soft in my hands when I pick it up. I hold my breath as I read, like any sudden movement will dissolve the light that points the way out of my tunnel of ickiness.

"Alrighty. Let's see what you need." I place my hand on the Tree trunk and look at my copy of *Healing: A Beginner's Guide.* "It says here I need to harvest the energy of the plant in question so I can help heal it. Do you have any idea what that means?"

The Tree obviously says nothing, but warmth flows through me instead. I tilt my head. "Uhh, what was that?" The warmth solidifies. Strangely, I now feel like I can do anything.

I frown. "I'm gonna say I'm reading too much into this." I study the book again. "Feel the plant speak to you as it tells you what it needs."

I shut the book. "Any of this make sense to you? Because it doesn't to me." I stop. "Unless..."

A vast field of brightly colored plants fills my mind.

I turn in the direction of the water's current.

A memory of me kneeling next to a dying seedling, whispering words of encouragement floods my mind.

The tendrils of my new plant from Mr. Weedle wrap around my hand, and I giggle.

My eyes fly open. "That's it!" I hug the Tree, and suddenly it feels like it's hugging me back. I bounce, jostling my stone in my pocket. "Thank you, Tree! I'll be back before you know it."

"Do you have books on the Tree different from the one I checked out?" My words tumble out as I look at the librarian.

She blinks. "Yes, I believe there are some scrolls in the back room you can look through." She frowns. "It's odd we don't have anything else. I guess all this time the Tree has taken care of itself."

"Thanks!" I speed toward the door on the left and push it open. Pain shoots through my eyes as I blink away spots from the sudden darkness. Is there a light in here?

A warm glow radiates from the corner, and I swish over to it, clutching my stone. Something hot shoots through my palm.

"Yikes!" My stone falls to the ground, bright as the neon green plants I keep hidden in my closet.

The exact same color as the glow coming from the corner of the room.

"You sure are my lucky stone, aren't you?" I kick it with my tail all the way to the warm light.

An orb in the center of a chest pours out light, and I lay my stone atop it, wincing as heat burns my skin. The second the two touch, torches on the walls flicker to life, bathing the room in a fiery glow.

I suck in a breath. "What is this place?"

Wooden chests line planked walls, their sides reinforced by a light silver metal.

The sand in here is thick as if it hasn't been used in centuries.

I open the closest chest next to me. A cloud of fine silt poofs when the lock is released, and I cough to clear my lungs. Inside, scrolls upon dusty scrolls lie untouched, the bleached seaweed that's surely thousands of years old free from wrinkles.

Delicately, I pick up a scroll, waiting for it to disintegrate in my hand, dooming yet another thing. The scroll unrolls without so much as a sound, revealing lines and lines of intricate script.

Is everything in here like that? Are all the scrolls filled with script and covered in magic that preserves them? Or are they just cared for in a way like no other?

I gently replace the scroll and scratch my head. I feel a tug to a chest on my left, and before I know it, I'm sitting inside and digging through the scrolls.

What am I looking—

Crack.

I fall through the bottom of the chest and land hard into more sand. I open my eyes to a vast room lit by a pale blue light.

Towers of scrolls fill the room, some stacked higher than my height.

What just happened?

I look up. The scrolls I was digging through hover over the broken chest bottom. *What in the sea?*

The tug in my gut gets stronger. I follow where it leads, turning left and right. I plunge into darkness the pale blue light barely touches. Just as my chest feels about to burst, I reach into a small gold box, taking in the ornate leaf designs engraved in its surface.

My fingers wrap around a scroll. I pull it out. It's as white as the day it was made, yet with edges begging its old age.

I slowly unroll it. I frown at first, then I'm practically bubbling over with excitement.

"Could this help save the tree?" I spin around, clutching the paper to my chest.

Drawn on the scroll is a giant tree with swirling seaweed and coral-like holes. It's our Tree—the one I've nearly destroyed. But that's not the only thing on the page.

Below it is a tiny sapling, barely reaching above the base of the Tree's trunk. It has a canopy of leaves instead of long seaweed, and its trunk is solid. It leans toward the Tree and suddenly, I'm reminded of Mom's hugs.

The Tree has a baby.

My heart wrenches. Is it possible the Tree is sad, and I didn't almost kill it? Can I reunite them?

My last hope is dashed when I read the script at the bottom of the page.

The Tree has an offspring protected at all costs by the Gardeners of Lanori. In any instance where the Tree becomes injured or dies, the Sapling is to be planted next to it to provide healing. Without it, Lanori will never survive. Protect the Sapling at all costs.

I inhale a deep, musty breath. Not only does the Tree have a baby, only the Sapling can save it.

If they're so important for each other, why were they separated in the first place? Where is the Sapling?

I roll the scroll back up and gently hold onto it as I swim back through the chest. My plan to save the Tree is now set. Now I just have to find the Sapling before it's too late.

"Theor!" I pull to a stop next to my new friend in the game room.

He looks up from his plant containers. "Wha—? Oh, hi, Malcolm! What can I do for you?" His hair is ruffled like he fell asleep scratching his head, and he has dark circles under his eyes.

"Do you know anything about the Sapling?"

"The what?"

"The Sapling." I unravel the scroll and show him. "It says if the Tree is hurt, its offspring can save it. But I don't know why they're separated!"

Theor frowns. "Where did you find that?"

"The little scroll room in the library. Have you never been there?"

He shakes his head. "I've never seen this before, but I have heard the ancient myth about the Lost Sapling."

I frown. "The Lost Sapling?"

He nods. "Growing up I heard a story of how the Tree had a baby and then it got lost. No one has seen it since."

"It can't be lost." I study the paper. "It says the Gardeners care for it."

Theor shrugs. "It's just a story."

Mhmm. And I'm a Fashion Designer.

There's no way it's just a story. Why else would an ancient scroll describe everything in such detail? And why would it have a perfect drawing of what the Tree looks like?

I shake my head and go to toss my stone. My hands close around nothing.

Where did it go? My mind drifts to the scroll room and the stone laying atop the orb. I rush back to the scroll rook and find my stone right where I left it. It immediately starts to cool when I pick it up.

"I gotcha, little stone. Sorry about that." I kiss it and then rush from the library.

It's time to find the Lost Sapling.

"Where do I start?" I lean against the bark of the Tree. "Your Sapling will save you, but where is it?"

A thrumming goes through my body. My mind drifts back to the library. Could it be there? No, surely I would've felt something if it was.

Wait. Since when did I start *sensing* the presence of things?

I shake my head and swim toward home, ready to write out a plan on my sketch pad.

"Malcolm, is that you?" Mom's voice drifts down the hallway, and I stop. *Should I ignore her?*

No, she already heard the door. I mentally slam my head against a wall and paste on a grin.

"Hey, Mom! I'm gonna go up to my room for a bit, okay?"

"Okay, honey! Just let me take a look at you." She comes into view dusting something from her hands. A smile stretches across her face, and her cheeks turn pink. "How's my little Gardener?"

"I'm fine. I, uh, need to..." My gaze drifts up the staircase, my fingers itching to hold my pen.

Mom laughs. "Go write your ideas!" She points to the scroll tucked under my arm. "What's that?"

I gulp. *Do I tell her the truth?*

"It's umm," I unroll the scroll. "It's something I think'll help fix the Tree." I show her the drawing, and as she reads, her eyes widen.

"Why, Malcolm, did you know that's just a story?"

"No, it's not. I think the Lost Sapling exists!" I shake my head and rush up to my room.

Surely it's not just a story?

I shrink in my chair as a heavy weight settles on my shoulders. Something thumps outside, and I bolt upward.

Mr. Weedle would know!

I open my window and look down at Mr. Weedle, who's humming while he pats soil around a plant. The soothing melody drifts up to my ears.

"Mr. Weedle!" I swim through my window to meet him. "I need to ask you something."

He turns around, and a smile stretches across his face. "Malcolm! It's good to see you. What do you need?"

My heart sinks like an anchor. I've barely acknowledged him the last... how long has it been? A week? Yet he still wants to help me. "I'm sorry." I hang my head. "I, uh—"

Mr. Weedle waits, and I reach out to touch the plant. Its leaves brush against my fingers, and a lightness flows through me.

"I stopped spending time with you because I thought I could be something else." I look him in the eye. "I wasn't sure I wanted to be a Gardener. But... I do."

There. I said it. And it's true.

"I love plants, and I can't stand not being around them. But when I hurt the Tree, I thought I couldn't possibly be a Gardener!" I throw my hands up, then let them fall to my sides. "So, I set out to fix it. And I found this."

The scroll feels smooth in my hands as I pass it to Mr. Weedle. I hold my breath as he reads.

Unlike when I told Mom and Theor about the Lost Sapling, Mr. Weedle smiles. He looks up at me with a soft glint in his brown eyes.

"You're so very much a Gardener, Malcolm. More so than any I've met in awhile."

I cock my head. "Really? But I hurt the Tree!"

Mr. Weedle shakes his head. "You did, but you also found something so hidden no merfolk has touched it since it was written." He rolls up the paper and hands it back to me.

"The Lost Sapling is a well-protected secret in this city. A group of secret caretakers tend to it to ensure its health and safety. No one else knows of its existence." Mr. Weedle sighs. "But you've learned when no one told you. I'm convinced it's because you're meant to be an amazing Gardener."

I frown. "Why is it hidden? Doesn't it need to be with its mom?"

The Gardener's shoulders sag. "It should be, but it was taken a long time ago when merfolk wanted to use its healing properties for themselves and their families. Without it, the Tree will die if it gets injured or sick, so the Sapling was brought to the caves and cared for away from where the merfolk could reach it."

My eyes sting, and my vision goes blurry. "It has to get back to its mom! She's dying." I suck in a breath to stop a sob from escaping.

Mr. Weedle pats my shoulder. "We'll go get him. I know where he is."

I blink the tears away. "You do?"

He nods. "Of course! I'm a secret caretaker. How else would I know about the history of our most precious plants?"

A laugh tickles my throat. "I guess you're right."

We're about to head toward the caves when I stop and glance at the smiling merman beside me.

"You didn't say anything about me ignoring you."

Mr. Weedle stops. "I didn't, did I?" He turns to me. "Well, Malcolm, I accept your apology. I understand where you're coming from. I felt the same way once myself."

"About what?" I wring my hands together.

The lines in his face deepen. "I was your age when I was told I was destined to be a Gardener, but I did not want it. Everything in me protested against it. Surely I wasn't meant for such a tender thing!" The lines disappear as his eyes grow brighter. "But the more time I spent around plants, the better I felt. I was a gentle spirit but never knew it until then. Gardening found its way into my heart, and grew a love of it from the roots that were always inside me. I wouldn't change a thing."

Suddenly I want to hug him, but I stop myself. "You feel better around plants?" *I thought I was the only one.*

He nods. "I'll let you in on a little secret. You're not supposed to learn this until you start training, but all the children of Gardeners seem to know it." He winks. "The reason we feel better around plants is because we help them photosynthesize. We release more carbon dioxide, and in return, we get more oxygen. It's a gift only Gardeners have. We make this water vibrant with the oxygen all of us need."

My mouth falls open. "Really?" No wonder I feel better when I'm around lots of plants!

Mr. Weedle smiles, the corners of his eyes creasing. "Well, we must get on with it if we are to save our beloved Tree before the end of the day. Shall we?"

We enter the Sea Tunnel and swim quickly into a corridor that goes up and up. When we reach the top, Mr. Weedle pulls out a seashell and inserts it in a hole of the same shape in the wall. A lock clicks and a door slides into the purple stone wall.

I gasp. "That's so cool."

Mr. Weedle laughs. "From the sound of it, my boy, you'll have a seashell key one day too."

"Really?" *Oh, that would be great. What if I could use my lucky stone?*

I look around, and my thoughts are immediately silenced.

Bags of fertilizer, tree food, and gardening supplies line the walls all the way up to the domed ceiling, where the column of water releases into the sea. In the center and all by itself, a tiny little tree waves its branches in the tiny currents surrounding it. Light shines off blue leaves the size of my pinky fingernail, and the trunk is white with brown splotches at the base of its branches. It's no taller than me, and when I reach out to touch it, everything in the world stops.

My heart seems to stop beating. My fingers freeze. I'm holding my breath. A single branch reaches out to me. Its leaves brush my cheek, and I let out a giggle. My anxious mind settles, similar to when I'm curled up in bed listening to Mom read a good book.

I'm safe. I'm loved. I belong.

"Quite something, is he not?" Mr. Weedle touches the leaves of the outstretched branch, and it curls around his arm.

"He's amazing," I breathe, stroking the aqua leaves.

"He likes you; I can tell."

I sigh. "Will he be safe out there?"

My friend nods. "He's grown much since he was out in the open waters. He can hold his own. Besides, he was destined for this. His time has finally come."

Bumps form on my skin. Maybe I was destined for this, too.

"Ready?" Mr. Weedle stops swimming and gently sets the pot on the ground. The Sapling's leaves stretch toward his mom, and she does the same.

I smile. "I'm so glad they found each other again." Mr. Weedle puffs out a breath, snapping me out of my daze. "Oh, sorry. Yes, I'm ready!"

I place a palm on the Tree's coral bark and begin whispering to it. "We brought you your Sapling. I'm sorry he's been gone for so long." I hug her, and when I flutter back, a rush of warmth floods my body.

"Put him right here." I swim to the other side of the Tree and hover above the correct spot. It's the first place everyone will see the Tree when they come this way.

Perfect.

Maybe the mom is guiding me.

I read Mr. Weedle the instructions on the scroll, and before we know it, the Sapling is tucked safely under the shadow of his mom's branches.

The Tree starts to straighten and stretch out its branches. Bits of seaweed poke through the rough bark, like the fuzzy hair of a nearly bald newborn baby. Translucent sap covers the sickly holes in the trunk.

The Lost Sapling is healing the Tree.

I restrain myself from clapping, resorting to bouncing and flicking my tail around.

"I'm glad you're getting better," I whisper. "Thank you, little Sapling." I pat its small trunk. A branch gently curls around my arm and squeezes.

"Good job, Malcolm." Mr. Weedle plants a rough hand on my shoulder. He smells of soil and sunshine.

"Thanks for your help." I look at the Tree and its Sapling. "I'm glad they're together again."

"You will make a great Gardener." A tear rolls down Mr. Weedle's cheek as I make eye contact with him.

For the first time ever, I actually believe it.

"I'm happy to be a Gardener." I grin as I stare at what my friend helped me do. "How can I repay you for your help? I was so rude to you."

Mr. Weedle grins. "Well, I think you would make a fantastic apprentice. How do you feel about being mine?"

"Really? Yes!" My voice cracks and I clear my throat. "I would love that."

"What happened?" Mom comes around me, her brow furrowed. "What is that?"

"It's the Lost Sapling. It's healing the Tree."

Mom's eyes widen as she glances between me and the Tree. "You did this?"

I look at Mr. Weedle, and a smile forms on my lips. "I had a little help."

Soon, a crowd begins to form around us. Merfolk murmur to each other, words like "Gardeners" and "useful" and "saved the tree" float around the water. Some people even point to me with wide eyes.

People don't think I'm weird after all.

At home, Mr. Weedle smiles encouragingly as I tell my family about the Sapling.

"That's my boy!" Dad smacks me on the back, and I wince. "Always knew you could do it."

I'm about to protest when Mom wraps me in a warm hug. I relax at the sound of her heartbeat.

"I'm so proud of you."

Heat rushes to my cheeks and I hug her back. "I love you, Mom."

"I love you, too."

"Uh, Malcolm?"

I look up and see Preston, his face pink.

What's he gonna say?

"So... I saw what you did the other day." Preston kicks his tail, and a cloud of sand rises. "Maybe being a Gardener is useful after all."

My insides warm. "Thanks."

I hover at my window, gazing at the plants outside. One of Hedgie's tendrils wraps around my finger. Leaves sway in the gentle flow of the water, and some flowers close up for the night while others open to begin their lives. I smile.

Nature is beautiful to behold.

A.A. ROLLINS

A.A. Rollins grew up with her hands in soil and head in the clouds, and is the proud best friend of not one, but two hummingbirds! Growing up with a disability means she knows what it's like to feel alone and misunderstood, so she writes stories that are a safe haven for kids like her, incorporating witty humor to showcase the positives in life. A.A. can be found reading, bingeing a detective show, drinking tea, caring for her roses, or training her service dog, Harley. She's always looking for another opportunity to make someone smile!

Achievements

- Written seven novels and two novellas.

- Was a founding graduate of The Author Conservatory.

- Received and implemented feedback from a professional edit letter for a novel.

- Owns a crochet small business, Crafting with Hope Shop, where she has grown her marketing and finance skills.

- Coordinates a group of volunteers for a prolife nonprofit.

- Will receive her Associate's of Applied Science in Paralegal Studies in May of 2025.

Pitches

- *When Sea Becomes Sky* meets *The Secret of Haven Point* in an upper middle-grade adventure novel about three disabled kids who work to save their place of belonging—the town's wildlife sanctuary—from destruction for oil drilling.

- *Ballet Shoes* meets *Leap* in an upper middle-grade contemporary novel about an injured ballerina who refuses to give up her passion after doctors tell her she'll never dance again.

- *Ranger's Apprentice* meets *Dragon's Green* in an upper middle-grade fantasy novel about a medieval archer with a gift for healing others, who must save his kingdom from a darkness that destroys creativity and imagination, while wrestling with his desire to avenge his father's death.

YOUNG ADULT
FICTION

THE SWORD ROSE
CALEB E. KING

P ierce faced his enemy. Through strands of dirt-blond hair, he locked onto the old hay bale sagging in its ties. His sword morphed into blurred silver, striking the side of the bale again and again.

High guard. Counterattack. Never remain stationary. Pierce's lips moved with the instructions in his head. Golden straws exploded into the air, floating away under the spring sun. He gritted his teeth, his lungs aching, begging for rest. *Don't stop. Keep fighting. They must never endure what you went through.*

His concentration drifted as exhaustion weighed his arms, but images flashed through his mind, renewing his motivation. His mother's face. Pale, hollow cheeks. Eyes the color of the sky, fast approaching dusk. The hundreds of days he'd toiled, working to afford her medicines. The letter, stating there was nothing more to be done. Hopelessness. Tears.

Snap. His thumb slipped as his hilt's leather wrap unraveled. He halted, gasping for air.

"Great." He turned away from the mangled haybale, now surrounded by hundreds of sliced stalks glittering in the meadow.

Blinking back sweat, he trudged through the tall grass. Time for yet another repair. How he longed for a new sword... Perhaps he could afford one, now that he and Da weren't paying for new medicines every month. The thought made him grimace.

His gaze rose to Coltonham, a quaint town amid rolling hills of farmland. He stepped onto the nearest road and traversed the familiar gravel lane.

"Hello, Pierce!" the town cobbler called from his shop's porch. "How's your ma?"

"She's all right, thank you." Pierce forced a smile as he passed, but a knot grew in his stomach. It was a repeated lie. He appreciated the townsfolk's care, but he didn't want to tell them the truth of his mother's unknown illness. Saying it out loud made it too absolute. Too real.

Halfway across town, the road opened into a square. A fountain bubbled in its center. Townsfolk usually loitered on the benches nearby, bent over a meal or catching up with an old friend. Now a luxurious awning shaded the fountain. A pop-up booth stood beside it, painted bright purple and trimmed with gold. Pierce had already memorized the words on the sign: "Coltanham Estate's Annual Sports Tournament—Enlist Now."

Dozens of men laden with packs and swords bantered while they waited in line. Even a week before the tournament, competitors arrived to prepare.

Pierce stopped to stare. Once, years ago, his father had taken him to the tournament. That very same day, he'd cut a stick to resemble a sword and practiced for hours.

Every year Pierce passed the booth. Every year he ignored the festivities and the thousands of spectators that flocked from miles around. And every year he promised himself that next year would be different. Next year he would compete. Next year he would become a traveling swordsman and make enough money to never struggle again.

But if I forever plan for next year, it will never come. What if I lose someone else?

He swallowed hard, forcing down the tickle of excitement and anxiety. *I'm ready.* He shoved a hand into his trouser pocket. Coins within the small leather pouch clinked. Just enough money for the registration fee.

He took a spot at the back of the line and over the next half of an hour, shuffled closer and closer to the stand until his turn arrived.

The official smiled at Pierce and twirled his feather pen. "Good afternoon, m'lad."

Pierce tugged the pouch from his pocket. "I'd like to sign up for the tournament."

I actually did it.

Pierce lifted his sword to his face as he jogged out of town, catching a glimpse of his own smile in its reflection. Everything felt possible now.

He passed a cluster of rose bushes at the road's edge, their buds swelling, ready to burst into multi-colored flowers.

He followed the forested road until a familiar log cabin rose into view. In front was a yard boasting two ancient sycamore trees and long, uncut grass. It didn't matter that he'd recently moved away. This would always be home. He loped down the path between the trees. The goats bleated greetings through their fence.

Voices murmured nearby, so he flicked his eyes to the shed beyond the house. Three shining faces could barely be seen behind the broad back of his father, Kane Doryu.

Pierce smiled and approached. "What's going on here?"

"Pierce!" Gwyndol and Mandy pushed past Da to hug their brother's waist.

Pierce laughed and returned the embrace.

"Ah, it's good to see you." Da laid a hand on Pierce's shoulder. His ring finger only protruded halfway before it ended in a stub, cut off in a carpentry accident years ago. "We hoped you'd stop by today!"

Pierce peeled his sisters off of him and lifted his sword. The frayed grip clung to the hilt like a dead rodent. "My wrapping broke. I thought I could fix it here since I haven't moved everything to my place yet."

The sparkle in Da's eyes dimmed. "I see."

"What are you doing in here?" Pierce eyed his family. "This looks like a conspiracy meeting to me."

Da's deep chuckle filled the shed, packed with carpentry tools and the strong, sweet scent of cut wood. "Aye, of sorts. Ma's birthday is in a few days. We're organizing a surprise banquet for her. Timothy, Mandy, and Gwyndol are making the decorations, and I've invited family from Lentrock and Pertim City."

Pierce locked eyes with Da. How had he forgotten Ma's birthday? And now they were planning a banquet, and Da was inviting relatives? He gnawed the inside of his cheek. Was it really a birthday celebration? Or a goodbye gathering?

"Will you help us decorate?" Mandy asked, green eyes sparkling. She grabbed Pierce's hand. "We want to hang paper chains on the ceiling."

"Yes, and flower baskets!" Gwyndol added, staring at Mandy as she also clutched Pierce's fingers. Seven years old and the youngest, she stuck closer to Mandy than her own shadow.

The sword in his other hand suddenly grew heavy. He wouldn't have time to train for his first tournament and help organize a party. But what could he tell them? He broke his sisters' grips by brushing non-existent dust from his tunic.

"We'll see," he mumbled, ignoring Da's questioning gaze.

"Well," Timothy said, his tone laced with mischief. "I still think Da should make a wood cut out of Ma and put it behind her door. That would be the perfect decoration!"

Pierce snorted at Timothy's prank antics. Mandy sniffed. "Be serious, Timothy."

Gwyndol copied Mandy's sniff while Da laughed again. "Trust me, Tim, I don't think a scare is your Ma's idea of a thoughtful present. We're going to do our best to make her day special. Because what is the Doryu rule? In all we do..."

"We do with all our soul," all four children chorused.

"That's right. Come on, you rascals," Da steered the children out of the shed. "We need to eat supper so Ma can go to bed. Pierce, you'll eat with us, aye? You can fix your sword after."

The family crossed the yard to the house. As Pierce followed inside, the smell of stew and fresh bread greeted him. He tugged off his boots and ducked into the living room, careful to avoid bumping his father's carpentry work lining the shelves.

Da left to help Ma while the children set out supper.

Pierce unclipped his sword and leaned it beside his seat. Mandy and Gwyndol rushed to sit beside him.

Their chatter stilled at a door's creak.

Ma and Da entered the room, Da heavily supporting his wife. Her feet barely touched the floor, but Pierce knew she would protest if Da carried her.

The lump in his throat thickened. So much for his appetite.

Ma sat and readjusted her dress before looking up. "Oh, Pierce! I'm glad you're here."

"Hello, Ma. How are you feeling?"

"Not too bad today." Her response was too quick to be convincing. Seconds after, a cough wracked her body.

"Are you okay, Rose?" Da clasped her hand. At Ma's nod, he turned to the family. "Let us pray, then we may eat." He bowed his head. Pierce hardly heard a word, his mind focused on his mother.

At last, the prayer ended, and Timothy made a lightning-fast grab for the stew ladle.

Ma cleared her throat. "Pierce, is that your... um, s-sword? Must you carry it everywhere?"

"The grip broke. I need to fix it."

"Well, could you... set it in t-the hall?" Ma gingerly sipped her stew with a shaking hand. "I don't like it a-at the table."

"Of course, Ma." Pierce took the sword and set it by the front door. He trudged back to his seat, scooting in between his sisters. No one spoke as they each tucked into their soup.

"Really, I don't see what you find in... sword fighting," Ma said. "I don't want you hurt over s-some useless hobby."

Pierce sucked in his breath. How many times had they argued about this over the years, the same cloud of disapproval in her eyes? Each time those talks ended with raised voices and slammed doors. But not this time. Not when she was dying.

Ma carried on. "So much popularity around t-tournaments the last few years. Fighters leaving their homes and families to fight other men. For what? Nothing but entertainment, ego, and prize money." She shook her head. "It's not right."

Pierce stared at his spoon, cheeks warming. Sure, the tournaments weren't for everyone, but they were exciting. They brought people joy. And it was the one thing he was good at. *The one thing I could excel at to help Da provide for the family once Ma...*

The thought turned the bite of soup in his mouth bitter. He swallowed, gritted his teeth and stood, his chair scraping back against the floor. "I'm going to fix my sword."

Reclaiming his boots and sword in the hall, Pierce retreated to the carpentry shed. The calming scent of pine eased his nerves, but he tensed again at the sound of the house door squeaking open. Da's boots tromped down the porch steps and to the shed.

Pierce reluctantly turned to face his father.

"Pierce," Da said gently, his eyebrows upturned. "I know you and Ma don't agree when it comes to your... interest in sword fighting. But could you try to understand? Especially when she's so sick."

Pierce nodded, focusing on a shelf Da had set aside for Pierce's sword-maintenance supplies. Whetstones, jars of protective oil, and other tools he'd collected over the years lay strewn across the shelf. "I'm sorry, I shouldn't have left." His words came off more brittle than the blocks of Da's carpentry wood stacked around him. "I'll come back in a moment."

Usually, Da might nod, sigh, and retreat, but his shadow remained framed in the doorway.

Pierce turned back around. Da massaged his temple with his injured hand.

"All this sword training," he said at last. "I'm not a fool, Pierce. I know the Coltonham Tournament is nearing. I might assume you had half a mind to sign up."

Pierce held his breath. What could he say? Could he deny it?

No, excuses wouldn't work this time. "I signed up this afternoon. I know I can win, and if I do, it could set up my career for great success."

Da nodded, his expression unchanged. "You've moved out, so I can no longer tell you what to do," Da began, which meant he would do just that. "But why now? We don't know how much time your mother has left. We want you here. And what about the birthday banquet?"

"I can't just sit here and wait for Ma to die," Pierce whispered, nausea rising at his own words. No use sugarcoating the truth, though. "Every time I visit, she's wasting away even more. I can smell it in the house and see it in Timothy's face, Mandy's, and Gwyn's. I never want us to go through this again. For you and me to work every waking second to afford medicines. Successful swordfighters make a lot of money, and I'm willing to be away from my family for a while to make sure you're all provided for."

"I understand where you're coming from. But could you not put off competing for a little longer? A tournament the week of Ma's birthday isn't well-timed..."

"Ma's illness wasn't well-timed either," Pierce muttered. "What if Mandy got sick before next year's tournament? Or Gwyn?" *I never want to feel so helpless again.*

Da didn't reply.

Pierce turned to his sword, selecting a roll of leather grip from the shelf. "The tournament runs on the thirteenth and fourteenth. If the banquet is on the fifteenth it won't conflict at all. I'm sorry I can't help with the planning. But I'll be there."

Da opened his mouth as if searching for a rebuttal. At last, he nodded. "I understand."

"Thank you." Pierce let out a silent sigh. He set to rewrapping his sword.

Da's boot creaked on the threshold of the shed. "Just remember, Pierce; focusing on life in the future could lead to missing life altogether."

His footsteps retreated to the house. Pierce clenched his jaw. Even his father didn't understand the importance of his vision. But when he gave them enough money to never struggle again, they would see it, and they would thank him. And it would all be worth it.

Pierce's armor rattled with every step down the road. Blue sky stretched to the horizons, promising a good day for Coltanham's tournament. He rubbed his sweaty hands together. *It's finally time.*

In the last two days, hundreds of people had arrived, packing the inns and staying with relatives.

Pierce didn't recognize a single face.

Banners advertising the event waved above the bustling streets.

Breaking free of the crowds, Pierce followed an open road down Coltonham Hill. A shallow vale sat beside the town, and Lord Colton's estate towered atop the hill across the valley.

The sight of the tournament grounds in the middle of the vale's meadow made him feel small. Purple and gold pavilions peeked over the tall canvas fence bordering the event. Rows upon rows of benches built on top of each other encapsulated the arenas and stretched to the sky, ensuring plenty of seating for the avid audience.

Already a crowd had formed at the front entrance. As Pierce approached, the excited congregation formed a path for him.

A tall man in a tight green suit beamed at him. His smiling upper lip nearly touched his narrow nose. He reminded Pierce of a river reed. "Greetings, sir. My name is Bord Fellair, the tournament host. Are you a contestant?"

"Aye. Pierce Doryu."

He was waved through the entrance and immediately found himself in a crowd of other armored men milling about. Trainers and nervous family members hovered around them.

As he passed, Pierce was painfully conscious that he came alone.

A tent door flapped open, and a tall, armored man ran into Pierce's elbow.

"Watch it, boy!" The man huffed, patting down his slicked-back hair.

"I'm s-sorry."

The man looked down at Pierce. A shorter, bald gentleman followed him out of the tent, mumbling as he studied a flurry of parchments in his hands. A manager, perhaps.

The contestant flashed a smile. "This your first tournament, friend?"

Pierce nodded. "Aye, it is." He extended a hand. "I'm Pierce Doryu."

"I didn't ask." The man sniffed. "My oh my. Mismatched armor, fraying at the seams? Let's hope your sword is in better shape."

Pierce's cheeks flushed. The man continued, "And put your hand away, friend. Not just anyone shakes the hand of Holton Rive, four-time lightweight champion from the Teragon Plains."

Lightweight? Pierce's hand dropped. That was his weight class. He was going to fight this man?

"Don't break your sword in your first match." Holton coughed out a laugh. "It looks a touch thin. And who did the wrap job on the hilt? An intoxicated goat?"

Chuckling, the contestant strutted away, his manager at his heels like a dog.

Pierce balled his hands and continued down the green. He found his assigned tent and dropped off his pack before stepping back outside. *Where to next?*

He lifted a hand to a passing competitor. "Excuse me, when does our division compete?"

"The first call was five minutes ago. I'm headed there now. Follow me, if you like."

Pierce gratefully fell into step beside the man. Thank goodness not everyone was as lofty as that Holton fellow.

Weaving through the ever-growing crowds, the two approached the nearest arena. Trumpets raised a fanfare into the sky, adding to the overwhelming hubbub around them. Pierce's guide looped around the arena to a small pavilion tucked in the rear. A sign above the door stated: "Competitor Access Only. No Spectators Admitted."

Inside, four rows of tournament officials registered competitors. They hurried Pierce through and directed him to the other side of the pavilion, which led into the arena.

An official filled him in on the way. "For the qualifiers, four matches will run at once. Your first fight is scheduled for the second wave. If victorious, return to this pavilion to await further instruction. If you fail a match, you will have a couple of hours to remove any personal items from your tent and sign out.

Questions?"

"No, thank you," Pierce heard himself say as he ducked out in between the packed seats and into the arena.

The first four matches were already underway. The roars of the crowd vibrated the floor, scattering Pierce's thoughts. He skirted the arena to where an official yelled instructions into his ear.

Pierce nodded. The rules sounded standard—nothing he hadn't expected. He turned to watch the current match nearest him and recognized one of the fighters to be Holton Rive.

His lofty attitude was not misplaced in delusion. The man's blue-and-gold armor flashed in the sunlight as he fought his opponent with the precision and balance of a hawk. He ended his match in seconds, scoring three points to none.

Pierce licked his suddenly dry lips. What if his first adversary far outmatched him? It'd been months since he'd sparred a real fighter. Maybe Da was right. Maybe he shouldn't have jumped at this opportunity. Maybe he should've waited.

Ma's thin figure rose in his mind. *No. I'm ready. I've done enough sitting around. I have to do this, for my family's future.*

The official near Pierce elbowed him. "You're next. Greet the referee for instruction."

Pierce entered the bordered arena through the nearest gate.

Holton passed him on his way out, grinning. "Good luck, lad! You'll need it."

Pierce scowled. *Stay focused.* He stepped into the square opposite his opponent.

"Next match! Doryu versus Sharpe."

Sharpe. Everything about the name matched his appearance—from his chiseled features to the point of his longsword. He stood ready, a lithe snake in smooth black armor.

The crowd's roar set Pierce's ears ringing.

With trembling fingers, he tugged his sword from its sheath and ran over the rules in his head. A tap to his opponent's armor counted as one point. Three points to win.

This was what he'd trained for.

His arms felt like honey, and his tongue stuck to the roof of his mouth. *A sip of water would be nice right about now*. He tossed his sheath from the square.

The referee lifted a hand and brought it down in a cutting motion. "Fight!"

Pierce moved forward cautiously. Sharpe struck like a viper. Once. A cut toward his arm. Pierce pivoted away.

Twice. A curving slice at knee height. Pierce stumbled back.

Three times. Pierce raised his sword, and the shock of steel on steel radiated up his arms. The blow brought back every sparring session he'd ever experienced. He regripped his sword.

Sharpe backed away, grinning. None of his strikes had found Pierce's armor.

Pierce grinned back.

The smell of hot steel rose from his sword, mixed with a tornado of kicked-up dust. He moved forward, blade high. Sharpe had strength, but his feet shuffled clumsily. Pierce directed a side cut, but he was too slow. Sharpe dodged and retaliated. A painful blow rocked Pierce's shoulder. The crack of the sword against his armor sounded like delayed thunder after lightning.

The crowd cheered.

The referee's hand rose. "One point, Sharpe."

Pierce trudged back to his side of the square, ears burning.

Sharpe had seen his attack from miles away. Rookie mistake.

He turned around, eyes locking with Sharpe's. It didn't matter. He knew his opponent's weakness. *Just don't overcommit again.*

The referee signaled. "Fight!"

The two met in the center. Sharpe slashed at Pierce's thigh. Pierce blocked his sword. Sparks flared. The crowd roared. On the rebound of the exchange, Pierce slid his sword up into Sharpe's breastplate. A second eruption of cheers. The referee's hand lifted toward Pierce's corner, and joy sizzled through his body.

Gone were the nervous jitters. He was going to win. For his future. For his family.

Sharpe's attempts to thwart Pierce were in vain. Swiftly obtaining his final two points with blows to the knee and shoulder, Pierce approached the referee, head held high. He flicked back locks of sweat-soaked hair and beamed at the crowd through heavy breaths. *I did it, I did it, I did it!*

"Pierce Doryu, winner!"

As Pierce returned to the fighter's pavilion, he passed Bord Fellair.

The tournament host gave him a short smile and a thumbs up. Pierce grinned back. It didn't get better than this.

"And now the semi-final match in the lightweight division, our final match of the evening. Heath Langley and Pierce Doryu to the arena, please."

Pierce approached the gate, unsticking his sweat-soaked tunic for the hundredth time.

After a full day of fighting, his aching fingers could barely hold his sword. Eight matches. Eight wins. One match remained to determine his future: become a finalist or return home with nothing.

He drew in a shaky breath. *You've come too far to lose.* If he won, not only would he win the first-place reward, but he would open doors to years of opportunity, larger tournaments overflowing with glory and riches for the best fighters.

A tall, lean swordsman faced him across the arena. Heath Langley. Though clean-shaven and boyish in appearance, he was nearly thirty and knew every trick in the book. Pierce had watched him not only defeat but humiliate his opponents throughout the day. *Not me, though.*

The referee's hand dropped between the competitors. "Fight!"

Pierce jumped forward. Heath dropped into a roll and rose in the middle of the arena, drawing gasps from the crowd.

Pierce's nose wrinkled at the unorthodox attack. He countered with an overhead cut, then swiveled and thrust. Heath sidestepped. Having missed, Pierce stumbled forward.

Heath stabbed at his shin guard. Pierce barely stopped the blade with his own. As he did, he felt his sword yield to Heath's. The blade clattered loosely near the hilt.

No, this couldn't happen. His sword couldn't break, not now.

A silver flash overhead jerked him back to reality. Heath's teeth gleamed white as his sword cracked down on Pierce's pauldron. The referee's hand lifted. One point, Langley.

A thousand curses rose in Pierce's mind as he examined his broken sword. The tang of the blade still lay inside the hilt, but it could bend or fall out at any moment.

He hurried to the referee. "My sword is damaged. I think I need a replacement."

The referee shook his head. "Weapons cannot be exchanged during a match. I'll give you two minutes to fix your sword, but if you can no longer fight, you'll have to forfeit."

Pierce stalked back to his corner, mind whirling. He couldn't forfeit. But how was he to fight with a loose sword? He fiddled with the blade, praying it would fix itself.

"One minute!"

One idea left. With trembling fingers, Pierce undid the clasp on his belt. He yanked it from his waist and tucked his sword between his knees, looping the belt around the cross guard and the base of the blade. Wrapping the last few inches of belt around his left hand, he gripped the bottom of the blade to keep it in place, his fingers protected from the razor-sharp edge by layers of leather.

The crowd, murmuring at first, now cheered as Pierce straightened, sword held high.

Heath's eyes darted toward the referee, but he only shrugged and dropped his hand between the competitors. "Fight!"

Heath unleashed heavy blows on Pierce's blade. Every clash sent painful vibrations up his left arm. Heath lifted both arms to strike. There. A perfect opening. Pierce lunged forward, slashing Heath's stomach armor.

One point! Cheers doubled.

Round three began. Pierce deflected Heath's attacks, searching for another chink in his opponent's guard. When Pierce backstepped a diagonal cut, Heath's left side remained unprotected. Stretching forward, Pierce stabbed his sword's point into Heath's arm. As he did, his left hand slipped up the blade, meeting steel. His skin split open, flowering a scarlet band of blood.

The audience gasped.

"I need medical attention," Pierce yelled, turning his palm to the referee.

Again, the man shook his head. "Not until after the match. Can you continue?"

One point remained. Pierce sucked air through his teeth and nodded.

"Fight!"

Pierce shoved his bloody hand in between his armor straps, burying it into his tunic.

Heath leaped on his advantage. One thrust, then again. Pierce crossed swords, but his loosened blade yielded. The sting of Heath's sword spasmed up Pierce's thigh.

"Final round! Competitors tied, two to two."

Pierce glanced at his hand. Splotches of red marred his cream tunic. He regripped his sword with sweaty fingers. *I can do this.*

"Fight!"

Heath ran to the arena's center. Pierce approached cautiously, his feet dragging like lead weights. Their blades crossed, but Pierce's loose sword shifted at the lightest pressure, forcing him back.

Heath swung downward. The blade split the air like a hissing snake.

It was now or never.

Pierce moved forward instead of back, ducking underneath the blade to come shoulder-to-shoulder with Heath. Swinging his sword behind him, the clattering blade glanced off Heath's back plate. The referee lifted a hand. The crowd leapt to its feet.

"Pierce Doryu, winner! Our new finalist in the lightweight division."

Pierce lifted his sword to acknowledge the crowd before a throbbing pain reminded him of his injury. As he exited the arena, two officials hurried him back to the competitor's pavilion.

"We need a healer!" one of the officials called. "It's one of our finalists."

After Pierce's hand was bandaged, an official handed him back his sword.

"We'll stow your armor in your tent, so you don't have to carry it home. Better fix your sword, though. You're going up against Holton Rive, the four-time champion."

Pierce had studied Holton's matches throughout the day. The champion had breezed past his competition, landing him comfortably in the finals.

Do I stand a chance against him?

As he exited the pavilion, a crowd of admirers surrounded him. Though he tried to be cordial, his hand throbbed, and exhaustion clouded his mind.

In only a day his entire world had changed. Pierce Doryu, the local boy always seen fighting hay bales, was now a tournament finalist.

Breaking free from the crowds, he hurried home. He ached all over, but becoming a finalist made it all worth it.

Along the road, bright red and yellow roses peeked out from their green shells.

Mandy and Gwyndol were playing in the front yard of the Doryu homestead when Pierce limped up the road.

Their mouths dropped open.

He chuckled. "Remember me? Your brother?"

They jumped up and ran into his arms. "Pierce! Did you win? You're so sweaty."

Pierce laughed. "I haven't won yet, but I haven't lost. I'm a finalist in tomorrow's match."

"And then you'll be here for Ma's..." Gwyndol lowered her voice, "for Ma's banquet the day after?"

"You know I wouldn't miss it," he whispered back. "How's decorating going?"

Mandy planted her fists on her hips. "I've done most of it. Gwyndol too, but Timothy hasn't done anything."

The chatter continued, and Pierce grinned at the warm comfort in his heart that he only felt around his sisters. A sensation the dozens of adoring faces in the tournament's crowds couldn't hope to compare.

"Pierce, you're back!" Timothy vaulted the porch rail and sprinted over. "I wish I could've watched the tournament. Did you win?"

Pierce laughed. "Tomorrow, I'm winning tomorrow."

The door opened and Da ducked his head out. "Pierce!"

"Pierce?" A faint voice trickled from the house. "Do I hear my eldest son?"

"I'm coming, Ma!" Pierce left his sword on the porch and walked inside. He stepped over decoration supplies scattered throughout the house, hidden from view of Ma's door. In the bedroom, the thick curtains blocked out the setting sun. The odor of illness mixed with the sickly-sweet scent of medicine roiled Pierce's stomach.

Ma smiled. Despite her pale skin and thinning golden hair, a twinkle in her eyes Pierce knew from childhood still held on. Pierce focused on them as he stooped to hug her.

"Wait, let me sit up," Ma protested. Her elbows quivered as she lifted herself off her pillows. She wrapped frail arms around Pierce, and he gently rubbed her bony back.

"Oh, it's good to see you. My, y-you're sweaty."

"It's hot outside." Pierce chuckled, crouching at the bedside.

Da stepped into the room. "Why Rose, you're sitting up! Don't overexert yourself."

"I had to hug Pierce. I'm... fine, Kane." Ma's eyes twinkled as Timothy, Mandy, and Gwyndol shuffled in behind him. "In fact, I'm feeling quite well. Better than ever with... t-the whole family together."

Pierce smiled, too, and heat stung his eyes.

He ducked his head. He couldn't remember the last time he cried. He must be dreadfully overtired.

"The whole family *is* together. Pierce is here too!" Gwyndol jumped on his back. He cried out and wrestled her off as everyone laughed.

"Careful, Gwyn. He's been competing all day," Da warned.

"Speaking of which." Pierce glanced up. "Da, something happened to my sword, I'd like you to look at it."

"Of course."

Leaving Ma to rest, they went to the shed together.

Da hummed loudly, fiddling with the loosened blade. "It's bad, Pierce. I don't think this is fixable in one day."

Pierce frowned. "It has to be. I need to fight tomorrow."

"I'm afraid the entire tang is bent. It'll need reconstruction. And as cheap as the sword is, it's probably not worth it."

"I did everything right!" Pierce pounded the shed wall. "I had a chance to change my family's life forever, and my own sword fails me. Perhaps another competitor would allow me to borrow their sword. Or my old tutor..."

The door creaked, and when Pierce turned, Da had retreated toward the house. He re-emerged minutes later, cradling a long, covered object in his arms.

"What's that?"

"Open it." Da thrust the package into his hands.

With careful movements, Pierce peeled back the folded cloth.

A gasp escaped his lips.

The polished sword glittered in the dim shed. He wrapped his fingers around the rouge leather grip, his thumb tracing the engraved silver cross-guard. The pommel was of the same metal, simple and round, but with a single rose engraved upon its flat face.

"What—how—why do you have this?" Pierce raised the sword until it tickled the ceiling.

Da smiled. "It's mine. Or it was. I retired it twelve years ago, when you were five."

"You owned a sword? You weren't in any wars, were you?" Pierce pulled his eyes from the weapon to his father's gaze.

"No. I was a tournament fighter. Like you wish to be." His voice grew wistful, memories lacing every word. "One of the best, too."

"Why didn't you tell me? I've wanted to be a fighter for years. Why make me find trainers when *you* could have taught me?"

Da lifted his left hand to stare at the scar running from his missing ring finger to his wrist. "Your Ma... she hated every time I competed. She worried herself sick and begged me to quit. When I injured my hand, I finally listened."

"You lost your finger in a competition? You said it was from a carpentry accident."

"Aye. The moment you showed interest in sword fighting, Rose asked me to keep it secret. As I said, we didn't want to encourage it. But we also didn't want to forbid it. We thought your passion would fade with age, but I guess sword fighting runs in our blood."

Pierce stared at the rose engraved on the sword's pommel. "The rose..."

"Ah, yes." Da's smile returned. "I thought it quite romantic. I even named the blade Rose. Dedicated to the love of my life, born in spring like the flowers. Your mother wasn't as enthusiastic, but I think she was secretly flattered. I had it done a week before our wedding, to appease her before I ran off to compete the day before."

"Why did you stop?" Pierce asked, lowering the sword. "Competing, I mean. Skilled sword fighters can make fortunes."

"It wasn't about the money, Pierce."

"Then what was it? If you'd kept fighting, we could've been rich. We could've had enough money for Ma's medicines and afforded better healers!"

"You don't know that. Do you think I never considered those what-ifs?" Pain bled from his voice. "Only God knows what might have been. But I can't go back now. And I don't regret my choice."

"Why? Because you didn't want to keep fighting? Isn't your family more important than what you want?" Pierce clenched the sword, knuckles white. "If you were so great, why did you quit?"

"I quit for you!"

The crickets' chirps filled the sudden void between them.

Pierce shook himself from his stupor. "What?"

"For you and Timothy," Da elaborated, softly. "Mandy was on the way. I missed the first several years of your life. I told myself it was fine, that once I made enough money I would quit. But I never did. I wasn't there for your birthdays or when Tim was born. I had a tournament scheduled for the day Mandy was due, but then I was injured. So I went home."

Da's voice cracked. "And I got to welcome little Mandy into the world. I held her minutes after she was born. And she was so beautiful. I knew I couldn't stay away any longer. I couldn't let my children grow up without their father home every night. So I put the sword away and turned to carpentry."

He lifted his scarred hand. "I thank God every day that I lost this finger. Otherwise, I might still be out there, instead of with you."

Silence filled the shed again. At last, Pierce spoke. "Is this your roundabout way of saying that I shouldn't be a sword fighter?"

Da took a breath and shook his head. "No son, it isn't. And I mean that. Because as thankful as I am that I retired, I'd never take sword-fighting back. I loved every moment. And as you can see—" Da ruefully gestured toward the weapon "—I still polish it from time to time. Maybe because I thought I might pick it up again, or because I hoped to pass it on to you. I want you to make your own choices. By giving you my sword, I'm letting you have this choice. Competing itself isn't wrong. But it was wrong for me. Being a traveling fighter came at the cost of being a poor father. One had to go; I couldn't be good at both. Because in all we do, we must do with all our soul."

Pierce shook his head, struggling to believe it all. With no more words, he stepped forward and wrapped his arms around his father.

A chill breeze sent shivers up Pierce's arm as he approached town the next morning.

Dull gray clouds stifled the sun's cheerful rays. Butterflies roiled his stomach, and his injured hand throbbed. When he crested Coltonham Hill, he overlooked a crowd even larger than usual outside the tournament green.

What was happening?

Bord Fellair, dressed in his bright green suit, stood on a small stool at the tournament entrance.

When more fighters arrived, the tournament host began to speak. "Welcome, all, to what was to be the final day of the tournament. However, we're expecting a spring storm by the time of the event finals. Therefore, I'm afraid we must call off the tournament until tomorrow."

Murmuring, the crowd cast black looks toward the darkening clouds.

"Do not fear! The competitors will be ready tomorrow. This is not a cancellation—simply a delay. I will see you all tomorrow, the fifteenth, to conclude this year's tournament!" Bord gave a tight smile and stepped down from his stool.

As if summoned, the wind strengthened, and thunder rumbled in the distance.

Pierce swallowed hard. He gripped the pommel of his sword, the rose emblem digging into his injured palm. The fifteenth. The same day a dozen relatives would arrive at the Doryu's doorstep to celebrate Ma's birthday.

Now what?

Pierce trudged back up the hill with the rest of the dissipating crowd.

The wind gathered strength and whistled around him. It tugged at his tunic as if taunting him. When he passed the Doryu household, he spotted Da herding the goats into their shelter. The chickens had already gathered in their coop, and the shed door was locked tight.

"Oy, Pierce!" Da approached the road. "Back so early? What happened?"

"They canceled the finals." Pierce sighed.

Da's eyes widened. "Completely?"

"No. They're rescheduled for tomorrow, once the storm blows over."

Da cleared his throat, breaking the silence. "You haven't forgotten about Ma's birthday?"

"No. That's the problem. I can't miss the banquet. I don't *want* to miss it. But I'm a finalist in my first tournament. And if I miss that..."

"That's a tough choice." Da crossed his arms. "And one you'll have to make."

Pierce meandered down the road toward his house, those parting words haunting his mind. At last, he reached a tiny property wedged between the fences of two farms. It boasted only a simple shack, but it was his. Shouldering open the front door, he trudged into the main room. He unbuckled his sword and tossed it onto the table before easing into a hard wooden chair.

"What am I going to do?" His only answer was the rain outside swelling from a patter to a roar. The first bolt of lightning lit the room through the covered window.

Pierce Doryu. A tournament finalist. How could he give up now? What was missing one special day in exchange for the opportunity to take care of his family for decades?

They would understand, eventually if not now.

He stared at Da's sword, reminding him of his father's missing finger.

Pierce studied his own injured hand. Underneath the many bandages, the cut still stung.

The rain had stopped by morning. Pierce pulled himself out of bed, groaning at the ache in his muscles.

He downed a tasteless breakfast, before buckling on Da's sword. *No point in delaying.*

Warm sun rays greeted him outside. The grass squeaked with dew as Pierce strode across his lawn and onto the puddle-strewn road. He passed his family's home and smiled. Colorful paper streamers lined the porch roof.

He noticed the carpentry shed's open door.

Da stood inside, watching Pierce from across the yard. His eyes flicked to the sword at his son's side. Pierce attempted a cheerful wave, but Da's stony face drained his resolve. Head lowered, he continued swiftly down the road.

As he entered the grounds filled with even more people than yesterday, excited eyes turned his way. He smiled and nodded to those he passed, still shocked that they all knew his name.

He retrieved his pack and armor from his tent and paused to stare at his name above the door. *I won't be seeing this tent again.*

He hurried to the fighters' pavilion and approached an official. "Excuse me—"

"Pierce! Oh, thank goodness you're here." Bord Fellair crossed the pavilion, his hands outstretched. "We're interviewing the fighters before the show. Come, it'll take but a moment."

He grabbed Pierce's arm and pulled him toward the arena. In seconds, Pierce was standing on a stage in the center of the stadium.

Holton Rive stood nearby, grinning.

"Ladies and gentlemen, I'd like to announce our youngest fighter, Coltanham local, and lightweight finalist. Pierce Doryu!" Bord lifted Pierce's arm as the crowd cheered. "He will be competing against the four-time champion Holton Rive for his shot at glory, honor, and this!"

Bord bent to unlatch the lid of a large silver chest by his feet. With a flourish of his arm, he threw it open, revealing the glittering pile of coins inside. "The grand prize! Well over a year's wages for the greatest sword fighter in Coltonham."

Pierce's eyes fixed upon the chest. *A year's wages!*

"Pierce. Are you excited for your fight? Ready to take on the champion?"

The crowd hushed, and for the first time, Pierce took in the moment. Hundreds of faces stared at him from every side. All he had to do was say a few words. Give the crowd an underdog story of a boy who'd do anything for his dreams. Who would sacrifice it all to become the next champion.

This is your time. Every day he'd sweat, wept, and bled for this. Every dream of comfort and wealth that kept him going. To never see his family struggle again. It was here. *And all you need to do is reach out and take it.*

His fingers gripped the hilt of his father's sword. His thumb rubbed over an engraving, and he looked down to stare at the rose shining dully on the pommel. A declaration of Da's commitment to his wife. To Ma. That he would always be there for her, no matter what.

Now Pierce carried the sword. And the commitment to those he loved that came with it.

"It is with a heavy heart that I must announce... due to another event at the same time as my final match, I am forfeiting the tournament."

Silence followed. Bord stared at Pierce, his jaw gaping.

A loud *boo* rang out from the crowd, followed by hundreds of jeers.

Bord blinked and spluttered, "But Pierce, you can't be serious. You're forfeiting? You'll lose your guaranteed spot at second place... you'll lose your chance at more money than you've ever seen in your life!"

Pierce shook his head. "There will be time in the future for all of that." *And time with Ma is too precious to give up.*

He made to step off the platform, but Bord grabbed his hand, desperation in his eyes. "Name your price to fight. I don't care if you win or lose, I'll pay it!"

Pierce peeled Bord's fingers from his wrist. "No amount of money is more important than this event. I'm sorry, Bord."

"But what of the crowd?" Holton Rive pushed past Bord, scowling. "You can't let these people down. Are you that afraid to face me?"

Pierce squared his shoulders. "Congratulations, Holton. But no, I am not. Come back to Coltonham next year and you'll see."

Holton scoffed. "Very well. You had best be training! If you had faced me today, I would have fenced circles around you."

The words fell on deaf ears as Pierce descended the stage steps, confirming his forfeiture, and started for home.

A roar of applause rose from the arena as the first match commenced.

As he continued down the road, each step felt lighter. No number of fans, prize money, or hopes of an unknown future could bring Pierce back. His heart yearned instead for the presence of his family, and the embrace of home.

Pierce broke into a jog, his armor rattling wildly. He only slowed to admire the roses by the roadside, glowing in their fully bloomed radiance. He stooped to pluck a handful of yellow ones before continuing onward.

His home appeared amongst the trees.

He ducked under the hanging streamers on the porch and shouldered open the front door.

His equipment crashed to the floor. He yanked off his boots and hurried into the living room, where the smell of blackberry pie tickled his nose. A merry fire crackled in the hearth where Mandy and Gwyndol watched over the food. Bright decorations hung across the walls and ceiling.

Timothy looked up from the table. "P-Pierce?"

"Hello, Tim!" Pierce clapped his back while his sisters rushed to hug him.

"You didn't tell us how the tournament went yesterday!" Mandy said.

"Did you win?" Gwyndol asked.

"No, I didn't." Pierce looked up to see Da leaning against the doorway, smiling from ear to ear.

"That's too bad!" Timothy snapped his fingers. "I wanted a champion for a brother."

Pierce grinned. "There's always next year."

Da gave Pierce a short nod, understanding passing between them.

"I'm not late, am I?" Pierce asked.

Mandy shook her head. "No one's arrived yet, and we're still preparing the food. Want to help?"

"I would love to. Is Ma up yet?"

Da nodded. "She just woke up and asked about all the commotion. Do you want to break the surprise and wish her a happy birthday?"

All four siblings exclaimed their approval.

Da stepped into the bedroom first, followed by the children and their cries of, "Happy birthday, Ma!"

Ma let out an astonished laugh, tears flooding her eyes.

Pierce stopped next to his father and watched his siblings flock around Ma.

Da patted his shoulder. "I'm glad you came back."

"I wouldn't have missed it for anything. Oh, and I believe—" Pierce unclipped Da's sword from his belt, "this is yours."

"You keep it." Da smiled. "I don't need it anymore."

"I thought if you looked after it, we could train together. You know, some other day."

Da studied the sword with thoughtful eyes. At last, he took it. "I'd like that, Pierce."

He set the sword behind the door. "For now, though..." He walked to Ma's bedside and gently grasped one of her hands. "Happy birthday, my love."

Pierce crossed to the other side and offered her the yellow roses, their vibrance beating back the room's shadows. "I wish I had something better to give you."

Ma's eyes sparkled, just like Pierce remembered before she'd fallen ill. "My men. My family. For what greater gift could I ask?"

Pierce blinked back the tears stinging his eyes. He rubbed Ma's frail fingers with his thumb. "I love you, Ma."

In that moment, with his and Da's scarred hands holding Ma's, and Timothy, Mandy, and Gwyndol filling the room with laughter, Pierce felt whole.

And he never wanted to let go.

CALEB E. KING

Having read Lewis and Tolkien's epic novels by age eight, Caleb E. King penned his first stories shortly thereafter. His head is constantly filled with swords, castles, and several flying dragons. His mission is to write tales that gift young adults the courage to stand up against darkness and ignite the warrior inside.

When he's not living vicariously through a thick tome with a steaming mug of tea at his elbow, Caleb can be found on adventures of his own. He loves exploring God's creation with friends, drawing cartoons, or puzzling over a particularly difficult rhyme in his next poem.

Achievements

- Completed eight full-length novels as well as multiple novellas and short stories.

- Received and implemented edits from professional editors.

- Networked with authors and industry professionals at The Young Writer's Workshop Conference in 2022 and 2023, as well as the 2024 Young Writer's Retreat.

- Built an email list of over 150+ subscribers.

- Has received in-depth training and coaching on business and marketing strategy through the Author Conservatory.

Pitches

- *Ranger's Apprentice* meets *The Knights of Arrethtrae* in a non-magical YA fantasy where a wounded young soldier stationed at a remote watchtower is the only one standing between an invading enemy clan and the land he knows and loves.

GHOST IN THE GARDEN

JULIA NAUS

W hen no one else wanted me, I could still dance with the flowers. Their petals welcomed me no matter what.

Spinning in a circle, a childish giggle escaped my lips as blossoms twirled around me. My braids, never quite as good as when Mother would do them, flew behind me, and I collapsed to the ground with a sigh.

Eyes squeezed shut, I tried to drink in the peaceful lull hanging over the garden. But a chill wind brushing past made my arms prickle. I opened my eyes. A dark patch of clouds mottled the sky over our house, swirling with foreboding.

Our brick manor towered like a sentinel amidst gardens overflowing with flowers.

I wanted to believe it was impenetrable. But as the wind intensified and brushed dandelion fluff through the air, I could almost see the shapes of ghosts flitting around the delicate gables and arching windows.

These were not the nice ghosts, not like the one I called my friend. Icy fear crackled through me. These ghosts ripped wallpaper and shattered mirrors and threatened to tear homes apart.

Laughter flittered across the lawn, shaking me from my thoughts. Gaping windows flung themselves open, exposing the dark interior of our living room to the patchwork of sun that pressed through the clouds.

I squinted at the distant shape of the couch lumbering out of the way. It crouched in the corner, avoiding a beam of sunlight. The tea table scooted forward on trembling legs, drinking up sunshine.

Mother sat to the side, braiding Twi's hair.

Unbidden thoughts rushed to mind as I imagined them talking about me.

"The house is so peaceful without Moon," Mother would say. *"I'm so glad she isn't bothering us today."*

In my mind, Twi laughed in response, echoing the sentiment they were surely all thinking: *Moon isn't wanted here.*

I dragged my gaze away. Deep inside, I knew my mother would never say those words, and Twi would never be so cruel. After weeks of silence from my entire family, though, I was sure they'd thought much worse things.

The grass around me fluttered, and a bright daisy dipped its head to rest softly on my knee.

I brushed it off with a scowl. "I'm fine."

A pang of guilt shot through my stomach as the daisy turned away, hanging its head.

"I'm sorry; you're right." I reached over to cup the flower in my hands. "I shouldn't have snapped at you."

A cluster of flowers scooted close, wrapping around me in a hug. Their soft leaves brushed across the bare skin of my arms, so delicate I couldn't even feel the petals.

I sighed. At least the flowers hadn't forgotten me.

They clung close, as if even they could tell something was haunting our house—something more than the peaceful ghost I'd befriended.

A shadow flitted across the lawn as our resident ghost-girl darted toward me. Barely visible in the day, Melissa quirked a smile as her curls bounced.

I sat up, tucking lanky, mid-growth spurt legs underneath me, and smiled back.

Alighting on the grass, she brushed flowers out of the way. They moved obligingly—whether Melissa could actually touch them, or the flowers were simply playing along, I wasn't sure.

The little ghost reached out, wispy hand poking mine and sliding right through it. My skin shone a pale white next to hers, nearly see through. I really did need to get outside more often.

Leaning back, I sighed. "Can you feel the sunlight, Melissa?"

She opened her mouth to respond, and I imagined I could hear the words. Poor Mel had been a ghost so long, even the memory of her voice had faded from the world. She'd been here as long as we'd lived at the house, and never had I heard her speak.

I bit my lip, shooting another glance toward the house. "It must be lonely to be a ghost."

Faint shapes darted around the roof again as the wind rose, just like the ghosts who tore through our hallways and shattered dishes and overturned tables.

They had attacked twice now, leaving chaos behind. Did Melissa know why they were here? "Mel?"

Her childlike eyes carried far too much sadness.

"Do you know what's haunting our house?" I whispered.

She bit her lip and glanced away.

"So you do know!" I leaned forward. "Mel, can you help me—"

The ghost sighed. Then her eyes shimmered with a playful spark. She covered her face with her hands and mimed counting: our universal sign for hide-and-seek.

Before I could protest, the girl zipped toward the house.

I had no option but to go after her. Abandoning my flowers, I trudged up the marble stairs until I stood face to face with the rusty lion embossed on our front door. It winked at me as the majestic door swung open, welcoming my soft footfalls with the creaking of its ancient hinges. Holding my breath, I tiptoed past the living room. Not that Mother would care.

A wooden floorboard squeaked as I passed the room's gaping doorway. My mother turned, and I froze. Her eyes passed right over me before she murmured to my little sister.

Swallowing, I ignored a jealous flush creeping up my cheeks and darted further into the house. The sculptures lining the walls watched me with skeptical stares, their marble eyebrows tilted upward.

"And just where do you think you're going, young lady?" The head of my great-great grandfather Charles spoke from his bust displayed on a table.

"If you're looking for the other little girl, she ran off that way—" A high-pitched voice chimed in.

"For heaven's sake, Miranda, you don't have arms. She has no idea where you're pointing." Great-great Grandfather frowned.

I scampered away before they could ruin our game.

The hallways spread out before me, offering endless places Melissa could be hiding.

The first stop was Mother's parlor, empty except for the chattering tea set and embroidered cushions. The teapot waved at me eagerly, but I ran past, knowing well the trouble I'd be in if I was caught there.

I climbed the stairs higher into the house. These hallways had once been so friendly, but I couldn't shake the feeling Melissa wasn't the only ghost here.

Father's library greeted me with its scent of fresh wood and old books. I longed to slip inside and disappear amidst the beckoning piles of books. Instead I hesitated in the doorway, peeking in for the vicious coat rack guarding Father's books.

It glared at me from the corner, so I opted to leave the library behind.

Climbing the final flight of stairs, I ducked to avoid hitting my head on the attic's low ceiling. The dust-filled air was warm and dry, rarely disturbed by our family.

I peeked into each nook and cranny, dodging between towers of boxes, old toys, and broken furniture. Still, nothing. I frowned, until something caught my eye up ahead.

A door.

Tucked behind an old rocking chair and a stack of photo albums, a door nearly half my height blended in with the wall's dusty brown panels. I crept toward it. How had I never seen this before? Surely I'd explored every inch of the place.

The door swung inward as I reached the threshold. A round window illuminated the tiny attic room. Crayon drawings covered the walls, accented with dried flowers and finger paintings.

Papers scattered the ground with scribbled drawings and handwritten notes with the big, halting script of a child. A teddy bear sat atop one pile, his head sagging downward and one eye threatening to pop out of its socket.

It should have been precious; childhood mementos living in this perfect, undisturbed room. A shrine to years lived long ago. Instead it made my skin crawl. I took a step back, reaching for the doorframe. I couldn't take another second in this room.

The temperature around me dropped, and instinctively I clutched my freezing arms.

"Melissa?" My voice shook more than I cared for. "Mel, are you here—"

I cut off as the window rattled, gusts of wind battering it.

Oh no. Not now.

I took another step back, but it was too late. The window flew open and a wild gust of air tore through the room. Childhood mementos flew around me. Papers caught in the breeze, teddies knocked from their perches, toys scattered across the floor.

I opened my mouth to scream, but no sound came out.

The ghost had returned.

I ran from the room, taking shelter in an alcove of the attic as the wind increased. It ripped through the house and tossed boxes like confetti. Squeezing my eyes shut tight, I hid as the ghost tore my house apart.

I pressed further back into the alcove, face covered, until the wind faded and gradually, the nightmare ended. The roof's violent shaking slowed to a stop, and I could hear the sounds of birds outside once more.

I cracked open an eye, taking in the destruction. The ceiling's wood paneling was nearly stripped bare, scattered across the floor along with toppled towers of boxes and shredded books.

Pushing to my feet, I blinked back the tears pricking at my eyelids.

A silvery figure dropped through the ceiling, and I let out a squeak of surprise. Melissa spun to face me.

"Mel!" My voice was practically a shout.

The little girl waved. A massive grin spread across her face, in direct opposition to the fear gripping my heart.

"You were supposed to help me, Melissa!" My anger sparked like the start of a wildfire.

The little ghost just gave me a big, triumphant nod.

"How is that helping?" I was very nearly shaking, hardly able to keep myself from shouting. "Look what the ghost did!"

But Mel pointed toward the little attic room, and I hesitated. As she darted inside, ducking under the tiny door frame, I stood outside and peered in.

"Is this you trying to help?" My voice softened, and Mel nodded once more. "Is this room—this belonged to the ghost that's destroying our house?"

One, final nod gave me a new understanding. And a new fear.

It crept into my chest, burrowing deep in my heart as I stared at the torn wallpaper, the childhood drawings ripped to shreds, the little teddy still perched in the corner. I shuddered, taking a step back, and then another as fear made way for repulsion.

I fled. The images of the room burned into my memory.

I was done with ghosts, and mysteries, and trying to solve whatever … this was. As the perpetual cold in my bones intensified, I decided maybe it was time to just forget about all this. Our home was a disaster, and this time, it was because of me.

Paintings were thrown from the walls, carpet ripped from the floorboards.

If looking for the ghost was only going to cause more attacks, maybe I just needed to ignore it altogether.

I burst into my room, bracing myself for a mess.

I was met with nothing.

The shelves that once held my most prized possessions—books—were empty. The walls where I'd pinned countless pictures drawn by both Twi and myself, were empty. The desk normally so cluttered in papers I couldn't see its painted pink surface was entirely bare.

Even the vase of flowers normally on my bedside table was gone.

"No—" My voice broke. "No, no, no—"

I flew through the room, throwing open drawers and tearing into my closet. Everything, empty.

The blank walls stared back at me.

They looked dead without the dozens of pictures, cards, and crayon drawings I'd accumulated in fifteen years of life. All the memories which made me *me* were gone, replaced by faded wallpaper and a few scattered thumbtacks. The rest of the room was almost painfully pristine, the bed perfectly made, the shelves dusted and emptied.

The image of that little attic room came to mind once more. I swallowed, meeting my wall's blank stare. This ghost wasn't just destroying my home.

It was trying to erase me.

The certainty seeped into my bones, haunting me as I tried to sleep, burdening my dreams until I woke in a cold sweat. By the time morning came around and the sun crept over the horizon, I had made up my mind.

The ghosts must go.

With no one else willing to even acknowledge them, it would be up to me. But the best mysteries aren't solved by a single person. If I wanted to ensure I got rid of the awful ghosts, I needed to enlist a sidekick of my own.

Thankfully, I knew just who to ask.

I stood before my mirror, ignoring the painfully bare walls behind it. Fidgeting with my sleeves, I frowned. When had I changed into this dress? The day before I had worn a frilly blue thing, but now I stood in my favorite lacy dress, adorned with little embroidered lemons.

"Going out today, dear?" The burnished frame of my mirror cracked a coppery smile at me.

"With Twi." I brightened, smoothing my skirt. "It's our monthly tea date."

"Oo-ooh!" The mirror hummed. She stretched out a long, spindly metal arm and brushed some hair out of my eyes. "We must get you dressed up, then."

My reflection in the mirror wavered for a moment. I rubbed my eyes until the blurriness faded. I swept my hair aside, combed the tangles out with my fingers, and waited until the mirror gave me a final nod of approval.

Waving a quick goodbye, I skipped out of my room in search of Twi.

The main floor was abuzz with life. Mother rattled around the kitchen, humming a song I'd heard a thousand times. The piano clunked along from the living room, trying to pick out the notes to accompany her.

"Twi and I are heading into town!" I hollered toward the kitchen. I poked my head into the living room, searching for my sister. "Twi?"

Nothing.

"Twi, it's time to go..." I bit my lip, waiting for a response.

Laughter echoed outside, and relief rushed over me. Of course. Twi was already outside, waiting. She hadn't forgotten.

My footsteps echoed in the hallway as I hurried toward the door. Beaming family portraits greeted me, tracing our family line from Grandma and Grandpa, all the way down to Twi and me.

The dark oak door swung open, and I hopped outside while tugging on the soft flats I'd saved for special occasions. "Twi, are you ready—"

I froze. "Twi?"

My younger sister skipped down the winding path to our house, arm in arm with her friends. Their laughter filtered back to me, drifting on the lazy wind. That wind pierced through me like ice, carving a wound I'm not sure I could fix.

I raised my voice. "Twi?"

One of her friends glanced back only to turn and pull Twi farther away. I stood in the doorway for far too long.

When I finally turned away, I had to blink back the tears. I kicked my shoes off and into the closet before tromping up the stairs. Portraits watched me with judgmental glares as I stormed, but I didn't care.

Shoving my hands deep into the pockets of my dress, I hurried past my room and climbed the stairs to Father's library. If Twi wouldn't help me, I'd do this on my own.

I scanned the shelves as I tiptoed through the library. Somewhere nearby, the rogue coat rack was hiding, ready to defend the library from anyone who dared to try and read its books.

I slipped through the shelves until I spotted the word "ghost" on one of the titles. It slid easily out from where it was nestled with dozens of other cloth bound books, letters embossed in gold and details etched into the fabric.

"Ahh, finally!" The book stretched its pages, letting out a long—and very loud—sigh.

I winced, hushing the book as I glanced around. Something shifted behind me. I turned just as the coat rack rounded the corner.

It halted, taking another hesitant step toward me, its branches quivering for a moment before it shrugged and trotted off in the opposite direction.

"Oh, sure." I scowled at it, blinking back a fresh round of tears. "You can just go ahead and ignore me, too."

I still wasn't taking my chances, so I snatched two more titles before scrambling to the top of the bookshelves, sitting with my head nearly brushing the ceiling as I cracked open the first book.

"It's about time!" The book yawned, its voice too pompous for such a small, faded cover. It shivered, dust falling from its pages. "I've been just wasting away up here."

"Hey!" The second one piped up with a shrill tone. "Don't forget about me! As far as books-about-ghosts go, I'm your best option."

That seemed to ruffle a few pages, and the third book quickly chimed in. I groaned and covered my ears, waiting until the ruckus died down, and the three books all turned to me, expectant.

"Well?" The first fluttered its pages eagerly. "What are you looking for? I'm sure my glossary can explain everything—"

The other two looked like they were about to comment, so I spoke up quickly.

"I need to learn about ghosts." I tucked my feet under me, drawing in a long breath.

The books chattered and flipped their pages open to faded words, sketched drawings, and inked illustrations. Each spouted off facts, narrating faster than I could keep up with.

"Ghosts: also known as spirits or specters—"

"They are known to haunt their childhood homes, often peaceful—"

"—unable to appear corporal, but they can affect some objects—"

"Wait!" I raised my voice, and my hands, to shush them. "I need to know about dangerous ghosts. The kind that destroy homes and erase memories."

The books fell silent for a moment, their pages rustling as if uncomfortable. Then, slowly, the first book flipped to an illustration of a house, paint peeling from its walls as a wild gust of wind and ghosts tore through it.

They could have stolen the image from yesterday's attack.

"You mean... this kind of ghost?"

I nodded eagerly.

The second book spoke in a hushed, nervous voice. "We don't like to talk about those kinds of ghosts—"

"But I think there's one in our house." I cleared my throat. "I need to know how to get rid of it. I think it's making my family forget about me."

The books shifted and rustled their pages once more. The third one finally spoke up in a deep, rumbling voice.

"Angry ghosts can do many things. It's possible there's a ghost making them forget about you..." It hesitated.

"What?" I pressed, leaning forward.

"When ghosts are in emotional distress," the book continued, "when they should have moved to the afterlife but they haven't, it can start to affect the world around them. It can destroy homes, sometimes even kill people."

Kill people? I couldn't let that happen.

"But how do you get rid of them?"

"Results are inconclusive!" This time the smaller book chimed in. "But popular theory suggests if you remove a ghost's ties to an area—mementos, pictures, that kind of thing—it will give them no reason to remain."

I swallowed.

"So... if I can figure out what is keeping the ghost here and get rid of it, they'll leave?"

The books quivered, pages fluttering in agreement, and I raised a nervous gaze to the ceiling. The attic room seemed to be calling to me, but my heart clenched at the idea of going there again.

"I don't really have a choice, do I?"

I drew in a deep breath, my jaw set. Tears trembled at the back of my eyes. I would do this, I would get rid of this ghost, and everything would go back to normal.

Something rustled above me, and moments later Melissa floated through the ceiling. She tilted her head, and I realized the tears had fought their way out and were now rolling down my cheeks.

"It's fine, Mel," I mumbled, rubbing a hand across my face.

The little ghost drifted closer, her face drawing into a frown.

"It's just—" I choked back a sob. "What if this ghost erases me—what if my family forgets me forever?"

The words echoed in the quiet library, as if to taunt me.

Melissa rested a tiny, ghostly palm atop mine. I stared down at our two small, pale hands next to each other and sighed softly.

"Thank you, Mel."

At least I knew she wouldn't leave me behind.

The girl flashed a little smirk at me, slipping from the bookshelves and toward the door. A new frown tugging at my face, I scrambled down the shelves after my one and only friend.

Melissa led me through the halls. She turned left where I usually went right, walking down a hallway which had fallen into disrepair years ago.

Ragged curtains hung over smudged windows, and puffs of dust exploded from the carpet under my feet. Where the hallway came to an abrupt stop, large red curtains hanging to the floor obscured the rest of the wall.

"What is this, Melissa?"

She gestured to the curtains. With a flourish, they swung open. Dust billowed off the wall, falling around us like snow. A family portrait sat there, eleven faces beaming at me with Melissa's bright grin.

I glanced from Melissa to the portrait. Two happy parents stood surrounded by their children. The mother held a baby while another little girl, barely five years old, tugged at her skirt. She may be a few years older now, but it was unmistakably Melissa.

"This... this is your family?"

The girl nodded, pointing to the parents, who waved back cheerily.

"They lived so long ago..." I brushed my finger against a tiny date inscribed in the bottom of the portrait.

The words from one of the ghost books ran through my head. *Ghosts often haunt their childhood home.*

I looked back at Melissa, my mouth dropping open.

"Mel… Do you know what ghost is destroying our home?"

The little girl nodded, eyes somber.

"Is it you?" The words came out strained and pinched.

Melissa's eyes widened, a hand flying to her chest. She shook her head angrily, a torrent of silent words falling from her mouth.

"You know I can't hear you, Mel." I sighed.

The ghost pouted at me, then gestured toward the portrait as if that would explain it all.

And as I watched, the painting began to shift. The family now surrounded a delicate gravestone wreathed in flowers. They held one another, shedding silent tears.

Melissa was the only one missing.

Invisible brushstrokes flew across the painting, replacing it with the image of a quaint little house. A wispy ghost girl ran through the flowers with siblings who could never quite see her. They laughed and played, growing up together and yet apart.

But the ghost girl stayed a small child as others moved on.

I gaped as the painting shifted once more. The family cowered as wild winds ripped through their home. Wallpaper shredded, books tossed from their shelves, cupboards ripped open.

In the center of it all, the little ghost cried as her home fell apart, her family moved away, and eventually she was left alone.

I looked to my little friend. Tears shone in her ghostly eyes, and she nodded softly.

"Oh Melissa—" My voice caught in my throat. "I'm so sorry—"

Melissa brushed her tears, nodding. Beside us, the painting was still changing as eventually a new house was built, a new family moving in. And still, Melissa was alone.

"So if you aren't the ghost doing all this, Mel... who is?" I bit my lip.

The look she gave me was entirely unamused, as though I should have figured it out by now.

"Is it someone else from your family?"

Again, she shook her head, bouncing from one ghostly foot to another. Then she pointed straight at me.

I frowned.

"Mel, I still don't know who it is."

The girl shook her head, gesturing toward me once more.

"Mel, what are you..." I trailed off.

A rush of heat flooded my body, and I shook my head. "Don't be ridiculous, Melissa. I'm not a ghost."

She continued to wave toward me.

"You can't just blame this on me to get away from the obvious fact you're the ghost doing this!" I snapped, hands balling into fists.

Tears sprang into Melissa's eyes, but I was too angry to care.

Spinning on my foot, I stormed from the room. The very idea that I was a ghost... It was ridiculous.

I was halfway to my room when I heard the crying.

Ducking into a nearby alcove to listen in, I held my breath as two pairs of feet creaked closer, followed by the soft murmur of Mom's voice.

"... darling, it's all right."

Twi sniffled. "I think I need to go up to the attic again."

"Again? Are you sure? I know that little attic room is cute, but—"

The rest of her words faded into silence as they moved further down the hall, their footsteps drowned out by the frantic blood surging through my ears.

The room.

Twi was going to go into the little room that started this whole disaster. My sister may be ignoring me, but I couldn't let her go there. Not when it could cause the ghosts to come again, and maybe even hurt her.

I raced for the attic. The door swung wide open for me. I watched it cautiously, slipping to the threshold. An involuntary shiver ran down my spine, but

I couldn't back out now.

Gritting my teeth, I ducked into the room.

Sunlight streamed in, bouncing off dust covered floorboards and a delicate mirror in the corner. I shoved down the churning in my stomach.

Outside, the wind growled.

The childhood mementos stared at me, as if they knew I didn't belong here.

Drawing in a trembling breath, I glared back at them. Once I'd thrown these all outside, once they were burned and gone forever, the ghost would have no reason to stay.

I picked up a doll from the shelf. Its head drooped to the side, half the stitches from its smile missing. Teeth clenched, I dropped it into a box. A pile of notebooks in the corner caught my eye. I snatched them off the floor, refusing to look at the leather covers as I tossed them next to the doll.

My hands shook as I grabbed toys and books and papers off the floor, piling them into the box. My movements were quick, scattered, frantic. The peace I expected to feel as I cleared out the room never arrived.

Instead, I just felt as empty as this little attic room, its walls stripped of a child's drawings. Only one thing remained: The teddy perched on the windowsill, looking at me with his lopsided smile.

I hesitated before it, one hand extended.

"What am I doing?" I whispered to the stuffed animal.

Teddy just sat there with his head tilted to one side, smiling.

Gritting my teeth, I yanked him off the windowsill. I couldn't allow Twi to be hurt by the ghosts now beating against the little glass window.

A memory slammed into my face.

A smiling little girl of barely eight years old, her... no, *my* hair up in pigtails, a gap in my smile where I'd lost a tooth. I was running through the house with Teddy, my best of friends. We did everything together.

But I couldn't keep Teddy with me forever.

Eventually Mom came, teaching me to braid my hair and dress like a grown up. So we put Teddy aside. He always sat on my windowsill, smiling at me, but I'd moved on. Teddy was now a memory, nothing more.

I stared down at his familiar little face, the place where Mom had to sew his ear back on after I'd chewed it off, the little patch over a hole in his left shoulder.

This was *my* Teddy.

"What are you doing up here, Teddy?" I whispered to him. I wasn't sure when it had happened, but I was sitting on the floor now, holding the stuffed animal up as I examined him.

What am I doing here?

I studied the room. The wallpaper covered in crayon drawings. The little circular window which made the perfect place to spy on the world. And the box of memories I had planned to destroy.

What was I doing? A creaking on the stairs shook me from my reverie.

The floor shifted and squeaked as someone approached.

I sprang to my feet. The attic still wasn't safe, not with the wind howling outside and the little window rattling as if it could burst open in a moment. I couldn't let Twi come in here.

I steeled my nerves, hands clenched into fists as I prepared to face my sister.

The door swung open. Drawing in a deep breath, I stepped up to block Twi's entry, opening my mouth to shout a warning.

My sister stood before me, staring right through my chest into the room beyond.

Drawing in a deep breath, she faltered, then stepped into the room.

Right through me.

For a moment, the world around me froze.

Twi... was Twi the ghost? But that didn't make sense—

Was Mel right after all? Was I...?

But that couldn't be true. I was a real, living, human girl.

Spinning around, I watched my sister move to the center of the room. She bent down to grab a box beneath the table.

"What—" My voice trembled, reaching a dangerously high pitch. "Twi, what's going on?"

Nothing. Just like every time I'd tried to talk to her for the past—

For how long?

I shook my head, huddled in the doorway. My memories were a muddled mess, days and weeks bleeding together until I found I could barely remember the past few hours.

Seated on the floor, Twi tugged a piece of paper out of her pocket. Unfurling it, she cleared her throat and began to read.

"*Dear Moon—*" Her voice shook, a tiny whisper struggling to be heard. "*I hope you hear this letter, somehow. Though if I'm being honest, I think I've been writing these more for myself than for you.*"

"Twi, stop it!" My voice rose to a shout, but she just kept reading.

"*It's been three months, and the house is still so quiet without you—*"

"I'm right here!" I waved my hands near her face.

"*Not much has happened since my last letter. But I think—*" She caught her breath, tears glistening in her eyes. "*I think you haven't really left. Something's destroying the house, Dad says it's a ghost.*"

My ears rang until I could hear nothing but the awful, all consuming scream growing inside me. I sprang to my feet, stumbling away from my sister.

"No—" My voice trembled, threatening to break. "Is this a joke?"

But still she didn't answer me. Where I should have tripped over a pile of boxes, I glided right through them. I stared down at my body, and what I'd thought was solid skin shifted to an eerie translucent glow.

With a sob, I ran from the attic. I still insisted on sprinting down the stairs like a normal person, imagining the sound of my feet slamming against the floor. As always, the house swung its doors open for me, letting me burst onto the main floor.

I sprinted down the hallway, stumbling to a stop as Mom stepped out of a room to the side, carrying a large cardboard box. The edge of a dress peeked over the top. My dress. My things. She was getting rid of my things.

They were erasing me.

Wiping furiously at my tears, I ran for the door. Portraits still hung on the wall, as always. Mom and Dad, smiling down at me. Twi, waving with a gap-toothed grin.

But my portrait was gone. Even here, they had removed any sign of me.

I was forgotten.

A gust of wind swirled through the hallway as a flush of rage warmed my cheeks. Blinking back ghostly tears, I ran for the door.

I sought refuge with the flowers, huddled in the gardens as wind tugged at me from all directions. Shaking, I squeezed my eyes shut and tried to imagine I was a real girl, that I could feel the soft dirt under my feet and the flowers clustered around me.

But that was only in my imagination, like it had been for the past... for however long I'd been a ghost. I'd been stuck in an imaginary world where I was still a real girl.

When I opened my eyes, I was simply hovering over the ground, flowers poking right through my translucent body. The wind picked up, brushing through me as though I wasn't even there.

The image of the hallway hung in my mind: three smiling family portraits, with mine removed.

Forgotten. I sobbed, burying my face in my hands.

My ghostly body still felt the growing cold that rolled out across the lawn. I raised my head, watching dark clouds form above me. Blocking out the sun, they cast my home into shadow.

I drew my arms in close, biting my lip. Shooting a fearful glance back toward the house, the shutters blown open, a wild wind tearing through my childhood home.

"No—" My voice cracked.

It was happening. Just like it had to Melissa.

I was the ghost destroying my home.

Shingles tore off the roof, whipped this way and that by the wind. The flowers around me trembled, ducking their heads as the wind threatened to blow them away.

Someone appeared at my side, her gleaming silvery gaze meeting mine.

Melissa mouthed words I still couldn't hear, but this time I knew what she was saying.

You can stop it.

She floated in front of me, completely undisturbed by the wild wind.

"How?" I pled.

She just watched in silence.

I was a ghost now. I would have to move on. Even if it meant leaving my family behind.

Biting my lip, I gazed at my home. Where I'd learned to read seated on Dad's lap, held little tea parties with Mom, and spent so much time with Twi.

I couldn't leave. Not now. Not ever.

The wind picked up, and with a resounding crash, the round window from our attic room shattered.

Glass fragments fell to the ground in a shower of sparkles. Melissa flickered at the corner of my vision. I couldn't let this happen.

Letting out a deep sigh, I stepped toward the house.

Though the wind barely seemed to touch Melissa, it tore at me. With each step it pushed me backward, whipping through my ghostly body as if trying to whisk me away. Teeth clenched, I took one step at a time, dragging myself toward my home.

Reaching the steps, I lunged to grab the railing. My hand slipped right through it, and I stumbled. Cringing, I forced my way up the steps. The front door was already blown wide open, and I managed to push my way into the hallway.

Wind whipped around me, swirling like the beginnings of a tornado. It slashed at the walls, pulled up the carpet, and tossed priceless family heirlooms around like sawdust. I wiped at my tears, lips trembling.

"I don't want this—" My small voice seemed lost to the wind. "Stop! Stop destroying everything, just leave it be!"

The wind continued to blow; more shingles ripped from the house.

Deep down, I knew the one thing that would protect my family, that would keep this house safe.

I sank to the hallway floor, wrapping my arms around myself.

"I'm not ready to go—" My voice shivered with the fear running through me.

A crack sounded through the air, and gaped as the wall before me tore open, a split running up the otherwise smooth plaster.

Shouts rang through the house, and I scrambled to my feet.

Mom and Dad stood in the living room, eyes wide. They clutched at furniture as if to avoid being blown straight out the gaping windows, all of which had shattered with the onslaught of wind.

"Twi—" Dad's voice rang through the air. "We have to get out of the house—"

A portrait ripped free of the wall, whizzing across the room and nearly slamming into his chest. I cringed, reaching out—

But what could I do?

I couldn't stop this; I couldn't protect them.

I wasn't even supposed to be here.

I backed away, walking right through the couch. Footsteps pounded down the stairs, and moments later Twi stood in the doorway, eyes wide. Her hair flew across her face, the wind ripping something free of her hands.

A piece of paper swirled through the air, almost pulled out the window before a new gust of wind sent it hurtling across the room. It landed at my feet. One of the tea table's legs reached out to hold it in place.

I hesitated, gaze darting from my terrified parents, to Twi's pale frightened face, to the letter at my feet.

Squatting down low, I squinted to read the words traced by my sister's delicate hand.

Dearest Moon,

It's been three months, and the house is still so quiet without you. Not much has happened since my last letter. But I think that maybe, you haven't really left. Something's destroying the house. Dad says it's a ghost.

I'm scared to go into our old attic room anymore. Mom says that might be what's disturbing the ghosts. But I need to read you these letters. I need to feel close to you, somehow.

I miss you so much, Moon. The house has been so quiet and sad since your accident. We all wish you were still here.

I've been taking good care of your gardens, I promise. The flowers don't like me as much as they liked you, but I've made sure they all stay healthy.

I can't believe it's been three months without you. I keep trying to live a normal life, but I don't think it will ever be that way again. I miss our trips into town, and our games of Sherlock and Watson.

But for now, whenever I miss you, I just come up to our room and write you a letter.

I hope you're doing okay without us, Moon.

I miss you.

Love, Your Sister, Twi

When I finally raised my head, the storm inside me was silent.

Around me, the wind fell to a faint summer breeze. Warm sunlight streamed through the space where our large living room windows once stood.

I reached up, wiping a faint tear from my ghostly cheeks.

"I love you too, Twi." My voice sounded like a whisper on the wind. But it was enough.

A faint mist began to fill the edges of my vision. I jerked my head around. The walls around me faded, becoming distant and surreal.

"Moon." Melissa hovered at the edge of the room, her voice now clear and distinct.

She held out a hand to me. Drawing a deep breath, I let my own glowing hand slip into hers.

"Is this goodbye?" I whispered, biting my trembling lip.

She nodded, and I cast a final look at my family as we stepped out of the living room. The three of them huddled together in a hug.

Twi raised her head as we passed, and for the briefest moment I felt our eyes meet. She whispered a soft, "Thank you."

I nodded, blinking back tears.

The hallway was just as fuzzy as the living room and growing ever fainter.

A blinding light shone at the front door, beckoning us both onward. As we passed the family portraits, I glanced up.

My face beamed back at me, a picture hanging in the spot that was empty not too long ago.

But this was a new picture, from just a few months earlier. I'm standing next to Twi, grinning as we pose before a garden bursting with flowers. I gazed up at the portrait and smiled. All fear, all sorrow, gone.

With a final look behind me, I whispered goodbye to my oblivious family.

Then, hand in hand with Mel, the little ghost girl who'd become my dear friend, I stepped into the light—and whatever comes beyond that.

JULIA NAUS

Julia Naus can't go five minutes in a crowd without making a new friend. After spending her teenage years as the odd one out, she endeavors to give everyone a place to belong. She writes fantasy stories that give readers the courage to find their place in the world—stories of found family that make fictional worlds feel like home. On a regular day she can be found drinking her fourth cup of coffee, wrangling her four siblings, and obsessively training Brazilian Jiu Jitsu.

Achievements

- Completed five novels, a novella, and multiple short stories.

- Received two full manuscript assessments on her novel, *To Defy Death*.

- Received interest in her novel from publishers and agents.

- Her novel, *To Defy Death*, won first place in the supernatural/paranormal/horror category of the Aurora Contest.

- Attended Realm Makers 2023 and 2024, Write to Publish 2023 and 2024, and Hope Words 2024.

- Started a social media marketing business and spent seven months as a marketing intern where she practiced social media, email, and ad marketing.

Pitches

- A 100,000-word fantasy novel about a Grim Reaper searching for his long lost sister, unaware she's been raised to kill him.

- *Ignite* meets *Mistborn* in a fantasy novel about a timid young woman, her audacious plan to steal from the gods, and the forbidden magic she's spent a lifetime running from.

THE RIVER'S LULLABY

MARYBETH DAVIS

How did his life fall to pieces so fast?

Averic dragged in a breath and squeezed his eyes shut. Maybe if he stayed put long enough, the shadows of the linen closet would keep him hidden forever, clinging to him like a blanket. Then he'd disappear and never have to face the nightmare outside again.

He stretched his achy neck until it cracked. It wasn't easy cramming his fourteen-year-old frame under the wide shelves in here. Still, it was better than listening to the baby's cries while Mama remained too exhausted to comfort her. The palace's stone walls sent those cries echoing everywhere.

His curled back pressed against one of them, the stony chill seeping through his tunic and darting down his spine. At least the linens and towels absorbed the worst of the sound. If he breathed loud enough, he could almost pretend not to hear it.

He shouldn't have heard his sister's first breath for another month yet. The news of Papa's capture came just yesterday, and Mama went into labor early. She and the baby barely made it. Although he'd only kept vigil from the hallway, no one could shield him from the sound ringing off the palace walls. Mama's *screams...*

The baby sent another wail down the hall. Averic gritted his teeth, nausea curling in his stomach. *Stop it. Please, just stop screaming.*

Papa's mission was supposed to be simple. As High Lord, he always led a team across the river into enemy land. The river was only calm enough to cross for a few days out of the year, so they had to be fast. But they'd done missions like this before. It was supposed to be quick. Straightforward. *Not dangerous.*

Papa, we need you back.

Shoes clicked across the stone floor outside. Averic held his breath. If a servant was on her way to get something from this closet, he was about to be in for an embarrassing explanation.

"Perhaps we should wait to carry out the funerary rites. Lady Eva hasn't recovered from the birth yet."

That was Father Fodar. Squinting under the door, Averic caught a glimpse of the man's white priestly garments swirling about his feet. Another pair of shoes strode beside his.

"Understandable," the other man's voice said—one of Papa's councilmen. "Yet it would be highly disrespectful to delay the rites of a High Lord too long."

Averic curled his fingers around his tunic, knuckles growing white as he held himself back from bursting out and yelling, "Papa isn't dead! He was just captured!" But it would be futile.

Averic had already begged the Council to rescue him—Papa was too principled to reveal his royal status to the enemy to save his own life. He would face torture and death before allowing himself to be used as leverage against his people.

The Council refused. It was impossible, they said. The river had returned to its year-round state of tumult, and trying to cross it now would be a deadly fool's mission. They would have to manage without the High Lord and appoint an older Council member in his place until Averic came of age.

How dare they?

"We won't delay forever, but for such a ceremony, the man's family must come first. I suggest we…" Father Fodar's voice faded as the men continued down the hall. Averic's fingers cramped from clenching his tunic so tight.

They're cowards. Abandoning their High Lord, just because of a stupid river? If anything was worth braving the dangerous waters, this was. Papa led them faithfully for years, and this was how they expressed their gratitude?

Maybe you should also stop hiding in a closet, coward.

Averic kicked the thought aside. It was better if he stayed far away from the baby. What could he do anyway? Even the nursemaids couldn't calm her down—only Mama could. Averic had never even held a baby before. That crying would send his nerves into a frenzy until his head throbbed. *Again.*

Could Papa calm her?

Mama was suffering from so much more than a rough birth. She couldn't hold the baby for more than a few minutes at a time. Averic sensed it was as much due to grief as her health.

Would she ever recover if Papa never came home?

The baby's cries once again echoed down the hall.

How could their family—their *country*—go on without Papa? Averic needed to learn so much more from him. Their country needed his leadership. Their family needed his leadership. *I still need my father.*

His brave eyes. His loud laugh. His huge, warm hands. He couldn't just be... gone.

He's not. The Council may be cowards, but you're not. Are you?

Averic licked his dry lips. Everyone else could pretend otherwise all they wanted, but the broken pieces would never be fixed without Papa. He was the knot holding everything together.

So Averic resolved to bring him back.

He stretched out a hand, feeling around for the doorknob until it clicked. Glancing through the crack in the doorway, he made sure the hall was empty before crawling out, stretching his cramped back. Then he ran down the hallway to his chambers.

Averic threw his door open and darted to his desk, shoving aside his neatly stacked study notes. Science would do him no good now. Instead, he rifled through the perfectly ordered bookshelves lining the wall, pulling out the first atlas he saw. He tossed it onto his desk and flipped through the thick pages. A map of both nations, a close-up map of the landing area—he tore them from the binding. He'd apologize for it later, after Papa was home. Right now, he—

"Averic, what are you doing?"

He whirled around with a start.

Father Fodar stood in the doorway.

Averic shoved the book and maps underneath his study notes. "I thought you were preparing for Papa's rites."

"They can wait for the moment. I was concerned about you."

Averic turned around and pretended to shuffle through his notes. "I'm fine."

Silence. The musty scent of old paper tinged the air as Averic ran out of pages to blindly flip past. He gritted his teeth and looked over his shoulder. "What?"

Father Fodar's eyes lingered on a spot on the desk. Averic glanced down. A corner of the map stuck out from under his notes. He shoved it aside, but it was too late. Understanding had already entered the priest's softening gaze.

"Whatever it is you're doing, I would encourage you to think things through. At times like this, it is vital that families stay close together."

How can we, without Papa? "I know."

Father Fodar took a step closer. "I've visited your mother and the baby several times in the last day, but I haven't seen you with them. Have you held Nadya yet?"

Averic's throat tightened. "What does it matter?"

"It simply seems strange to me. You've been so excited to meet the child, but now that she's here, you won't go near her." A smile lifted the priest's lips. "I'm sure your presence would comfort her. With all those lullabies you and Lady Eva sang, Nadya must know your voice nearly as well as her mother's."

Averic turned away, rubbing the sweat off his palms. His eyes traced the cold stone walls, the floor-to-ceiling bookcases that at any other time felt like old friends.

"I'm no use in there."

He'd been helpless to stop Mama's cries; how could the priest expect him to stop the baby's? If Mama was to get better—if the baby was ever to quiet and rest—Papa was their only chance.

Father Fodar's voice softened even further. "You will always be welcome at the Shrine if you need a listening ear. Grief is a wretched thing, and there's no simple way to handle it. But if you're thinking of doing something reckless, I advise you to consider why you're doing it."

Just leave me alone.

"Are you really trying to help?" The priest's voice grew quiet. "Or are you just running away?"

He glared at Father Fodar. "I didn't ask for you to come after me. Just go prepare Papa's rites like you're supposed to!"

Father Fodar raised his eyebrows. Averic expected a retort or lecture, but the priest only closed his eyes for a few seconds, almost as if in prayer. He dipped his chin and turned away, shutting the door behind him with a soft *click*.

Hot air rushed shakily from Averic's lungs. *What are you doing, Averic? You never talk to anyone like that—much less a priest!*

The baby's pitched wail echoed down the hall. Averic flinched.

He snatched the blanket off his bed. He shoved it with the maps into a satchel and yanked on his boots. Throwing a cloak around his shoulders, he glanced down the hall and slipped out.

The cries grew louder with every step he took. His jaw tensed. *It'll be over soon enough. Once Papa's back, all that screaming will—*

It stopped. Averic's brow furrowed as he drew near to Mama's room.

On the other side of the door, her soft voice shushed the baby.

She must have the strength to hold her again. His throat tightened as she hummed a tune—haunting, sweet, and flowing, like rolling foothills in a sunset's shadow.

She'd sung that lullaby to Averic when he was a child, and all through this pregnancy, he sang it with her to the baby inside her. It was as familiar as breathing. Even as he hesitated by her door, the song nearly slipped from his own throat.

Saving Papa is going to take a while, days at best. You disappearing will scare Mama. With everything else she's dealing with, would this really be...

A weary sigh and indistinct murmur slipped past the door. Cloth shifted, and the baby's cries pierced the air once more.

Tension seized Averic's limbs. Yanking his hood over his head to muffle the sound, he ran.

Averic slowed as he rounded a bend in the gravel path through the mountains. His lungs burned, but the palace was behind him now, and with it, the greatest risk. He'd avoided prying eyes on his way out. Now, with rocky slopes rising on either side of him and the pine forest looming ahead, he had the space to plan.

Stepping off the path, he crouched behind a boulder and pulled the maps from his satchel. He traced a finger along the soft paper. If he followed this path through the woods, he would reach the boat shed in a matter of minutes. No ordinary person wanted to go near the river, so there shouldn't be any locks. If he could drag just one small rowboat out, the current should take him down to—

Gravel crunched around the bend.

Averic held his breath. Surely no one would be looking for him already. Still, he didn't need anyone asking what he was doing out here.

Pressing a hand against the lichen-covered stone, he peered out as two soldiers came into view.

"I still say it doesn't sound like Lord Averic."

"It was only Father Fodar's suspicion. The boy may be fourteen, but he's too smart for something that reckless."

So the priest had said something. *Telltale.* He held his breath as they passed by.

"Still, I'd expected better of him. Going missing at a time like this? As if his poor mother doesn't have enough to worry about."

Averic's stomach twisted as they left earshot. No one told her he was gone, did they? He wasn't trying to make things harder, he just...

The phantom sound of Mama's cries rang in his ears.

Averic gritted his teeth, pressing his hands to his temples. *Once you find Papa, this will be worth it. She won't be upset after that, and the baby will have her father.*

He shoved the maps back into his satchel and looped it over his shoulder. Now he just had to wait for those soldiers to come back from the riverside and return to the palace. Then the path should be clear.

His ankles cramped as the minutes dragged by. Finally, the skitter of pebbles signaled their return. The instant their heads disappeared around the next bend, Averic clambered from behind the boulder, brushed off the dirt and gravel clinging to his palms, and burst into a sprint.

Brittle twigs snapped underfoot with the rustle of pine needles. Wind whipped past his face. Soon, the rush of the waters blended with the wind in his ears.

There. Just past the tree line, the boat shed sat a safe distance fifty feet from the shore. Averic aimed straight for it. As he'd hoped, no locks held the large wooden doors shut. He pulled them open and stepped into the darkness.

The smell of mildew hung in the air like cobwebs. Wrinkling his nose, he waited for his eyes to adjust. He reached for a paddle hanging on the wall, tucking it under his arm. He shoved his hands under the rim of an upside-down rowboat and strained to pull it out the door. *Are boats always this heavy?*

Once outside, Averic dragged it backward toward the shore.

His foot slipped in the mud, throwing him onto his backside. *Should have packed extra pants... no matter.* He rose and kept pulling until the water lapped about his feet. With a deep breath, he turned around.

Oh.

Papa once told him that even calm-looking waters could hide a treacherous current. This river wasn't bothering to hide anything. The waters tossed in waves, white foam arching down like teeth, dripping with saliva. Averic swallowed hard.

"The boy is too smart for something that reckless."

The soldier's words rang in his ears. Was this really a stupid idea? If something went wrong...

No! You're Papa's only chance. If you don't save him, no one will.

He could handle a rough ride. Even angry waters would still take him west to the landing point in enemy territory. All things considered, this wasn't even the hard part. Averic's fists tightened. He shoved the boat into the water and hopped in.

A frigid spray hit his skin. Averic gripped the sides of the boat. Beneath him, the river felt more like a herd of bucking, stampeding horses. The boat shed passed his view in seconds.

Averic pressed his knees on the sides to brace himself and took out the paddle to push himself farther into the torrent. It nearly ripped out of his hands the moment it hit the water. He stiffened and paddled anyway.

It's fine. You're going to make it. Papa is—

A wave seized the boat and threw it into the air for a breathless instant. Averic screamed. The paddle dug into the water as he landed, jerking him to the side and—

Cold!

Freezing water wrapped around his limbs. It swept over his head. Darkness and light spun above and below him. He grabbed at the light... wrong way, now it was... not there either!

He grasped for anything. Rocks. Air. The surface tumbled out of reach. The rocks slipped from his grip. His lungs burned.

His vision darkened. A scream built in his chest.

Help me!

The current threw him backward.

A bony arm wrapped around his chest and yanked him up. He gasped—

—air.

He coughed violently. Sparks flew through his spotty vision as someone dragged him up onto the muddy bank.

"Breathe, Averic!" A familiar voice filtered through the buzzing in his ears.

Averic spat water onto the ground and dragged in a breath.

"That's right, get air in those lungs. You'll be all right."

Averic wheezed and looked up. Father Fodar patted his back, apparently uncaring of the mud smearing his white vestments.

Rising shakily onto his elbow, Averic glanced back at the river. If the priest hadn't caught him, the current could have taken him for miles.

I almost died.

Tears mingled with the water streaming down his face. Trembling overtook him. *I really almost died.* He glimpsed trees in the corner of his eye. He'd never have gotten to climb one again. Never taken a book with him to the highest branches to hide from his tutors again. No, he almost never got to breathe *air* again. *What was I thinking? I could have ended up in the bottom of that river forever. I almost ended everything right there!*

What had ever made him think he could do this?

Father Fodar's hand stopped patting Averic's back. "Are you all right?" he asked quietly.

Averic shuddered. What was he even supposed to say?

The priest wiped a dripping strand of hair away from Averic's face. "Thank heaven I came to check for myself. You hid from those soldiers rather well, didn't you?"

Too well. The Council was right, curse them. This was never anything more than a fool's mission.

You knew that all along, though, didn't you?

Averic stared at his mud-streaked hands. *Warm and alive, not cold and stiff.* What would he have even done once he made it there? Fought the men who took his father? What could he have done that Papa wasn't capable of doing already?

Why did he even do this to begin with?

"Are you really trying to help? Or are you just running away?"

A vision of Mama, alone in her chambers...

He'd almost left her grieving Papa *and* him.

"I'm sorry," he whispered.

Father Fodar took his shoulders and looked him in the eye. "I won't waste my breath telling you how foolish that was. I think you're well aware already." His gentle gaze brought tears to Averic's eyes. "To say your mother is worried would be an understatement."

Averic wiped his face with a water-soaked sleeve. "I need to..." *To quit being an idiot. To fix things. To be there, even if Papa can't.*

The priest nodded. Averic pulled away and stumbled to his feet. He paused.

To leave Father Fodar here alone would be rude, especially after he'd just saved Averic's life, but—

Father Fodar smiled. "Go to her."

Averic ran.

Pine needles flew from his feet. Tears and river water blurred his eyes.

I'm sorry. I'm sorry. I'm so sorry, Mama!

So what if the cries twisted his insides into knots? She needed him home. Nadya needed him home. *They need me alive!*

Pine needles gave way to gravel. He ran toward the road, past staring commoners, back to the palace. Scattered soldiers rose a shout. He came to a wheezing halt by the great wooden door in the stone wall.

"Lord Averic!" one of the guards snapped. "Where have you been? We've all been—"

"Mama," Averic gasped. He stared up at him through strings of dripping hair. "I need to—"

A woman rushed over, tangled hair flying in the chilly breeze. One of Mama's attendants. "Lord Averic!" she cried. "Where in the—what *happened* to you?"

Averic wiped the mud from his face with his sleeve. "Please tell me she's okay."

She sighed, harried expression softening. "Come along."

Averic followed her inside and up the grand staircase, silently begging her to go faster. She didn't seem upset. Surely nothing could have gone too wrong? The shock of Papa's capture and giving birth had taken such a toll on her. What had Averic's disappearance done?

The woman led him down the hallway, past his chambers, past the dark linen closet...

The moment Mama's door came into view, Averic ran past the woman and threw it open.

Sitting up against pillows, Mama sat with her pale hair falling in messy strands over her face as she cried. She raised her head and gasped.

"Averic," she breathed, reaching out her arms. He rushed over and held her tight. Was the shaking from her shoulders or his? It didn't matter.

"I'm so sorry." His voice wobbled. "I was—I was being stupid, and I was scared, and..."

"There, now," she whispered. "Just breathe."

Averic cried. The neck of her robe grew damp with his tears, and she held him closer.

"I know you're afraid. I'm afraid too." Her voice shook as her hand rubbed his arm. "I still hope your father will make it back to us somehow. But until then, now more than ever, we have to stay together."

Averic squeezed his eyes shut and nodded.

A small wail pierced the air.

Averic expected to flinch or even to run out of the room, but instead he only wanted to see his sister. To touch her even.

Mama sighed wearily and glanced into the cradle by her bedside. She pulled away and reached for the baby.

"Um—if you're tired, maybe... I can hold her?"

Averic swallowed hard as soon as the words were out of his mouth. Mama's warm smile made them worth it.

"You'll have to change out of that shirt. We can't risk her getting sick, with her being such an early baby."

The midwife's assistant stepped into the room and handed Averic a fresh tunic. Dazedly, he pulled his muddy one off and wrestled the new one over his head. Tying his dirty hair back, he wiped his hands and reached into the cradle.

He barely heard Mama's murmurs to be careful, to support the baby's head. How could he, looking at her?

Nadya was wrinkly, red, and so loud his head throbbed.

She was the most beautiful thing he'd ever seen.

He drew the wailing little girl close to his chest. His throat tightened, and his eyes blurred with threatening tears. Papa should have been the first man to hold her. Should have been able to comfort Mama in her labor pains.

Averic might never see him again.

And yet...

He cleared his lumpy throat and hummed a soft tune. Haunting, sweet, and flowing, like rolling foothills in a sunset's shadow.

Nadya's wail caught. Her blue eyes peeked up at him. He held a finger against her hand, and her tiny fingers wrapped around his.

His sister needed him. If Papa couldn't be here, Averic would be.

Papa, I still hope you return to us. But if you don't, I'll love and protect her in your stead. And I'll look out for Mama.

Whatever happens, I swear I'll stay by their side.

MARYBETH DAVIS

As a kid, Marybeth Davis created stories out of cotton balls in her bathroom sink. Having since wrestled through the throes of religion-focused OCD and come out the other side, she now writes intense stories that take her audience back to their "reading under the covers" days as kids, but with the complex biblical truths they're ready for as young adults. When she's trying to avoid her manuscript like the procrastinator she is, you can find Marybeth pranking her friends, talking to her cat in Japanese, and reading found family fanfiction until two in the morning.

Achievements

- Completed four novels and over ten short stories.

- Received in-depth feedback from award-winning authors and professional editors.

- Received interest in her projects from multiple agents and publishers.

- Gained experience in marketing and project management through running a successful housecleaning business with multiple employees.

- Attended the Write To Publish and Realm Makers conferences in 2024.

- Gained her first 200 email subscribers in less than two months.

Pitches

- *Avatar: The Last Airbender* meets *The Blades of Acktar* in a YA fantasy about a young assassin with magic healing blood who wants to escape his line of work, but is forced to choose between completing one last kill and losing the only family he has left.

- *The Scarlet Pimpernel* meets *Red Queen* in a YA fantasy about a teenage boy with destroying mist magic who must evade a tyrant to save his best friend, knowing his friend would kill him if he knew about his powers.

- *The Wingfeather Saga* meets *Mistborn* in a YA fantasy where a dying princess's only hope for a cure to her mystical illness lies with a man imprisoned for trying to kidnap her.

WILLOW, ZILLOW, AND SMITH

ESTHER PIPKIN

The tiny potion bottles look like little soldiers all in a row on the empty bookcase, the liquid inside swirling in different shades of blue, green, and purple.

"Where are we going to hide them this time?" I glance around at our back room littered with stacks of yellowed books and boxes.

"We've got to think of something. She nearly found them last month." My sister, Zillow, presses her mouth in a thin line as she finishes braiding her brown hair. She keeps it much shorter than mine. Always the practical sibling.

"Mrs. Milburn won't be here until tomorrow, and Mr. Tatterval will be by later to pick up a healing tonic for his wife. Smith will have plenty of time to hide them in one of his spots in the woods," I say.

Our landlord, Vanessa Milburn, had started giving monthly inspections when she discovered we used to sell potions before magic was outlawed. Now we just sell them to a select few customers behind her back.

Because the last thing we want to do is find ourselves in jail, again.

Zillow rolls her eyes. "Honestly I'd almost rather her find out instead of always sneaking around."

"You don't mean that. Do you want to end up in prison?" I glance at a village's local paper lying on a crate of books. The top reads: "*BAKERY CLOSING DUE TO OWNER'S ARREST!*" Mrs. Milburn had given it to us during her last visit as a reminder that she had evicted one tenant and reported another for doing business with elves.

I've been in prison before. As soon as I cause conflict with our landlord, I run the risk of ending up there again.

Zill has always been the fearless one. When we were kids, she once punched a boy in the nose for saying my face looked like a toad.

I had just nodded and agreed with him so as not to cause trouble.

When magic was first outlawed, I'd tried to fight it. I was thrown in jail for my efforts while my siblings nearly starved with no income.

Now, I just keep my head down.

Zillow shrugs and picks up a box of cookbooks, blowing a stray strand of hair out of her face. "I'm going to put these up before we open."

"I'll be right behind you." I shut the cupboard. *Why did we make so many potions this month?* We really should stop, but they do so much good for those who need them.

Zillow yells from the front room, "Willow, come look at this!"

I hurry across the wooden floor covered in a light layer of dirt from my younger brother Smith running through with his boots on. I brush aside the yellow, onion-dyed linen curtain. My sister stands in front of the *Biographies* section, holding up a chunk of an oak floorboard.

"I nearly fell through the floor." She points to a hole in between her feet. It definitely was *not* there a moment ago.

"Oh no." I sigh. What else could go wrong with this place? The floor was creaky and saggy, and seemed to worsen every day, but Mrs. Milburn had assured us it was nothing to worry about. Just like the stove, the leaky roof, and the hole in the window we stuffed with rags...

I look around the large room. Bookshelves and tables create makeshift aisles for customers to browse and get lost in as soon as they enter. The early morning sun shines onto the window seats. Cushions and blankets invite anyone to cuddle up with a new read and enjoy the scent of old paper. From the outside looking in, our shop looks quaint and cozy, with maybe a little bit too much dust on the top shelves. I make a mental note to remind Smith once again to clean them.

If only our customers knew what we do to keep this place from falling apart at the seams.

I look down at the floor and tap the opening with my foot. I *don't* think wood is supposed to bend that much.

"We're opening in an hour, Willow. We need to do something." Zillow crosses her arms, her mouth twisting to the side. I can almost hear her thoughts. She could say a thousand things without speaking a word. And she's telling me to listen to her.

"We'll ask Mrs. Milburn to fix it." I push back my long dark hair behind my ear.

We're used to her monthly investigations. Except when she rubbed all the disrepair in our faces. She knew we couldn't do anything without getting thrown out. "You know my husband died from a bad potion he bought. You know I'm only doing it out of the goodness of my heart," she'd said.

If only she had some goodness to spend on fixing the place. She owns it after all.

"How many times have we asked, and she hasn't done anything about it?"

"I know. But…" I look around and notice a wooden crate of children's books next to the *Health and Remedies* section. "We can put a blanket and that crate over it in the meantime, so customers don't trip. It'll be fine."

She raises her eyebrows, but agrees and walks to the back, returning with an old calico blanket.

"Aww, I haven't seen that old thing in forever." I grab the other half, and we lay it over the weakened floor boards. "Smith used to take it with him everywhere."

"Where is he, anyway?" Zill steps back and picks up one side of the crate.

"I'm not sure. He told me he was going out this morning." I move over to help, and we set the crate over the blanket. Thankfully, it doesn't weigh too much, so it shouldn't be too much for the rotten boards to handle.

"Probably off saving another stray cat or something," she mutters.

I chuckle. The entire village knows he can't resist anyone in need, especially animals. If our landlady didn't strictly forbid pets, our shop and quarters above would be full of abandoned cats and dogs.

The back door bangs open, the sound reverberating through the entire shop.

"Willow! Zill!" Smith yells, sounding out of breath.

I march toward the curtain leading to the back room. I move it aside, revealing a floor covered in piles and crates of unsorted books.

Smith's cheeks are red, his dark hair unkept and windblown as always.

One look at his wide eyes, and I know something isn't right.

"What's wrong?"

"Hi!" A little girl peaks around his legs and waves at me. She clutches his hand and smiles, blue eyes wide as she looks up at me. She can't be more than three.

"Smith..." A million scenarios run through my head. Is she lost? Injured? She doesn't seem injured...

"Blazes, Smith, who is this?" Zillow steps out from behind me.

"So, this is Rosie. I think. She's hard to understand most of the time." He avoids looking me in the eye.

Rosie lets go of Smith's hand and hops to the nearest box, her curls bouncing around her head, showing her ears. Her *pointed* ears.

"She's an elf," I whisper.

He runs a hand through his hair. "Look, I know this isn't great, but I found her in the woods, clearly lost. I had to do something."

Zill pinches her lips together. "So you brought her here? You know how bad this looks! This isn't some stray cat you can nurse to health and set free. This is an *elf*."

I close my eyes. Smith might be sixteen, nearly a man, but his habit of bringing on trouble will send me to my grave far before my time. And this one is far worse than anything he's ever done. Elves were bidden unwelcome in our country since they naturally wield magic. If anyone, *especially* Mrs. Milburn finds we've been harboring an elf girl, we'll be sent to jail. Rosie will likely be carted off to the capital for questioning, and we will lose the new life we've built after shutting down our potions business.

What could I do? If caught my siblings will know what jail is like. The one thing I've promised to never let happen.

"I know what she is!" Smith says, stepping in front of the girl. "But if you think I was going to just leave her there, you're wrong."

"It's all right, we can fix this." I hold out my hands. A full on argument between my two younger siblings is the last thing we need.

"How? By turning the girl in?" Zillow looks at the girl sitting on the floor with a dictionary of bugs lying open on her lap.

"Pwetty!" She points to a sketch of a monarch butterfly.

I shake my head. "No. There's a sanctuary near Badger that harbors magic-wielding races. We can take her there and no one has to know she was ever here."

"Brilliant! Good thinking, Willow. But not before I get her something to eat. What do kids eat, anyway?"

"Um, the same thing you eat," Zill says, but her shoulders relax as Smith walks up the stairs to our living quarters.

"Just remember to cut her food in smaller pieces!" I shout up to him.

"Food?" Rosie drops her book on the floor and looks at me.

I kneel beside her. "Yes, honey, are you hungry?"

She rubs her stomach. "So hungwy." Her blue dress is stained and torn at the hem, indicating she traveled a long way.

Where did she come from?

"What's your name?" She points at me with a tiny finger.

I smile. "I'm Willow. This is my sister, Zillow."

The girl giggles, her plump cheeks dimpling. "Funny names."

Zillow shifts from one foot to another in the doorway.

I laugh. "That's what I told my parents when Smith was born. Can you guess what I wanted to name him?"

She shakes her head.

"I thought he should be named Watermelon," I whisper.

"That's so silly!" She squeals, rocking back. I laugh with her; her joy is so infectious.

Two quick knocks come from the front door.

Zillow and I look at each other. We're not open yet. If we just ignore them maybe they'll go away.

"Too-da-loo! Anyone home?" A husky, yet deceptively cheerful voice calls from the front room.

Blazes.

"How did Vanessa get in?" Zill hisses.

"I didn't lock the door after I swept the front porch this morning." I stare at the child. We've got to do *something*, but my mind goes blank.

"Siblings? Are you up and about?" The floorboards creak in the next room, telling me she's headed right for us.

"Hide her. I'll distract Mrs. Milburn." I clasp my shaky hands together as I walk through the curtain into the front room.

An image of the potions lined up in the bookcase flashes in my mind. I run back and fling the cupboard door open, cramming them in my pocket. I take a breath, and walk back into the front room.

Mrs. Milburn is standing on her tiptoes, running a finger along the top of a cabinet, her dark purple skirts brushing against her skinny ankles and fine black leather boots. Her brown leather bag is next to her on the ground.

"Good morning," I say, my voice thick and wobbly.

She straightens and turns around, lowering her hand. "Why, hello, Willow. I must say, I'm quite surprised by the amount of dust you've let accumulate over the past month."

I smile politely, holding my tongue. She always looks for the smallest things to critique, searching for any possible sign that we're still selling potions. Are there any secret compartments behind our bookcases? Any potions underneath the floorboards?

I reach into the deep side pocket of my dress, clutching the few tiny vials. She won't find anything, as long as she searches just the house.

"We weren't expecting you until tomorrow."

She laughs, batting a hand at me like I'm a child asking a foolish question. "I thought I'd come a day early as tomorrow turned out to be a very busy day for me." She glances down the aisle of shelves of crusty, weathered books and the couple of potted plants sitting beside them.

"Oh, I see." I breathe in and out, trying to remain calm. Why did she have to choose today to give a surprise inspection? Have we been anything but good tenants?

Zill steps out from the back room, nodding in my direction.

We can do this. If we can just satisfy Mrs. Milburn, we can get Rosie out and all of us to safety.

"I'll just do my usual poking around. Feel free to go about your business." Mrs. Milburn smiles and continues to peer at the bookshelves.

Thump, thump, thump.

Smith's quick, heavy footsteps descend the stairway from the apartment. A moment later he pops through the curtain, holding a steaming plate of carrots, mashed potatoes, and beans. Our leftovers from last night.

I stare at him, my expression saying, *Don't do anything stupid.*

Mrs. Milburn tilts her head at him. "Didn't eat dinner last night, did we, young Smith?"

"Um, no, it's not for me, I-I just..." he stammers.

Zillow kicks him in the shin.

Mrs. Milburn raises a thin eyebrow.

"He's a growing boy. He eats more than his fair share of leftovers." I laugh, staring Smith down. "Why don't you eat that in the other room?"

Mrs. Milburn shrugs and goes back to prodding the beams of the ceiling with a stick she'd found in the corner.

"Why is she here?" Smith mouths before he returns to the back room.

Mrs. Milburn smiles and claps her hands together. "Well! This room looks fine enough, besides the occasional dust pile. Why don't I move on to your back room next?"

My heart plummets to my toes.

She marches toward us, her smile obviously fake. "Come on, move aside. I'll be up and out of here in no time at all."

I freeze, my feet glued to the floorboards as Mrs. Milburn brushes past me. Zillow looks at me, her mouth in a thin line.

Praying Smith read my warning and hid the child, I swipe away the curtain to find Mrs. Milburn standing over Smith. He's sitting in front of the cupboard, holding an empty plate in the corner of the dimly lit room.

I take a shallow breath of air. If Rosie is in that cupboard and Mrs. Milburn finds her, we'll all end up in jail, no questions asked.

With her hands on her hips, Mrs. Milburn says, "Well, you wiped that plate clean. Don't your sisters ever feed you?"

"This isn't going to work, Willow," Zill hisses in my ear. "Maybe we should confront her before she finds Rosie. Tell her we've got her here and are taking her away. If we stand our ground she might leave us alone."

"No." I whisper back. "We can do this without having to fight her."

"Why don't you stand up, dear, I'll need to get to that little cupboard sooner or later," she coos to Smith.

He looks at me like a rabbit staring at a coyote.

"Tree!" He shouts, dropping the plate in his lap.

"Pardon me?" Mrs. Milburn tilts her head, her thin lips twitching.

"There's um, a tree outside that you need to see. It has very good apples in the fall, but it is close to the back, and any rain storm could knock it flat, you know."

She purses her lips. "Oh, I see. I don't recall it being close enough to be a threat, but..."

"I'll show you." He jumps up and steps over a box before running out the back door.

Zillow and I let out a breath as Mrs. Milburn follows him outside.

"Quick, let's get her to the front," I say the second the door closes.

I open the green-painted door, revealing Rosie with a carrot stained dress.

"Come on, honey, we need to take you somewhere else for a little while, all right?"

She nods as I take her grubby hand.

We walk to the front room as fast as her chubby legs can go. Zillow empties the basket of blankets by the window seat, and I lift the little girl inside.

I place my hands on my knees and look into her brilliant blue eyes, sparkles of light glimmering on her cheeks. I haven't seen an elf in so long, I'd almost forgotten how their faces glow. "Can you sit down quietly for me until the lady is gone?"

Rosie nods, and I cover her with two quilted blankets as Zillow stuffs the other ones under the window seat.

Someone taps the front door, and I flinch.

Zillow throws up her hands. "Who else needs us before we open?"

I peek through the window. It's a short, hunched man with snow white hair. He leans on a cane in one hand and holds one of our book baskets in the other.

My shoulders relax. "It's Mr. Tatterval." I move to the door and grasp the handle. "We're close enough to opening time, we might as well let him in."

"Maybe that'll motivate Vanessa to move along," Zill mumbles.

"Good morning Mr. Tatterval!" I raise my voice just slightly, making sure he can hear me.

"Why, hello." He totters in, swinging his basket unsteadily as he crosses the threshold. "I know I'm a bit early this mornin', but my wife was doing some spring cleaning and said I was up and under her feet." He winks at me.

"I see," I laugh. I'd never met his wife, but from his stories she sounds like she's quite a character, even with the sickness she's suffered for over a month now. I reach in my pocket and bring out a purple potion, gently placing it in his basket without a word.

He nods. "You don't mind if I sit and finish my book, do ya?" He points at the window seat where Zill is standing.

"Of course, but..." I can't think of a reason to say no.

My sister and I both glance at the blanket hamper as Mr. Tatterval settles on the brown cushion.

Zillow shakes her head and moves to a crate of books.

"Willow!" Mrs. Milburn struts from the back room, Smith following behind with his head bent like a disobedient dog.

Can't this day just be over with?

"That apple tree is nowhere near the house, and you have nothing to worry about. Lucky you," she twitters.

"Oh, how wonderful." I can almost hear the eye roll in Zill's voice.

"Well, I'm moving on upstairs after I finish this back room. Holler if you need me." She flashes a smile and goes back to her usual business of poking through our every possession.

I sigh and turn back to Mr. Tatterval. Rosie has poked her head out of the basket and is smiling at the elderly man.

"Oh, Rosie!" The words escape my mouth before I can think.

Mr. Tatterval cocks his head at me. "Who is this young lady?"

"A friend. Why don't you come with me, honey?" I lift her out of the basket. We can't afford to make mistakes. If anything happens, it'll all be my fault.

"Willow!" Mrs. Milburn yells.

I freeze. I can hear her footsteps on the stairs.

"I'll hide her." Smith picks the girl up under the waist and speeds behind a bookcase the moment Mrs. Milburn reemerges.

I clasp my hands together, forcing on a tightlipped smile.

"Now, who is this? You have all sorts of people here today." Mr. Tatterval chuckles.

"This is Mrs. Vanessa Milburn, our landlord." I gesture to her.

Mrs. Milburn nods politely. "One of your customers, I assume?"

Zillow eyes everyone in turn from her corner.

"Yes, indeed I am." He taps his cane on the ground. "And I must say..." He clears his throat. "I have been so impressed by these siblings and their shop. You must be so glad to have them renting from you."

She laughs, her typical fake, throaty laugh. "Well, I'm sure they're even more glad to have a landlord who will take them after their previous history with magic."

My cheeks burn. She uses this jibe often enough, but never in front of a customer. One of our most loyal customers.

He looks at me, and our eyes meet. He furrows his bushy eyebrows.

"That is not a kind thing to say," he says slowly. "I could use some strong words for someone who would say such a thing in front of their own tenant. But I'll refrain, if you apologize."

Mrs. Milburn's mouth drops. "Oh! I..." For once, she seems at a loss for words.

He winks at me.

She smoothes out her skirt. "Well, I am so sorry for any sort of misunderstanding. I didn't think my statement would be taken that way."

I nearly smile, my respect for Mr. Tatterval cemented. He stood up for me, boldly, without a second's thought.

I look at Zill, still watching from the other side of the room. She's never been afraid of conflict, but I've always believed keeping the peace is better.

"Well, I think it's time I picked out a new book." He leans on his cane and stands. "What have you got for me, Ms. Zillow?" He walks over to her, floorboards creaking under his feet.

"Hmm, I suppose it's time to take my leave. Everything seems in order." Mrs. Milburn glances at the crate covering the broken floor is as she heads for the door. She gives a less cheerful: "Ta-ta," than normal as she closes the door behind her.

I nearly collapse onto the window seat, the soft cushion springing up under me.

She's gone.

Mr. Tatterval leaves a minute later, two new books in his basket. Zill sits beside me, returning a stray strand of hair behind her ear.

Smith pokes his head into the room. "Did she leave?"

"Yes." We are free of her for another month. But, somehow, this doesn't feel like a victory. Next time she might come down on us twice as hard after being embarrassed by one of our customers.

Rosie follows Smith into the room, clutching onto the hem of his brown tunic.

"Bad lady gone?" The girl whispers, lip trembling.

Smith kneels down and takes her hand.

"Yes, honey." I put on a smile. "And we're going to get you to a safe place."

The front door swings open, and Vanessa Milburn walks in.

I grasp the seat cushion. Zillow shoots upright. Smith's eyes widen as he hugs Rosie close.

Mrs. Milburn sets her eyes on Rosie standing in the middle of the shop, surrounded by books and bookcases, her elf ears in plain view.

"What is this?" she sputters, her cheeks reddening. Her eyes travel from me to the child standing next to her brown leather bag sitting in front of the bookcase.

I force myself to stand and face Mrs. Milburn when all I want to do is run. But I can't think about escaping. My first and only duty is to protect my siblings and the child.

"We are taking this child to where she will be safe, because she has done nothing wrong. I'm asking you to respect that decision, as your tenants who have respected you in *every* way since the moment we started renting from you." My hands shake, and I shove them in my pockets. The potion bottles bounce against my hand, cold and smooth.

"Ha! So you think you can just disrespect all of my rules and expect me to go along with it?" She steps toward Smith and Rosie.

I place myself between her and Rosie. I look intently into Zillow's eyes.

"Get Rosie to where she needs to go," I say.

Zillow was right; we need to stand up for ourselves.

Mrs. Milburn's eyes might as well be full of fire as she glares at me and steps around me toward Rosie.

Zillow runs on the other side of me, cutting Mrs. Milburn off. I reach out to grab her arm, but miss her bony elbow by a mere hairsbreadth. Smith snatches up Rosie, clutching the wide-eyed girl to his chest.

"Get her out!" I scream.

I reach inside my pocket, grasping the tiny flask full of wispy blue liquid. I throw it on the ground, shattering it.

A dense fog swirls from the remains, filling the room and obscuring everyone's vision within seconds.

"I knew it! Magic!" Mrs. Milburn screams. "Have you no respect for my dead husband? Don't you believe there's a reason magic has been outlawed?

Feet scamper across the floor, and I can only assume Smith and Zillow make it out.

I turn in circles, trying to find Mrs. Milburn. If I can distract her long enough, perhaps they'll have enough time to get away.

Yet I may have just given up everything. Already I envision being shackled and led to jail. Again.

"Where are you?" Mrs. Milburn screams. Items thud to the floor, and I hear a scraping sound, like a crate being moved.

"You couldn't believe how harsh I was on you, and I was right. Keeping an elf child under my very nose! After all I've done for you."

"No," I say, sounding much calmer than I feel. "You haven't been good to us. We've had to piece this place back together with you not listening to anything we had to say just because of our past. You have been anything *but* fair to us."

My eyes fill with hot, angry tears. Anger I've kept inside me for so long, building with every belittling comment and jibe, every failed effort to take care of her property.

"Well, I never... Never had anyone so ungrateful..."

The blue fog thins just a little, and I can make out the tall woman's frame standing in front of the crate and blanket covering the weakened floor.

"There." She shakes her finger at me, stepping back. "Your magical tricks won't work on me." She stamps her foot, hard. Boards creak.

"Mrs. Milburn..." I start, reaching toward her.

"Don't you say anything more." She crosses her arms. "You are in a whopping mountain of trouble. I'm going straight to the authorities to see you thrown in prison."

The mist is practically gone now. The front door opens behind me, but I can't risk turning around.

"Please step away from there," I say, moving toward her.

"Why? So you can cast a spell on me? I don't think so."

The floor caves, boards cracking and splintering under her weight. She screeches, arms flailing as she falls through.

"Oh, my!" A man's voice says behind me.

I rush forward to grab her hand, but she only falls through to her waist, her face red and eyes wide.

"What did you do to me?" she screams.

The man steps forward, grabbing her other arm.

"Don't panic or move. We'll need to make sure the wood isn't lodged in you."

I look at him for the first time. "Mr. Tatterval! Don't hurt yourself, I'll get her out."

He just laughs as Mrs. Milburn glares at him.

"Don't worry about me," he says as he lifts her out of the hole with almost no effort. I study his frail arms. *How did he do that?* I think.

Mrs. Milburn just stares, her skirt torn and a little blood seeping from her right thigh.

Mr. Tatterval turns to me. "I've been watching your shop for some time, Willow. And Mrs. Milburn's treatment has not gone unnoticed."

"Why, I *never*. Did you just see what she did to me? She used magic, for goodness sakes! I'm going to go talk to the Mayor right now, and..."

He throws back his head and roars out a laugh. Then, he reaches into his tattered coat pocket and pulls out a vial of yellow potion. One I certainly *hadn't* given him. As soon as he drinks it, his face begins to change. The lines and wrinkles in his cheeks disappear, his white hair darkens, and his eyes turn from blue to gray.

"Oh!" Mrs. Milburn's eyes widen. "Mr. Mayor, I..."

I'm equally as shocked as she is.

He chuckles, corking the empty bottle and placing it back in his pocket. "I apologize for the shock, ladies. You see, I recently signed a treaty with leaders of the surrounding towns to petition the royal council to reinstate magic. I have gone undercover, scouting out different businesses I believed have secretly been producing magic to help those like my wife who has been gravely ill." He looks at me, his eyes soft and grateful.

"Why, how *could* you?" Mrs. Milburn sputters. "Don't you know my husband was killed by magic?"

He frowns. "What happened to your husband was the cause of one greedy man. These children do not deserve the slander you've spread against them." He studies the hole in the floor. "And, by the looks of it, you haven't been a very good landlord, either."

"Why, I'm afraid my tenants haven't quite looked after the property like they should." She pastes on a smile, pushing back a lock of her frazzled hair. "Why, if I had known this floor had gotten so bad, I would never have..."

"Really?" He raises an eyebrow. "Is this true, Ms. Willow?"

I try to answer him, but words refuse to form in my frozen brain.

Silence strings on for way too long. I swallow. "No-no, sir. We told her many times about the floor and other things, but she's done nothing."

"I see."

"Why, the girl's lying! Can't you see? She's used magic to bewitch you, and…"

"Madam Milburn! I suggest you hold your tongue and come with me. I'd like to question you further at the courthouse."

Mrs. Milburn's mouth opens wide, and a tiny squeak escapes.

I have to work very hard not to laugh.

I turn over the faded and yellow "CLOSED" sign on the door, looking out into the darkening streets. Two children bounce a ball down the road, laughing as they hit it back and forth, their cheeks sunburned by the summer sun.

I hope Zill and Smith are holding up and get Rosie to where she needs to go. I smile as I look at the sign above the door that reads: "Willow, Zillow, and Smith" in curlicue letters with a stack of books next to it.

I step inside and wipe my boots on the brown mat. It's so quiet, even with the soft chirp of crickets outside.

"Willow!" Smith yells as the back door slams against the wall.

He bounds through the curtain, stopping short as he sees the bent and broken floor.

Zillow bumps into his back. "What happened?"

Her eyes grow wide when she sees.

I laugh. "Mrs. Milburn might have taken an unexpected trip into the crawl-space."

"Wow," Smith whispers. "I wish I could have seen that."

Zill steps closer, peering into the giant hole. "What did she do to you?"

"Tell me about Rosie first." I suppress a grin. I'm going to keep my secret for a moment longer.

Zillow crosses her arms, her eyes narrowing. She knows I'm hiding something. "We found the sanctuary."

"After getting lost twenty times. But then we found her parents there!" Smith's face is shining, looking like he just returned a baby bird to its nest.

"They nearly got caught while traveling through Woodbane forest and were separated," Zill adds.

"Her real name's Rosella. Isn't that a funny name for a little girl?"

My heart swells. I couldn't be more proud of all of us. We'd risked everything for Rosie. And I will be forever thankful she gave me the courage to stand up to our landlord.

"I have some news, too."

"What are you hiding? You look... different." Smith crosses his arms and raises an eyebrow at me.

"Maybe I am." I laugh. "Quite a bit has happened while you were gone."

"Oh, just spit it out, Willow."

"Welcome to our shop." I gesture in a big circle.

Smith looks around. "Um, I think it was our shop before. It's just a little more broken."

"Mhm. And it's about to get even more messed up when we replace the floors."

"Vanessa is making us do it?" Zill clenches her fist like she's ready to punch something.

I shake my head. "No, Mrs. Milburn is out of the picture for good. We're going to do it, because we own it now."

"What?" Smith says as his arms drop to his sides.

"You're joshing."

"Why did she give it up?"

"How did she end up through the floor? Did you push her?"

They fire off questions before I have time to answer. I just laugh as they both sputter off ideas for what happened to the old woman. I can't remember when my heart has felt this light.

I clutch the last potion bottle in my pocket.

It's amazing what can happen with just a little bit of courage, and a tiny vial of magic.

ESTHER PIPKIN

Esther Pipkin grew up on a farm in Missouri, where she spent her childhood in the woods playing with Peter Pan and the Pevensies. At 15, she moved away from everything she'd known to a strange new world called Massachusetts, which started her journey with mental health. She draws from her experiences to write YA stories full of hope and home for weary souls like her. When she's not writing, you might find Esther baking snickerdoodles and singing showtunes, playing with her cat, or going on adventures (like visiting bookstores) with her husband.

Achievements

- Has written three novels, two novellas, and two short stories.

- Has received and implemented two developmental assessments on her novels.

- Has received positive feedback on her work from agents and editors.

- Has attended conferences for three years, including Realm Makers and Write to Publish Pre-Conference.

- Received manuscript requests from multiple publishers.

- Currently a Fiction Instructor for Kids Write Novels.

- Grew her email list to 150 subscribers within two weeks.

Pitches

- *A Forgery of Roses* meets *The Raven Boys* in this YA fantasy where a boy is cursed with *tragic love* and any girl he falls for will die within twenty-four hours.

- *The Little Mermaid* meets *Caraval* in this YA fantasy where a magical healer who's afraid to heal is hired to restore the princess' voice, only for him to discover she's a Siren.

LOST IN THE LIBRARY

LIBRARY

J.A. ROSE

*W*hen books can talk for themselves, you'd think they'd be able to write themselves, too. But they can't. And that's exactly my problem.

The straps of my backpack dig into my shoulders, and they ache in protest. I glimpse the cracks on the sidewalk where weeds poke towards the sky. Their dreams of growing big and tall will likely soon be trampled.

I awkwardly hop over one of the fragile shoots and nearly trip.

Walking beside me, Shasta, my brother, lets out a chuckle as if to say, *that's what you get for not paying attention to me.*

It's not that I don't want to talk to him, but I can't focus on him. The slip of paper in my backpack seems to get heavier with every step.

"I see all the passion that you put into your writing, but it has been less than stellar. Put some work in over the summer, and I hope to see you again next year."

A sugar-coated way to tell me that I had failed the class, was below the level of my peers, and all of the books I wrote deserve to be burned.

Insecurity had already told me all of that. The problem now is that my little sister, Olive, needs me to write, so she can get what she's always dreamed of...

But I am destined to fail her.

The castle-like gothic building looms into view. A giant oak tree twists towards the sky from the center of the roof. It is the only place that can help me now. Shasta and I ascend the short steps to the library door.

A large sign reads, "Do not enter if you are not properly informed of the dangers of strong magic."

Shasta catches the handle and leans back to pull the wooden door open. It's twice as tall as Shasta, and one could easily drive a small car through it. It always makes me feel like I am entering an establishment for giants.

As a kid, I was always frustrated that the door was too heavy for me to open. Now I know that it's probably a good thing. Small children shouldn't come running in here on their own.

Inside, the roots of the oak tree twist and reach down to the floor, weaving into a giant, haunting maze. There's an unoccupied librarian's desk to the right and a bunch of tables for reading or studying to the left. A few people are seated, studying or reading, but no one nears the mass of roots and books.

Signs are posted in every direction stating, "DO NOT WANDER!"

Because people get lost in here. That magical maze of literature is a trap that only librarians can escape. That's what they say, anyway. But they also say that if one explores deep enough into the maze, they will be granted a wish.

"Thank you." I duck my head, feeling my brother's gaze on me as I march ahead.

I glance back at him. His eyes glint at me, making me suspicious. Before I can place the look, my backpack comes to a sudden halt as if the handle had been caught by a hook. Two hands on my shoulders steer me to the left, almost pulling me off my feet.

"Hey!" I dig my heels into the worn carpet, but it makes no difference.

Shasta pushes me like a rag doll towards a table beside the large cathedral-like windows.

"Why are you so *grumpy* today, Reagan?" His teasing voice is low enough not to disturb anyone.

"I'm not." I try—and fail—to shove him away.

He tips his head, a smile barely peeking through his melodramatic pout. "Is it a '*girl thing*?'"

"Shasta, *stoooop*." I squirm away.

He flops into a chair at an empty table, tossing hair out of his eyes. "You can just tell me if you don't want to help."

I shrug my backpack off and square my shoulders. "I want to help."

"Good, because this writing thing isn't my area of expertise."

That stings, even though he means it as a compliment. According to my

English teacher, writing isn't my area of expertise, either.

After casting me a suspicious glance, Shasta pulls a packet out of his backpack.

I wince at the sight of it.

It describes an extracurricular creative writing competition with a cash prize. A cash prize that will buy Olive a couple months of dance lessons which my parents can't afford. The money would fulfill her biggest dream. Shasta and I decided we couldn't continue to watch her lose hope in it.

He surveys the contents of the packet, sliding it over to me once he is done.

Oh no.

A name on the front page sticks out like a glaring light. One of the judges is none other than my English teacher herself.

"You can do it, right?" Shasta asks.

I swallow a hard lump in my throat and force a smile. "I hope you've been hiding some really fantastic creative writing skills from the world, Shasta."

His brow furrows. "Then we'd have two fantastic writers in the family. Sounds like overkill to me."

Shasta is the only person who tells me my writing is any good. I've already disappointed my teacher. I might as well have failed the competition before it even starts. But that's why I'm here. I won't need to try and fail if this library can give me what I need.

"I can do my best," I concede. "But if we still don't win?"

Shasta looks out the window. "I'll get a job."

"You don't have time. Not with your internship after school."

He crosses his arms. "If that's what needs to happen, I'll quit the internship. It's not a big deal."

But I know it is. It's his one step forward to achieving *his* dream, and I won't let him give it up.

I lift the pamphlet and look over the rules again.

"We'll make it work somehow."

The "somehow" I'm thinking of probably isn't what my brother is picturing. But it's my only chance.

The prompt on the packet states in bold letters to "Write an alternative ending to an existing story of your choice."

I cringe.

"How about you think of some books we can use for the prompt, I'll go find some help."

"Yes, ma'am!" Shasta salutes and dives into his backpack. "Just be careful."

I glance towards the shelves. "I will."

"And don't talk to anything in there!"

I roll my eyes.

There's nothing in there.

Signs all over proclaim to not to go looking for a book without a librarian, or you might get lost. Except I don't see a librarian in sight.

Good.

One would certainly stop me, and I never quite got over my old fear of them. Long term effects of magic exposure does strange things to people.

I head towards the center of the building where the tree's roots weave towards the ground. The "shelves" are made of just those roots, curling back and forth to create alcoves for all the books.

I stop at the first aisle labeled "How-To's" with a woody arch. Only candles light the passageway, giving them a dim, almost eerie appearance. Books are packed in every little alcove, and the roots seemed to have purposefully grown to cradle each and every one.

I run my fingers along the perfectly aligned spines, skimming the titles to appear as if I am doing what I told Shasta I would.

I eye the archway and rub the back of my neck. The many signs whisper that this is a bad idea.

It's feasible. I tell myself. *This isn't a maze; it's just a library. As long as I'm smart about it, I should be fine.*

Every step I take causes my every muscle to twinge with a desire to turn back, and I keep a close eye on the archway. Shasta turns to me, so I pull a book from the shelf and flip it open.

A monotone, croaky voice greets me.

The book drones on, audibly reading the words of the opened page. The paper rustles, as if by a breeze, but the air is still.

A flutter in the corner of my vision catches my gaze. I turn my head, but the dim hallway is empty.

I return to the book, close it, and place it back on the shelf. I lay it on its spine so it sticks out from the others.

If I just make enough bookmarks, I'll be able to find my way back, no problem.

A long white feather drapes over my hand. It sticks out of a round, fuzzy face with black raindrop eyes, each the size of an egg.

"You look bored." An inhuman voice comes from a perfectly curled proboscis.

I slap my hand over my mouth. The feather or rather the antenna flicks away. The creature squeezes out of a space nearly too small for its bulging abdomen and climbs up the shelf. It has six legs and dusty white wings the size of my head. A moth.

A giant, talking moth.

This can't be real.

I've only ever heard Shasta mention creatures in the library. I thought he had made it up just to scare me.

The snow-white insect pivots its head towards me.

"Are you always so quiet and bug-eyed?" Its voice sounds as if it came from a breath of the wind, muffled and earthy, like dust behind a bookshelf.

Funny. You're *supposed to be quiet and bug-eyed.*

"I didn't expect company." I steady my voice and put my hands back at my sides.

The large insect climbs along the roots. "I live here. Where else would I be but the densest collection of magic in this entire city?"

"Where are you going?"

Just one of the many questions going through my mind.

"I have something that I think you might like." The creature flutters its large wings and hovers in front of me.

Does it know how to find the wish?

"I-I don't want to get lost."

"I can show you the way." The moth's wings send small puffs of air against my face.

I glance back through the arch at the table. He's hunched over the table, paying me no mind.

I'll just keep leaving a trail, just in case. Following this moth may be my best chance.

"People say the library can grant a wish, and I want to know how to write really well so I can help my sister. Do you know how I can get it?" I follow the moth, rotating a book onto its spine at every turn.

Moss and lichen peek out from behind books as we travel through the dim corridor. We walk past a small bench made of a split log. Now I notice the gaps just big enough for a large moth. They're likely able to navigate the maze better than anything my size.

"Are there more of you?" I ask.

The moth lands on a shelf. The books in this area have leather covers and some look well-used.

"Yes and yes," it says as it meanders to a thin book with red and gold binding. It expertly pulls the book out of the shelf and passes it to me with its fuzzy legs.

I turn the book over. This is not what I expect a wish to look like.

"I think this will be exactly what you're looking for." The moth rubs its feet together.

"The wish?"

"That would be a book. I think you'll find it insightful. After all, if you want to write well, you best know how to read well." The creature carefully folds its wings back into their resting position.

In embossed gold letters, the title of the book reads, *Violet.*

Except it isn't a writing book, and I didn't come all the way back here for a story. The moth has to know what it's talking about, but can I trust it?

"Thank you, but I need to find that wish. I don't have any time to waste." I hand the leather-bound story back to the moth. Even if the book can help me, I don't have time to learn how to write the hard way.

"The book is small," the moth says. "It won't take you more than twenty minutes to read, and it has far more magic than the one you held earlier. I have no doubt it will get you much closer to finding your wish. And it is *very* important to me that you read it."

The moth expands its wings once again and dives into the air, wings fluttering. It slips through the roots above and disappears.

"No, wait!" I call after it, but it does not return.

All books have the same amount of magic, don't they?

I look at the book in my hand. Its simplicity entices me for a reason I can't fathom. Books just don't look like this nowadays. If what the moth says is true, then this book could have special magic. Could it really be the step I need to take to find the wish? What would a library want more than for me to read its books?

The logic makes more sense than to keep wandering.

I slide my finger under the cover of *Violet*.

I glance back towards Shasta. I can't see him anymore, but I know what direction he should be. If I could fulfill both my siblings' dreams, I would do anything.

This could be worth it.

I open the book, and it bursts out in a sweet, musical voice. It sucks me in as if the words are magic themselves, putting a vivid picture in my mind of the story from the first page.

If only I could write like this.

A chapter goes by, then another, and then I lose count of how many I have read.

Before I know it, I turn to the last page. The voice stops in mid-sentence, and the picture slips out of my mind. My eyes focus on a white, empty page.

My stomach knots in disappointment, deeper than I know is reasonable.

I look up with a faint hope that the moth has returned to explain why it gave me an unfinished book.

My skin prickles in unease.

I haven't looked up since I opened the book. I need to stay alert in this place.

Still clutching the little red book, I tiptoe down the corridor, following my bookmarks.

No archway. The curve of roots and books only continues on.

I thought this hallway was straight.

The exit can't actually be far. I can still find my way out.

Yet my unease digs through my skin and into my guts.

A short jog just brings me to a jumble of branches so tightly woven together I can't even see through it.

Did I miss a bookmark?

That seems hardly possible when I haven't gone far. The faintest bit of movement in the corner of my eye makes me whip my head around.

Moth?

What I find makes my jaw drop open. I feel goosebumps prickle the skin on my arms. One of the smallest roots is slowly growing around a bright yellow book. If not for the book's bright color contrasting with the tree, I might have missed it.

The roots are moving.

My breaths start to come in quick gulps.

"Hello?" I call through the branches. "Is anyone there?"

No answer.

I spin and run back to the shelf where the little red book belongs. I put it back on its spine.

My bookmarks are still in place. Which means *I* didn't move, the shelves did.

Just behind that dead end must be the archway. I can't climb over because the roots above me are too thick, but at least I know the right direction. At least I hope I do.

I take another book off the shelf and set it on the ground, the top of it facing the direction of the archway. And my brother.

Now if I lose my sense of direction, I can come back here.

Calm down, Reagan. This is where you want to be anyway.

The only thing left for me to do now is to go the other direction and find that wish. I can find another way out after that.

I put a determined foot forward.

Ivy curls around the shelves, and the warm light is almost cozy.

A cavern opens up in one of the shelves ahead. My hopes soar, but it's only a small table and a chair made of roots with a plush pillow. A steaming mug of tea sits atop the table with a pen by its side. I stop as a cool breeze brushes against my cheek, carrying the tea's fragrance of honey, cinnamon, and chamomile.

Where did that stuff come from?

"Reagan!" My brother's voice breaks through my thoughts, shattering the quiet, dream-like stupor of the library.

"*Quiet.* What have I told you?" A moth's voice rebukes him.

I push a few books aside to peer through the roots. Shasta is marching his way down an aisle beside mine.

Shasta points a finger at the insect. "*I told you* that I would shut up when I found my sister. You haven't exactly been much help."

The creature buzzes, rubbing its legs together. Its voice is higher pitched than the moth I had met. "Wouldn't it be nicer to stop for a moment and read? You have a project, don't you? It could—"

My brother glares at the insect. "If you're not going to be of any use then go away. I know what I want."

"Shasta!" I call to him.

He whips around, turning a full circle.

"I'm behind these roots!" I try to squeeze my hand through, but it's too tight. I still manage to push a book off of the shelf on his side.

Shasta walks over, swipes the rest of the books away, and leans down to peer through the roots.

The moth lets out a shriek of protest, but Shasta ignores it.

"What are you doing all the way back here?"

"Ummm... finding something to help with the project."

Shasta makes eye contact with me through the branches, and I can tell he's worried.

"I'll find a way to get to you, and we're getting out of here." Shasta takes a step back and looks around.

"I'm okay!" I protest.

"Then you know your way out?"

I bite the inside of my cheek, "Not-not exactly. But I left a trail. I won't get too deep, and I'm sure I'll be able to find an exit." My hands grip the root-shelf tighter. "You should get out before it closes *you* in!"

He shakes his head. "This isn't safe, Rae. If the shelves are moving, there is no way to safely navigate."

I don't want to admit it, but I know he's right. *I'll need to find another way. Maybe a string? And if I move something to block the entrance, maybe it won't be able to close.*

The aisle continues ten paces before veering right. I see nothing from here that will connect us.

"Fine... but what if we can't get to each other?"

"I'll backtrack, and we'll think of a new plan."

I nod, sighing.

"See you soon." Shasta runs off, and soon I can no longer see or hear him.

I sit in the little nook and dare to sip the cup of tea. The flavor smooths me, and the warmth trickles down my throat.

Maybe, since I'm in here, I can learn more about the wish.

I stand and peruse the shelves for anything that could give me a hint.

Shasta's moth returns all the books he had thrown onto the floor back in the care of the roots.

"Hey, quit that!" I run over and push the books back out of place. Shasta needs some marker to come back to. The moth protests, but gives up shortly.

So much for my bookmarks. They're probably all put away by now.

"Do you know anything about the wish?" I ask the moth. I look up just in time to catch it disappearing through a hole in the shelves. "Wait! Come back!"

The moth does not return, so I decide to spend my time looking around the books and between the roots. The search yields nothing, so I plop on the floor and hold my head in my hands.

All I can do now is see who finds me first. Shasta, or my moth. One of the insects will have to return eventually to put away the books that I had knocked on the ground.

I notice all the books have illustrations on the front. *The Golden Girl and the Hare* with a picture of a small town. *Stone Heart* with a picture of a gleaming suit of armor. *Guarding the Mist* with a picture of various insects on the cover.

What makes these books so special to be kept in a library instead of being deemed unnecessary and disposed of anyway? What made Violet *so special when it is nothing but a simple story that doesn't even have an ending?*

I picked up the book with the suit of armor.

That moth wanted me to read, well, here you go. You better show up.

I sit at the small table and pick up the pen, instinctively spinning it between my fingers.

A cool breeze blows through the passageway, and I flip the cover open. The book springs to life straight away in my hands. Its words burst to life as if they'd been held back for years behind the cover.

The voice of the book is so rich, deep, and so real that I feel like it is written just for me. It's as if whoever wrote it had put every ounce of heart into their words. But is something like that enough to make a book worth reading?

It seems to be enough for me.

It's about a knight and his mission to save a damsel. In his heart, he loves her dearly but missions and adventures have gone by. He's seen terrible things and slowly feels himself hardening. To protect himself from the horrors, he closes his heart behind walls of stone. When he rescues his beloved, he is no longer the same man that she loved. He worries that he is not able to love with all of his heart anymore.

The knight reminds me of Shasta, with how much he strives to protect the people he cares about. But Shasta would never give up on himself like that... not unless it meant taking care of us.

The story becomes hardest when the knight has nearly returned with the damsel saved, but the villain comes back. The damsel leaves him, and our knight is all alone.

My heart goes out to him, trying, trying, trying, only for the person he cares about to leave him when he needs her the most. Then a horrible thought crosses my mind.

What if I'm the person who leaves?

Could my unwillingness to try actually be abandoning my family when they need me the most?

I never thought my writing could be important, but if I don't write well and with all my heart, I'll have failed Shasta and Olive. And yet I know I'll still fail if I do.

I turn the page, the tears pooling in my eyes. I long for a happy ending, but the voice stops.

Blank?

The book can't be over yet! I flip through the remaining yellowing pages.

Empty.

This isn't fair! How can this stupid library be full of half-written stories? I want to throw the book, but my respect for it stops me. I will just go back to the librarians and get answers. Or find one of those moths!

Ah... How long have I been reading? Where is Shasta?

I take in my surroundings. My cup of tea is empty. The books I had left on the floor are gone. The gap in the shelf where Shasta had been before was gone. Have I been wrong about only the shelves moving?

Oh no. I can't have moved deeper into the library... can I?

Chills climb my spine, and I jump out of my chair.

I won't be able to find my way back! Shasta will be lost as well. What will our family do without him? I've already failed them!

"Shasta?" My voice cracks.

"*Shasta! Where are you?*" I scream.

"Quiet, child."

A moth-like voice from above stops me from bolting down the aisle.

"This is a library. *Some of us* are looking for some peace and quiet."

I look up, wiping moisture out of my eyes and shooting the moth a deadly glare.

"Are you doing this?" I demand, not bothering to lower my voice. "Are you moving the shelves?"

"Heavens, no." The moth flutters its wings. "I wouldn't care to do much but read. Say... you've been reading some lovely titles yourself. What do you think of them?"

I bang my fist on the shelf under the moth, but only successfully rattle my bones. "I'm not enjoying them much considering they keep sucking me deeper into the library before the book cuts short *without an ending*. And I haven't gotten any closer to that wish!" I cradle my throbbing hand to my chest.

"You can't blame the books." The moth seems almost offended; if I could even tell what an offended moth looks like. "Besides, you're plenty close to your wish."

I frown. "I am?"

It twitches an antenna. "Closer than you think. Read another book or two, and you'll have it."

I begin pacing.

How can I believe anything the moths say? There's no way for me to know if they're telling the truth.

"I need to find my brother. Can you help me do that at least?" I rub my temples against a sudden headache.

"That boy? I wouldn't be surprised if he is out of the maze already. I heard he didn't pick up a *single* book."

I wince. *Of course Shasta could make it out of here by himself. He isn't "less than stellar."*

"He wouldn't leave me." Just because he can doesn't mean he will.

The creature makes an irritated squeak. "It may be for the best, you know. It will be much harder for you to get your wish with him around."

I furrow my brow and turn to face the creature. It's fluttering right in front of my face, clinging to the bookshelf.

I step back. "Why's that?"

"Magic is dying in your world, you know." The moth gazes unblinkingly into my eyes. "No one notices. Even fewer try to replenish what was once there. Every new book that comes into this library has so little for us to feed on. So few care to write words that are greater than themselves."

My mouth goes dry. I don't know why those words seemed to carry so much weight.

Magic is dying?

"How does that answer my question?"

The moth holds oddly still, only its proboscis twitching as it talks. "You know that words are the most powerful thing in your world, child? They always *affect* the things they reach. Not all of them are used to their full potential, certainly, but they are what makes your library such a powerful place. Although, it must stay active. People must use it. People *must* read and write, or the magic fades away.

"It's rare that someone comes back here and starts picking out books for their magic alone as you have. If *you* keep reading those books. You could replenish the magic of the library."

I shake my head. "That won't get me my wish. That won't help Shasta or Olive!"

"You would already have your wish."

I sigh, running my hand through my hair. I pull it away with a jolt. There is something in my hair! Twigs? I gingerly feel my head again. No, they felt like feathers.

My eyes widen as the moth's feathery antennae twitches towards me. It watches me closely.

My hand shakes as I bend the feathers towards my face. Two identical white antennae are sticking out of my own head.

"What is this?" My voice shakes worse than my hands.

The moth's proboscis curls as if amused. "Your wish."

I reel backwards, bumping into roots behind me. "I don't want this."

"Oh, but that's been all you can talk about. Isn't that what you want? If you're like me, you'll never have to try and fail again. You can stay here forever and read."

Understanding dawns on me. The library is not a genie that can give me whatever I want. It's the magic. The dense exposure changes people. It gives the only thing the hopeless desire. Escape.

Stone Heart slips out of my grasp. The moth flares its wings just before the book slaps against the ground, landing open on its face.

The sweet voice of the book speaks, but is muffled against the ground.

"Sorry!" I exclaim, stooping to pick up the book. The words becoming clear when I turn it back towards me.

"...*The knight gazed up at the stars, his heart filled with wonder. 'Is it not worth living just for this one moment of beauty? Is it not even more so to live for the next and the one after that? To push through my countless blunders and heedless mistakes for a moment's peace.' A deep sigh escaped the knight's parted lips. 'If a moment like this awaits beyond the great chasm of darkness that I face, may I suffer through a thousand such futile efforts.'...*"

I close the book, although the thought sticks in my mind.

A moment's peace worth a thousand failures.

It reminds me of the stories I wrote for Olive to help her work up the courage to go to school, reading them for her in the kitchen while Shasta made dinner. She always had the biggest smile, and even Shasta would take his time so we could read for just a little longer.

The stories certainly weren't any good, but my siblings delighted in my heart. The heart that wrote out of love. It gave the words value. It gave them magic.

That's why this moth is wrong. Even if it thinks it wants me to stay here forever and read, once I become a moth, I will no longer be able to replenish the magic... only eat it, and the books will continue to collect dust.

"Rea!"

I whip around, relief soaring through my chest. Shasta jogs down the aisle towards me.

He tackles me in a hug, and this time I don't mind him manhandling me. When he lets me go, he looks around in obvious confusion.

"This isn't where I left you, is it?"

I smile thinly. "Honestly, I have no idea. But I shouldn't have gotten lost to begin with. I'm sorry."

"Don't worry. Someone will come looking eventually." Shasta goes to ruffle my hair and stops. "Ummm..."

"I know. I'm turning into a moth!" I press my antennae flat onto my head.

Shasta looks the rest of me over. "I'm sure it will go away," he says slowly, not seemingly convinced himself. "Someone will know what to do."

He furrows his brow, muttering, "I should have brought a librarian. This could have been over *so* quickly."

"Why didn't you?"

Shasta looks away. "I might have panicked a little." He slips a hand into his pocket and pulls out my report card.

My stomach clenches. *Less than stellar.*

"I got worried that the moths would convince you to stay, and we'd never find you again." I notice his hand shaking just before he stuffs it back in his pocket along with the card.

Clearly, he hadn't been wrong about that.

Tears prick my eyes. *I'm so sorry, Shasta. I won't let it happen again.*

"How do you know about that?" I wipe moisture out of my eyes.

"The same thing nearly happened to a kid in my class. No one saw him for weeks..."

My eyes stray towards the pocket where he hid my report card.

"So you know, then... that I can't help us win that money?"

My brother claps a hand on my shoulder. "That's a matter of opinion." His forced optimism grates against my ears.

"It's *all* a matter of opinion." I shove his hand away. "But it's their opinion that matters. I don't have what it takes to win them over!"

"That's not true."

I shoot him a glare.

"You won me over." He crosses his arms. "With all of those stories you wrote for Olive, and how you encouraged her to try and make friends. You showed her that she is loved through those words, and you showed me, too. You could do the same thing with anyone else if you stopped worrying so much about failing."

Two itching spots on my back put one word into my mind. *Wings.*

"I *already* failed, Shasta."

"You only fail when you don't try."

Tears drip uncontrollably down my cheeks. *He's right. I know he's right.*

He wraps me in another hug, and the itch seems to abate a little.

"I'll give it my all," I promise.

"Let's get out of here first."

I follow my brother as he leads the way through the maze. He seems to have some kind of system, but after a while, it doesn't lead us anywhere.

Shasta hesitates at his next turn. "I don't actually know where I'm going."

I press my lips together. He's right. We need to try something else.

As we continue, we pass by another cove with a little table in it. A pen rests in the center of it.

Shasta looks around. "Do you think that if we do what the moths want, they'd show us the way out?"

I shake my head. "I don't think the moths understand what they really want. They're desperate. They want me to read, but reading will only turn me into one of them."

"Well, I suppose they only know the way out through those stupid holes anyway." Shasta stuffs his hands in his pockets. "The library itself is probably the only thing that knows the way out, but I don't think we could persuade it to tell us."

I looked up at the twisting roots, each winding its way down, reaching to cradle every single book.

What does the library want?

"It would want us to write."

I explain to Shasta what the moth had told me about the magic of the library.

He smiles. "That book you're holding, is that what you want to finish for the project?"

I still held *Stone Heart*. I nod, looking down at it.

What if I ruin it?

The thought makes me hesitate. I am not as skilled as the original author. What if my words don't have enough magic?

I sit down at the table and a cool breeze tickles my cheek. The library itself goes quiet when the book speaks, but I am a little better at listening now. It reminds me that every true word has magic.

I take a deep breath.

Shasta sits across from me, his grin giving me courage. "Just tell me if you need my help."

I open the book to the first empty page and poise the pen in my hand.

Shasta turns away, so I have nothing else to do but write.

Writing the first word on the page makes me smile. The moment waiting for me may not be success, but it will be the sense of accomplishment when I write another story that Shasta and Olive love. As long as I put my heart into this, even if Olive doesn't get her dance classes, it will be worth it.

"Rea. They're shrinking." Shasta points to his head and winks at me.

I grin.

The words flow easily in this quiet place. My focus doesn't waver. The wisdom and creativity of the books around me seem to seep into my pen. The *magic* guides me.

Shasta browses the shelves, but never reads anything. He does peek at my story from time to time, though. After a while, Shasta sits down again and rests his head on his arms.

My internal clock tells me that it's been about an hour before I write the words "The End" at the bottom of the last page.

A smile grows on my face. Those two words fill my chest with fireworks of joy.

"Shasta!" I reach out without taking my eyes off the book to shake my brother's shoulder. "I did it! I'm done!"

My fingers close on air. *Was the table always this big?*

"Quiet in the library, please." A voice whispers behind me.

I jerk my head back, taking in my surroundings.

A librarian walks by with a cart full of books. She stares at us with eerily unblinking eyes. The afternoon sun through the blinds makes me squint.

We're at our old table! We made it out!

Shasta raises his head and blinks sleepily. "You finished the book? Let me see." He holds his hand out, and I give it to him. His eyes widen as he looks around.

A small shimmer on the title of the book draws my attention, and I gasp.

"Look!" I point at the title page.

Behind the author's name is a new addition. *My* name.

My brother grins. "It looks like a congratulations are in order. Your first published book."

My cheeks heat.

"Let's just get back home. It's almost dinner time."

Shasta packs up his backpack saying, "I'll go check out the book. You've done your part. I'll write it all out on paper so that we can submit it. Oh, this is yours."

He slides my report card over to me as he stands up.

I shake my head at it and stuff it into my backpack. *Less than stellar.* I chuckle. *This less-than-stellar writer just put her name on the title of a real book!*

I follow after Shasta, hoisting my backpack onto my back.

The librarian had just finished scolding Shasta for getting a book by himself. He shrugs and apologizes before she hands it back to him.

We speed out of the library, bursting into laughter the minute the door closes behind us.

"Let's go get some ice cream." Shasta shoves a thumb at the place across the street.

"For dinner?"

"For dinner."

J.A. ROSE

J.A. Rose is an introverted daydreamer with a passion for sharing the hopeful and inspiring stories that have shaped her imagination. She lives on a farm in Idaho and her best friends are her cats and miniature goats. A lifelong vow to maintain her sense of wonder and creativity drives her writing, as she aims to inspire that same sense of magic in her readers with engaging and imaginative stories that are undeniably hopeful even in the face of darkness.

Achievements

- Drafted over ten novels.

- Implemented professional feedback on two of those projects.

- She has experienced marketing and launching a small business.

- Graduated from The Author Conservatory.

- Completed Nadine Brandes' *Self Edit Your First Draft* Course.

- Attended Write to Publish 2024.

Pitches

- *Give Me Gray:* A YA Fantasy novel about Drew, a girl who must save her father from his own grief and the gray that spreads from his touch because of it.

- *Magpie:* A YA Sci-fi Superhero novel about a bird-obsessed teen who is trying to win an inventing competition with a pair of robotic wings.

THE JOURNAL IN THE ATTIC

KIRA ROSENGREN

"You see, Adanaya, I never said she killed the bear."

I hung on my grandmother's words as she read the fight scene she wrote about River Tombs and the snow bear.

"What happened next, Grammy?"

Grandma smirked. "Why, River Tombs pushed the bear down the mountain and watched as he rolled away."

I laughed. "Grammy! Couldn't he stand back up?"

"Oh hush you. It's a story. Let a story be a story."

I grinned and climbed into her arms, and she wrapped me in a tender hug.

"Can we travel one day, Grammy?" I nestled my head against her shoulder, playing with the tassels on her worn out shawl. "Like River?"

"Without a doubt, my little butterfly. Without a doubt."

The wind blows in through the window, ruffling the papers on my desk. Goosebumps rise on my arms, but I don't shut it, embracing the fresh air it brings.

I run a hand over my face, then rest my chin on my desk, staring at my open laptop. Grandma Mary's handwritten to-do list sits next to it.

To Do's Before The Redwoods:
- *Get suitcases*
- *Pick a date*
- *Find an Airbnb*
- *Book the flight*

Rushed handwriting but still elegant—despite the fact she wrote stories daily, she never bothered to make her handwriting consistent. Switching between cursive and print, uppercase and lower.

I remember giving her grief for it once, to which she responded, "You can't teach an old dog new tricks, Adanaya. Don't you go trying."

My fingers hover over the keyboard as I stare at my screen. I have so many tabs open it's ridiculous, everything from Airbnbs to plane tickets to gas prices—all to see the Redwood trees.

This morning, an email arrived in my inbox announcing dropped ticket prices.

But now, as I stare at the screen, I find myself sweating despite the fresh air wafting from the window.

I can't travel, no matter how much I want to. No matter how scared I am of being stuck in Prescott, I can't go without her.

"Elias, where are my cigarettes?" Dad yells to my brother from down the hall. "I swear, if you are hiding them, you aren't playing your Xbox for a month!"

I smirk as my younger brother and Dad go back and forth, until a gust of wind rushes in through my window. The gust rips some of my pinned papers off the wall and into my open closet. The floor creaks as I kneel to grab the papers, I try to ignore the mess; I don't want to know what's underneath all the loose clothes and junk.

I pick up the last paper. In the back corner sits a suitcase.

"This one. This is the one." Grandma had said. *"It's the right size for you.*

There's plenty of space for stickers!"

"Stickers?"

"Why of course! You have to get a sticker from every place you travel."

"But Grammy, there's not gonna be enough space if we are going everywhere River goes!"

Grandma laughed and kissed the top of my head. "Then I guess we'll have to get you another suitcase."

I grind my teeth, fighting back the tears as I stare at the dusty suitcase. Unused, unwanted, and unneeded. Then I shut the door, leaving it to sit in the dark where it belongs. I push the thought of travel out of my mind.

Not without you.

Within seconds of me sitting back in my chair, Mom bursts into the room. I slam my laptop shut, wiping away a stray tear.

"What is it?" I ask, trying not to sound too snippy.

Concern is etched in Mom's face as she looks between me and my closed laptop.

"Are you ready to go? Your dad and brother are in the car." She smiles slightly as the smell of green bean casserole wafts into my room.

That's right. It's Thanksgiving day.

The second Thanksgiving since Grandma Mary passed away.

When we pull into the driveway, I still almost expect to see Grandma sitting on the front porch swing, waving at us when we walk in. Or in the attic window, watching us get out of the car with her mischievous smile, making it seem like she knew something you didn't.

Fighting against a wave of grief, I plaster on my best smile, straighten my maroon sweater, and take the green bean casserole out of Mom's hands. She loads us all up with the rolls and the sweet potato casserole before we walk up the pumpkin-decorated porch steps.

The warmth from the oven hits me like a wall as soon as I walk through the door, and I am immediately aware of the most wonderful smells of roasting turkey and baking pumpkin pies. I can smell the buttery mashed potatoes and the Au Gratin potatoes before we even go into the kitchen, and my mouth waters. Christmas music plays on a vinyl record in the corner of the living room. My family has debated over whether or not it's okay to listen to Christmas music on Thanksgiving for years now. Grandma Mary decided it was so long as it was Frank Sinatra or Bing Crosby, so every year we switch between the two singers.

Everyone is already all here. My youngest cousin, Penny, squeals as Grandpa Charles tickles her. Haley, my oldest cousin, is sitting on her phone in the corner, looking pissed off as usual.

"Hey, Grandpa." I smile as he stands up and gives me a bear hug. He almost pops my ribs out of place when he hugs me, but I wouldn't have it any other way.

"So glad y'all could make it," Grandpa says as he hugs his son. His voice is deep and gravelly from all the years of smoking, and he has a thick southern accent, which I'm still convinced is fake. "Jessica and Mark are in the kitchen. Y'all can set your stuff down there."

I follow Mom and Dad with Elias trailing behind me into the kitchen, where it's hotter than Satan's bathwater.

"Ivy!" Aunt Jessica hugs my mom, grinning wide. She was always an overly happy and loud person. But it didn't really bug me until a year and a half ago.

"Oh my gosh, Jessica," Mom gasps. "That turkey looks amazing!"

Jessica smiles, draping a towel over her shoulder. "Thanks, you want to know what I did?"

Mom nods, and I tune them out as they discuss the precise way to make a moist turkey. I set the casserole on the island and excuse myself from the crowded kitchen.

I look around the living room, empty of anyone I connect with, but full of reminders of Grandma. Everyone is talking over the music, which is much louder than Grandma would have allowed. My sweater is sticking to my skin, and it feels like it's tightening around my throat.

I tug at my collar. It's loud and hot and there's too many people, and Penny spilt grape juice on Grandma's flower-print couch. The couch she sat on so many times with a book in her lap and, in her last year, an oxygen tank at her feet.

Tears prick at my eyes. Without a word to anyone, I slip down the hallway and up into the attic.

I take a deep breath as I look around. It's dimly lit, and a draft blows through, making a slight whistling sound.

Grandma Mary's desk sits untouched against the wall near me. A thick layer of dust sits on it, showing how long since no one's come up here. Including me. Maybe especially me. Grandma would have wanted me to use her writing room, I know. If she could see it now, she would be in a tizzy, demanding that I help her clean it. She'd scold me, tell me to stop crying and pull up my big-girl pants and fix this. To be strong. To be better.

But I'm not strong. I'm not better. And she isn't here.

I step towards the desk. Boxes of books and journals sit all around it. The rest of the attic is filled with random furniture, decorations, and boxes, covered in cobwebs and dust.

Everything is covered in dust.

My hands shake as I stand up straight.

This room used to be whimsical and bright. The lights strung along the rafters would twinkle, candle flames would dance, and it was clean and filled with bean-bag chairs and bookshelves. Everything Grandma needed for writing. She had a mini fridge at one point, but Grandpa insisted on taking it out because "if that woman doesn't need to come down for food, she'll never come down at all."

I smile at the memories. This place was our oasis. Whenever I came up here, I stepped into another world. The fictional world of River Tombs and her many great adventures that I very much wished I could escape into. I had always thought River to be a boy's name, but I like how Grandma saw the earthy, flowy name to suit the heroine of her stories.

She wrote the stories for me. To encourage me when I was depressed and lonely. She wrote River Tombs to show me how to be brave, how to have faith, how to be strong.

Obviously she didn't do a good job, because as soon as I heard she was dying of lung cancer, I fell apart. And now, a year and a half later, I'm still not okay. No matter how hard I try. I can't forget about her.

I can't erase the memories of her pale and sickly, struggling to breathe, struggling to walk. I wish I could erase it from my brain and only remember the good days. But now all the bad is souring the good. Every time I think of something that makes me smile, it's followed by something that leaves me feeling empty.

How much time will pass before all of my memories are tainted?

Why am I the only one who can't seem to get over this? Still unable to take that stupid suitcase out of my closet and go somewhere?

Grandma would be so disappointed in me.

I squat in front of the boxes, ignoring the tears streaking down my cheeks, and open one. The first few papers are articles about the beginning of Indiana Jones movies, books by authors like Jane Austen and Shakespeare and Charlotte Brontë.

And a photo album. I don't bother opening it. I know what's in it. I know I don't want to see it.

I open the next box, and it's full of her journals. The thinnest was the first story she wrote. The thickest was the most recent.

The smallest one's leather is fading from dark brown to a lighter tan and beginning to peel. The strap is wearing thin, threatening to break. The biggest journal is at least an inch and a half thick, and a foot long. Its leather is still clean and oily.

I run the thin strap between my fingers, sitting crisscross applesauce on the attic floor. A strong gust of wind hits the side of the house, blowing the dust around me. I cough, closing my eyes, and hold the journal close to my chest, protecting it.

When the dust settles I loosen my grip on the journal. As I stare at it, I can almost hear Grandma speak to me.

"Open it, butterfly. Be strong."

I bite the inside of my cheek and slowly untie the old strap.

I turn the pages carefully, barely touching them. Grandma's handwriting fills the journal.

River Tombs, the island god, the jungle temple. Her stories jump out of the book, reminding me of all the hours I spent listening to Grandma's raspy voice as she read to me.

She quit coming up here since she got the oxygen tank and wasn't able to climb the ladder anymore. When she became weak and all her hair fell out. When she was confined to her bed. When she would sleep all day.

By the time she died, I hardly recognized her.

I slam the journal shut and stuff it back into the box. My chest feels tight; my hands tremble. Tears stream down my cheeks as I climb out of the attic and rush into the nearest bathroom.

I lock the door behind me and stare at my reflection in the mirror. My eyes are puffy and red. I look pathetic.

Stop crying, I scold myself. *She's dead. You know that. You had your time to grieve.*

I take a deep breath, then splash water onto my face.

You're fine. I tell myself. I repeat that over and over again until my breathing returns to normal, and the redness leaves my eyes.

"Dinner!" I hear Mom call from downstairs, so I make my way to the kitchen.

Mom and Aunt Jessica stand by the kitchen island and assemble all the dishes. More than once they yell at their kids to not destroy the china or the fancy silverware. I never understood why we didn't use paper plates and cheap silverware. Especially with the little kids. They are bound to break *something* on Thanksgiving. Then again, it wouldn't be Thanksgiving without that.

After dishing up, we all sit around the long oak table. Grandpa leads us in prayer, and we go around saying something we're thankful for. I decide to stick with a joke as an answer instead, and say I'm thankful for the green bean casserole.

"So Mark, how's work?" Grandpa asks, his mouth full of food.

My uncle Mark swallows. "Great. I made some really good commissions last month. And I heard a rumor that the holiday bonus is going to be really good this year. Our new owner really knows how to treat his employees."

Dad chuckles. "And I'm sure you're planning on blowing all that money the first second you get."

Mark's eyes flash a twinge of annoyance, but he keeps a strained smile plastered on his lips.

"I'll be treating the family, of course. A vacation is in order. But I'm not wasteful, if that's what you're suggesting."

"He sure isn't." Aunt Jessica smiles, setting a hand on her husband's arm. I can tell she's trying to defuse the upcoming fight that happens every time the brothers are in the same room. "Since Mark's been making more money, I've been able to travel some. I just got back from a trip to the redwood trees in California."

I freeze, my eyes darting up to look at Jessica.

The redwoods? She went?

"They were beautiful. I never imagined there could be trees that big," Jessica continues, shaking her head. "It really makes you think, when you see something like that."

"How so?" Mom asks.

Jessica stirs her mashed potatoes with a fork, a half pout on her lips where she so delicately applied her red gloss. "Just think about all those people who don't get to travel. Or the people who have no desire to do so. They're missing out on so much."

Don't you dare continue that sentence.

She can't hear my thoughts, and since she's always oblivious to my emotions, she keeps talking.

"It's so tragic Mary never wanted to travel further than her own front door. She had such a long life, and yet she missed out on so much."

I slam my fork down, and Mom gasps.

All eyes turn on me. Jessica holds my gaze, obvious pity seeping from every pore. She isn't upset at me or scared of me; she thinks I'm being childish and grieving.

I'm not grieving. I just want her to shut up.

"Naya," Jessica reaches to set her hand on mine.

I yank it away. "Don't talk about my grandma like you knew her, because you didn't. She may have been your mother-*in-law*, but she was nothing more than that to you. You didn't even like her."

Heat floods to my face as silence covers the table. No one says anything. And here I am, center of attention, face beet-red, making a fool out of myself.

My chair screeches on the tile floor as I push away from the table. I leave my food untouched. I can feel my family stare as I storm out of the room.

I grind my teeth, trying to fight the onslaught of tears.

I don't want to feel like this anymore. Everyone else is fine. Why can't I be?

The crisp November air hits me as I step outside, a sharp difference from the sweltering house. The winter air cools the heat on my face and helps calm me down. The sun set not too long ago, and someone switched on Grandpa's lights. They wrap around the banisters and crisscross over the top. I sit on the porch swing, pulling my legs under me, and look up. The soft yellow lights almost look like stars blending into the night sky. A breeze blows my hair back, kissing my cheeks and making me shiver. I close my eyes, letting the cold and silence wrap around me.

I can hardly hear my family talking or the music.

My breath hitches as I try to take a deep breath. A tear slips down my cheek, and I swipe it away.

Jessica doesn't know. None of them know. Grandma never talked about the plans we made. She never talked about her dreams or how she wanted to travel but was never able to. They don't know she gave up her dreams so she could get married and be with her sons, who struggled with mental illnesses all throughout their childhood. She never talked about any of it to anyone but me. She once said she and I had similar spirits, and she didn't want me to make the same mistakes.

We were going to do it. We were going to fulfill her dreams.

Then she got sick.

We should have gone as soon as she got the diagnosis. But she didn't want me to "be bogged down by a sick old lady."

I should have done more.

She died, having never accomplished her dreams.

My hands shake, and I pull my sweater around me. After about ten minutes, I can't feel my nose. But I can't go back inside. I want to go home. Maybe I should walk. Except it's a thirty minute *drive* back to my house, and I'm a sixteen-year-old girl, and it's Thanksgiving night. There's bound to be drunks on the road.

Yeah, not one of my brightest ideas.

Light from the house spills across the porch as someone opens the back door and steps out. Mom is holding a piece of pie and a steaming mug, and a soft blanket hangs over her arm.

"Hey, Naya," She holds the pie and mug out to me. "Can I sit with you a while?"

I purse my lips, then nod and take the items from her. She sighs, getting comfortable and adjusting the blanket to cover our legs. Once she's settled she takes the pie onto her lap and gives me a soft smile.

"Apple cider," she says as I sniff it. "It's too hot to drink. I'd wait a minute."

I nod, staring at the wooden flooring of the porch. Sirens blare in the distance, but other than that—and the faint sound of music and talking from inside—the night is quiet.

"What's going on, Naya?"

"Why does something have to be going on?"

She smirks. "Honey, you yelled at your aunt and stormed out of the room without touching your cheesy potatoes. That's unnatural."

I laugh through the threat of tears. Mom knows I never let anything come between me and my potatoes.

She wraps an arm around my shoulders, pulling me into her warm embrace. "What's going on in that head of yours?"

After a minute or so, I sigh. "It's... about Grandma."

Mom waits silently.

"We were going to go to the redwoods. Before she got sick." My voice is so quiet I'm certain no one but Mom can hear me. I try to hold back the tears. "We didn't tell anyone. She didn't want anyone to know how much she wanted to travel, because she didn't want anyone to feel it was their fault that she didn't. So when Aunt Jessica brought up the redwoods and said how—well, you heard her. It made me mad. She didn't know what she was talking about."

"You're right, she didn't. You can't blame her for that, Adanaya. I know you're upset, but we need to make things right with Aunt Jessica." She paused. "We don't have to do it right now, though."

After a few seconds of silence, Mom takes a deep breath. "Talk to me, Naya. What brought this up?"

I shake my head, rubbing at my eyes and sniffling. "I went into the attic. And I went through one of her journals. Or, I tried to."

"What do you mean?"

"I couldn't do it." My breath hitches. "Why does it hurt so much, Momma? I want it to stop hurting."

"Oh, honey," Mom pulls me into her arms again. I burrow my head against her chest, soaking her flannel with my tears. She smoothes down my hair. "I know... I know. Is that why you haven't wanted to travel at all since she got sick? Is that why you haven't gone on any of our family vacations?"

I take a shaky breath before nodding. "I'm sorry. I couldn't do it without her. I *can't* do it without her. Not when she didn't get to."

"Naya." She tucks my hair behind my ear. "Grandma may not have gotten to do everything she wanted to, but she still had a wonderful life. She would have wanted you to— "

"Stop. Please," I interrupt her, fighting back another sob. "I can't, Mom."

"Let's start with something smaller then."

"What do you mean?"

Mom points to the small window of the attic. "Let's go read her journals."

I shake my head. "No, Mom, I'm serious, I can't."

"Yes, you can." Mom sighs, squeezing my shoulders. "Don't you want to read her stories again? Don't you want to be reminded of the good things? The good memories, before she got sick?"

"I'm not—I'm not strong enough."

"I'll come with you." She takes my hands in hers. "That way we can be stronger together."

The ladder creaks as we pull it down. Mom lets me go up first, and I turn on the lights. Grandma and I had strung up the off-white lights all around the rafters and walls, so they would cast a dim glow. Bright enough to read by anyway.

"Which one should we read?" Mom opens the cardboard box full of journals. She picks one with a vintage pen tied to the end of the strap.

"I don't remember that one very well." I pull the beanbag next to the next and sit by Mom.

"Then, let's see what River Tombs is doing here." She carefully opens the storybook, then searches my eyes. "Do you want to read it?"

I hesitate before I nod and take the book into my lap. This feels impossible. But the alternative isn't working. I have to start moving forward. I can't keep going on like this. I have to process through my grief.

I look at Mom again as she smiles comfortingly. Then I begin to read.

River Tombs never meant to get involved with the Russian mafia, but here she was. Racing along the side of a cliff on a black stallion, gun fire flinging past her ears and clanging against the mountain side.

I guess you could say she was stuck between a rock and a hard place, except in this case she was stuck between a cliff and a mountain side. Which is worse? I'm not sure.

River's heart raced faster than the steed beneath her. It pounded in her temples and made her head light with the rush of blood.

She made a sharp turn into a canyon. Quickly she realized she ran herself into a dead end. Her pursuers followed in after her, sly smirks on their ignorant faces as she looked between the six men and the rock wall that seemed to stretch up to the sky.

"Nowhere to go now, Miss Tombs!" the leader said, his Russian accent making it hard for her to understand him. She got the gist.

River wracked her brain, desperate to think of how she was going to get out of this. She wasn't going to die in this canyon, at the hands of the Russian mafia. Not after everything she'd been through. Not after everything she had survived.

No, today was not the day she was going to lose.

With a new determination coursing through her veins, River pulled out her whip, adjusted her hat, and hopped off of her horse.

"Come at me," she said, and the six members of the Russian mafia charged at her...

My fingers trace the letters as I read the rest of the story: River fights them off and wins the day, like every other story Grandma wrote.

I run my fingers over the words "The End" that Grandma traced over and over when she was trying to think of new story ideas.

Her stories were cheesy and predictable and weird, but I still loved every single one of them.

"I don't remember that one," I whisper, not wanting to disturb our comfortable silence.

Mom rubs my shoulder. "You should take these home with us. Then you can read them whenever you want."

I shake my head, rubbing the edge of the paper between my thumb and index finger. "I don't know."

"Why not?"

"Because," I pause, my throat starting to tighten. "It hurts."

"Maybe if you spend less time trying to forget the bad stuff and more time trying to remember the good, it will start to get better." Mom smiles. "Grieving isn't easy, baby. It never is, for anyone. And we all handle it differently, but it hurts for everyone. And it's a long process. But you're never gonna get through that process if you keep pushing it all away."

"You handled it so well."

"Oh, I handled it horribly. I was a mess. For a long time."

"You were? I never saw you upset."

She purses her lips. "I know. I hid it from you because I was trying to be stronger for you all. But I definitely felt it. And I miss Mary so much. You weren't alone in grieving her, Naya. You *aren't* alone. I'm sorry I ever made you feel that way."

Tears fill my eyes. If she feels it, too, she can help me get through it. We can help each other.

Before I can say anything else, Grandpa calls. "Girls? Jessica and Mark are getting ready to leave."

"I guess that's our cue." Mom kisses the top of my head.

Her way of telling me it's time to apologize.

As we leave the attic, my eyes catch on the newer dark brown journal on her desk. I grab it and chase after Mom. She is standing at the bottom of the stairs, hugging Aunt Jessica. When she pulls away she turns and gives me *the look*.

I take a deep breath. "I'm sorry." I tell Jessica, quiet at first but then I speak louder. "I shouldn't have acted like that. You didn't do anything to deserve that."

She smiles, pulling me into a hug. "I miss her, too."

My room is warm from the fire in the fireplace, and after I plug in my fairy lights, they cast a dim glow. Stuffed animals that I refuse to get rid of are piled on top of my bed.

I set my mug of eggnog down on the end table and crawl into bed. The journal I grabbed from the attic sits on my other end table, waiting to be read.

After talking to Mom and reading that story, I feel stronger. Like I'm not falling apart. When I open the journal, I'm not as afraid of what its words may do to me.

This book is thicker and filled with small, messy print. The leather feels new, and the pages are still slick, not having withstood the test of time. Most of the stories here I have never heard before. Grandma never dated her pages—which didn't bother me as a child, but now I wish more than anything she had.

I read the stories, handling the pages gently, until it comes to an abrupt end. About twenty pages are left empty.

I sit up. Grandma wouldn't have left this unfinished. River hadn't defeated the bad guys yet; she didn't win the day.

Where is the ending? Why didn't Grandma write the end?

Realization sets in, and the tears pooling in my eyes spill over my cheeks.

No, no, no. This can't be it. This can't be all she wrote. There has to be more.

I flip through the last pages, almost ripping them in my frantic state.

When I come to the last page, it's empty. I wanted *something*. A letter would fall out, or she would have written something for me. Something to say "it's okay, I love you," or "goodbye."

Nothing but emptiness. The last words of a dying woman who didn't get to finish her sentence.

Sobs wrack my body as I pull the journal to my chest and cave in on myself.

Mom's words come to me then. *"Grandma may not have gotten to do everything she wanted to, but she still had a wonderful life. She would have wanted you to have one too."*

I wonder if Grandma really *was* happy, even if she didn't get to do everything she wanted to.

I wonder what she would think if she saw me now.

"Stop crying. Would River let some old lady dying drag her down? No. River would keep her head up, charge forward, and win the day. You can be like River, my butterfly."

I smile. Grandma was tough, and she always tried to teach me how to be tough, too.

A knock startles me from my curled up position, and I wipe my eyes before Mom peeks her head in. Her eyes go straight to mine, and then the journal in my arms.

"Hey, Naya." She smiles. "I wanted to check on you."

I sniffle, trying to speak but the words seem stuck in my throat. Mom sits next to me, draping an arm around me.

"You read another journal, huh?"

I nod, staring down at it as my tears drip onto the front cover.

"What was in this one?"

I shrug and clear my throat. "More stories. Not ones I had read before. She, uh, she wrote this one more recently."

"Is that why you're crying?"

"Kind of. She didn't... get to finish it."

Mom takes a deep breath, rubbing my back.

I close my eyes and focus on the strength of my mother's presence.

"A lot of things are left unfinished when someone passes away," Mom whispers. "No one knows the exact day they are going to be with God. You can't plan around that. There's always going to be something left unfinished."

"Grandma had so much left to do."

"Naya, she did so much. I think you're forgetting that."

I pull my long sleeves past my hands and rub at my eyes. "I wish she could have traveled."

"*You* can."

I stare at my mom.

"I know you wanted to go with her, but we can't change the past. Grandma would want you to be happy." She grabs my hand. "And Naya, maybe this is a way you can move forward."

"You think I would be happier if I went on the trip?" I shake my head, staring into my mom's eyes. "I can't do that, Mom. That would be—I don't know, dishonoring her memory? Disrespecting her? I was supposed to do it *with* her."

"But you can't. And I can guarantee you if she could talk to you right now she would tell you not to let her death stop you from living." She shakes her head. "That would break her heart."

Grandma's face appears clear in my mind. If she were here right now, she really would be heartbroken to see how many trips and opportunities I've turned down since she passed.

"You don't think it's dishonoring her memory or betraying her?"

"No, baby. I think it would make her smile down at us."

I look at my closet, the suitcase Grandma had given me still sitting there, untouched. Waiting for its stickers.

"Okay." I nod. "Let's do it."

When winter break came around, Mom and I set off.

We decided to drive to the redwoods instead of fly, because it worked out to be cheaper. It was a seventeen hour road trip from Prescott, AZ, and every minute was filled with long talks with Mom. We brought some of Grandma's journals, and we read through them, we listened to music and audiobooks, and we stopped at an absurd amount of tourist attractions to take pictures.

While we both cried many times over Grandma not being with us, we still felt her. I know she smiled down at us.

All I could think was how happy this would make her. To see that I didn't let her death stop me. I was living my life again. I was finding my joy again. And I was doing it with Mom.

Now I wander through a gift shop, searching for a sticker.

My eyes catch on one that says "Redwood National Park" with big trees arching along it. It will fit perfectly.

When I step outside, the bell on the door chiming, I stare in awe at the view before me. The trees stretch so high into the sky I wonder if they could kiss the stars. I can't even comprehend the sheer magnitude of the forest. Not only are they taller than the giants in storybooks, but there are so many of them, stretching out for miles and miles. This truly is one of the most magnificent places on Earth.

December air blows through the pine needles and makes my cheeks go rosy. My nose is frozen, and my lips are chapped, but I don't care.

I smile, my eyes watering as I stare up at where the trees kiss the sky, fiddling with the sticker in my hands.

"I wish you were here," I whisper as a single tear falls down my cheek.

The words hang in the air as everything seems to go still.

The clouds part, making way for the sun to shine through. I close my eyes and lift my face skywards, letting the warmth soak into my skin. I hold my breath for a long time, and when I release it, a large weight lifts off my chest.

The weight of grief.

I take a deep breath of fresh, pine-tinged air, and I'm once again filled with joy.

KIRA ROSENGREN

Having experienced a tragic loss at a young age and also undergoing a full spinal fusion in her teens, Kira Rosengren loves writing stories of strength in dark times that show you you're not alone in your struggles. When she isn't working at her housecleaning or tutoring businesses or plugging away at homework, Kira is listening to any and all kinds of music or binge watching a period drama or mystery television show.

ACHIEVEMENTS

- Completed four full length novels and four short stories.

- Received and implemented a professional edit letter.

- Completed drafting and self edits on a 50k novel in seven weeks.

- Ghostwritten a book on marketing for WritingMomentum.

- Volunteered at Havok Publishing in submissions for three months.

- Attended Write to Publish and received interest from a publishing house.

- Started two successful businesses in order to hone her skills in business.

- Co-organized the 2022 YDubs Retreat.

PITCHES

- This YA Contemporary novel is a classic summer road trip gone wrong story about a girl learning to forgive her sisters and falling in love.

- In this YA Contemporary novel, three kids are sent across the country for the summer, unaware that their long lost father lives in the area. *Bumblebee* meets *Secondhand Lions.*

ADULT FICTION

(not objectionable for younger readers but written for an adult audience)

EVERY SECOND WITH YOU

SAVANNA AMMONS

C erise Cartier pushed the cafe door open, and the buttery aroma of fresh-baked croissants mingled with the scent of newly fallen rain.

The shop, aptly named "Crumbs," bustled this time of day, Seattle residents seeking a warm sandwich or barely-out-of-the-oven cookie for lunch. Cerise checked the time on her cell. *Thirty-five minutes left.* She could still finish her lunch break on time and return to her graphic design project.

No biggie.

As the person in line ahead of her moved forward, Cerise followed suit, tapping her fingertips against her thigh.

A minute later, the woman behind the counter smiled. "What can I get for you today?"

"A baguette, please."

"That'll be $4.50. Can I get a name for the order?"

"Cerise." She swiped her debit card as the worker scooped a loaf into a brown paper bag.

When she looked up, the barista was peering at her, brows lifted in... recognition? "Cerise, you said?"

"Yes." Her name was somewhat unusual, so people often thought she'd said "Clarisse," "Clarissa," or some variation. "Or you could just use my last name, Cartier, if that's easier."

"Actually," the woman pulled an envelope from beneath the counter and held it out, "I have something for you."

Huh. Cerise couldn't remember seeing this girl before, but that didn't mean she hadn't. She wasn't great with faces.

"Oh?" Cerise took the bread, then the envelope, turning it over in her hands. "What is it?"

"You'll have to open it and find out." A hint of a smile tugged at the girl's lips. "And I'd do it before I left if I were you."

Cerise raised an eyebrow and tucked the envelope beneath her arm. "All right, thanks. Have a good day."

"You, too!"

Frowning, Cerise returned outside to the drizzling rain and dropped the loaf into her bike basket. Scootching her bike beneath the mint green awning, she slid her finger beneath the envelope's flap, tearing its seal.

She pulled out a piece of stationary with multicolored iridescent circles slightly raised along the thick paper. *What in the world?*

Squinting at it, she scanned the words written across the page.

Find the place where air inflates, where what is flexible becomes fragile, where the broken can be restored, and where scorching heat makes a thing of beauty.

Huh?

Pulling out her phone, Cerise called her mom's cell. She held her phone between her shoulder and ear, still examining the words, and muttering each phrase to herself.

Mom answered, "Hello?" and her cheerful voice momentarily lifted Cerise's confusion.

"Hey! So, the lady at the bakery gave me a riddle. Do you know anything about this?" Mom had sent her here, after all. Who else could be the culprit?

"A riddle?" Mom's voice went up an octave, as was her default when she tried to act innocent. "What sort of riddle?"

Cerise read the note aloud. Mom waited a few seconds before speaking, her tone still high-pitched. "Oh, interesting. And the barista gave it to you?"

Cerise resisted the urge to roll her eyes, a smile creeping up her face. Okay, she could play along. "Yeah. I got your loaf of bread, and she handed it to me. Am I supposed to follow it?"

"It sounds fun to me. Maybe you should."

"Mom, I have work to do." Cerise stole another glance at the letter. "I have all those graphics to finish, and my lunch break ends in half an hour."

"I think work can wait, don't you? Aren't you curious to see where it leads?"

"Of course I'm curious, but I have *deadlines.*" Although she was on track to finish the project two days early, the idea of not following her schedule made her a little queasy.

"Plus," she added, "I need to bring this bread home, and doesn't this whole situation seem a little... odd?"

"I don't need the bread until dinnertime, and there's more to life than work. Go find out what the riddle means. *I think you'll have fun.*"

What if Mom had planned this? She commented more than once at how overwhelmed Cerise had been for the last few months. Even when Titus, Cerise's boyfriend, was in town, she sometimes spent more time on her work than with him, despite the sting of guilt she felt over it.

Deadlines were deadlines, though.

The gentle rain pattered on the awning as her thoughts swirled. If Mom had planned this, she'd be sad if Cerise didn't at least try to solve the riddle. And she couldn't deny the niggle of curiosity.

"Fine." Cerise straightened. "But I'll be home in less than an hour. I can shift my schedule that much, but that's it."

"Have fun, honey." Mom's smile came through the line. "I love you."

"Love you, too. See you soon."

Cerise hung up and dropped her gaze to the paper, now crinkled from gripping it too hard. One riddle. She could be home in less than an hour. Maybe forty minutes.

Find the place where air inflates.

That could be anything. Balloons? She could see how balloons would connect to the first two phrases, air inflating and becoming fragile. Balloons were stretchy, after all, and popped easily once inflated. But she couldn't connect how it would relate to brokenness being restored, or how heat could make it into something beautiful.

A few words drifted through her, whispering of Bible verses about passing through the fire to be refined. Like gold, heated and purified until it shone, until you could see your face in it. Maybe it had something to do with gold.

Her eyes caught on the bubbles on the paper. Prism-like, almost. Or—

Glass.

She scanned the words again. Yes. It had to be, right? When glass broke, it could be heated into *flexible* glass. When scorching hot, it could be shaped into whatever shape before hardening again. She and Titus had found that out on their date to the blown glass studio—

Blown. Air inflated it.

It had to be blown glass. The blown glass store. Probably the same one she and Titus had been to on their first date.

What if this wasn't Mom's doing, after all?

A sizzle of excitement rose within her. What if it was Titus? She hadn't heard much from him today, but they usually talked more after work. What if he'd planned something? What if he enlisted Mom to help?

Then again, he said he couldn't visit for another month. So maybe not.

Dropping the note and the bread in her bike basket, Cerise straddled the seat and raised her kickstand. The bike ride to the glass shop would take ten minutes. She'd go there, find what she was supposed to, and get home in time to finish her work.

She pushed off and peddled to the heart of Seattle, flinching as the rain pelted her skin. The buildings gradually stretched into skyscrapers, and the smell of exhaust intermingled with the salty tang of Puget Sound as she entered her favorite part of the city.

Despite the many tourists, she adored Occidental Square. The art hub of Seattle, where, on some weekends, markets and art shows flooded the tree-lined brick path and courtyard. If someone needed a respite from the city, a nearby wall hid Waterfall Garden Park, a charming courtyard with a man-made waterfall.

Soon, the Glasshouse Studio stood ahead of her in all its brownstone, industrial glory. Cerise leaned her bike against a conveniently placed handrail and locked it to the rail. She tucked her note into a pocket and pushed open the door.

Golden light flooded through the room from glass pendants. All around her sat objects she didn't feel qualified to touch and would probably break if she did. Plates spiraled with flowers and images of the sun, aquamarine vases held flecks of greens and darker blues and purples, and lamps flared into fluted bottoms like a salsa dancer's skirt in motion, twirling and flicking.

She could stay here for hours.

She might've forgotten her time crunch, and mission, if someone from the back of the shop hadn't called, "Welcome in!"

She started as a middle-aged man exited the workshop area.

"Hi there," she called back, unfolding the paper as they both approached the cash register. "This will sound silly, but do you know of a scavenger hunt happening here? I have this note, and I think it was meant to bring me here."

He smiled. "So you're the girl I heard about."

Before Cerise could respond, he pulled a vase from beneath his station and set it atop the counter. Cherry blossom pink with clear and magenta swirls, it sat slightly askew, with a mouth barely wide enough for a small bouquet.

And it was the prettiest piece of glass she'd ever seen.

Cerise brushed her fingers against the lip, tracing the curve of the vase down to the base. Only then did she see another piece of paper sticking out the top.

"It's all yours," the man said, breaking through her wonder at the creation. "Your boy made it. And it's paid in full. Would you like me to wrap it up?"

"Yes, please. Do you have bubble wrap? I'm on a bike."

"Sure do." He stepped into another back room.

While she awaited his return, Cerise pondered the vase, then gently lifted the paper out and unwound it.

It was plain paper this time, decorated with hand-drawn... mice? Along with another riddle.

Cerise glanced at her watch as the man reappeared and swaddled her vase in bubble wrap. She didn't have time to solve another clue and follow it to its destination. The afternoon was ticking away, and she only had fifteen minutes before the end of lunch.

But... she did want to see this through to the end—and really wanted to find out what Titus was doing.

Your boy made it, the man had said. So it must be Titus.

Right?

The man finished packing her vase, and she thanked him before slipping back outside and placing the package in the basket. Using one hand to protect the paper from the rain, she reread the riddle.

Go to where wrinkles fade and backs straighten, where laughter dings and eyes light, where the rain cannot reach and reality cannot register. There, the robin will give you your next clue.

Huh? This was even more convoluted than the last. How did Titus expect her to solve another riddle before she finished lunch? Her stomach grumbled, reminding her she hadn't even eaten yet. No matter. She could eat when she got home, while she worked.

Where wrinkles fade and backs straighten. That sounded like Botox and chiropractic care. But why would he lead her to a chiropractor or to get Botox? He often told her he loved the laugh lines already forming around her eyes. Had kissed the spots more than once. She smiled at the memory, and a shiver ran down her spine.

Concentrate, Cerise.

If it wasn't Botox or chiropractic care, then maybe he was saying it made someone younger. Was there a spring or water source nearby that people joked was the fountain of youth?

She couldn't think of one off the top of her head.

Her stomach growled again. Sighing, she dug into her purse, pulled out a granola bar, and took a large bite.

Maybe the other part of the riddle would spark something.

Where laughter dings and eyes light, where the rain cannot reach and reality cannot register.

Where the rain cannot reach.

She smiled as a memory appeared in her mind's eye.

She and Titus were walking through the rain when a strong gust of wind swept their umbrella up and out of their hands. They chased after it, slipping on the slick streets before reaching its final resting place, stuck upside-down against a small awning on the corner of the sidewalk.

Titus grabbed it and pulled it back over their heads, only to dump the rainwater collecting in it over them, drenching them further. After sputtering, she laughed. He looked like a drowned rat, with his hair the color of a sky aflame plastered to his face and his clothes clinging to his body.

She knew she looked the same or worse, and it was simply unfair that he could look so adorable sopping wet.

"Sorry," he said, his voice sheepish. Then his eyes locked with hers, and he reached out, sweeping a strand of her soggy hair behind one ear. His hand lingered on her cheek. "How are you so beautiful, even when you're soaked?"

She laughed, cheeks heating even as she shivered. "We should go somewhere to get warm."

They looked across the street to a tall building with an arched entrance., Displayed in the window were toys.

So many toys.

They glanced back at each other, and Cerise knew he was thinking the same as her. "Want to escape reality for a little bit?"

He grinned. "Who doesn't want to be a kid again?"

He seized her hand, and they ran into the toy store.

The memory faded, and Cerise clutched the note to her chest. Yes, that had to be where he was leading her next. Rain couldn't reach them, and they'd seemed to grow younger as they played with the toys together, which wasn't reality.

What was the shop called again? She glanced back at the paper, studying the mice again.

Right. *Magic Mouse Toys.*

Within five minutes, she coasted to a halt in front of the toy store. She entered and gaped like a child, taking in all the colors, toys, books, and games.

She approached the counter, and the girl lit up. "Hi, welcome to Magic Mouse Toys! My name's Robin. May I help you today?"

"Hi." Cerise smoothed a wrinkle from her flowy green top. She paused. "Wait, did you say 'Robin'?"

"Yes."

Cerise smirked, wishing Titus was here so she could tease him. A Robin to help her was the last clue. Good thing the girl hadn't called in sick today. "Wonderful! You're who I'm looking for. I've been following these riddles—"

Robin's face brightened even more. She dug into her pocket, pulled out a red plastic key, and handed it to Cerise.

"This is your next clue," she said. "And another hint: don't take it from the shop."

"Got it." Cerise accepted the key and examined it. "Thank you."

She stepped away and wandered toward the games. Where would it go? A wind-up soldier? A jewelry box? A diary set with a lock?

Her phone's alarm jarred the quiet space. She dug her cell from her pocket and switched it off—but not before she saw the words on her screen. *Get back to work!*

A reminder that lunch was over.

She gripped the key tighter.

She would find where the key fit, then go home and finish her graphics.

There weren't as many toys with keyholes as she'd expected, but whenever she came across one, she tried the key—but none matched. How would she find the correct item in this massive, multi-floored emporium?

She descended into the basement level, pulling the previous letter from her jacket. Maybe it gave another hint.

Go to where wrinkles fade and backs straighten, where laughter dings and eyes light, where the rain cannot reach and reality cannot register.

She'd thought the clue was only leading her to the location, but maybe not. Was there a toy here that matched with rain? Or laughter? Or eyes? Or youth? Or—

Where laughter dings. *Dings* was an odd word choice. Laughter didn't ding. Maybe he was alluding to something else. Like a piano, or a xylophone.

She took the last step, and her eyes landed on a display. One doll stood at the counter, its hands on a mini shopping cart filled with books and games. The other stood behind the counter near the cash register.

Where reality cannot register.

Register.

Cerise pressed a palm to her forehead, and a giggle tripped from her lips. Cash registers made a dinging sound, too. Would he be that sneaky?

She walked to the display and held the key up to the keyhole of the cash register. It looked about the right size, so she inserted it and turned. The pink plastic drawer popped open with a chime.

Yes!

A blank piece of paper and a miniature flashlight, not any bigger than a penlight, lay within. Setting the paper on a nearby table, she pressed the flashlight's button. A prick of blue light shone on the table. Wasn't blue light special somehow?

One way to find out.

She slid the light across the blank paper, and words appeared beneath the beam. *Clever.* She dug a pen from her purse and traced the words. The message read:

> *"Fill in the blanks:*
> *Thy word is a _____ unto my feet, and a _____ unto my path."*

Cerise smiled. He'd either run out of complicated riddle ideas or decided to go easy on her for this one.

In empty spaces, she wrote the words she knew by heart.

> *"Thy word is a <u>lamp unto my feet</u>, and a <u>light</u> unto my path."*

Combining those simple words and the pattern of the other clues, she knew exactly where Titus was spurring her. Lamplight Books, her favorite used bookstore, smack in the heart of the Pike Place Market.

As Cerise set her pen back in her purse, her eyes caught on a row of costumes and masks at one end of the room. A grin tugged at her lips.

When they'd been here together, she perused the picture books for Titus's nephew. As she combed through the stories, a presence sidled up next to her.

She'd turned and laughed.

Titus stood there, a pair of too-small plastic glasses attached to a large nose and mustache atop his real glasses. He peered at her through the fake lenses and raised one of his thick red eyebrows at her. His hair was drying, but a bead of water ran down his temple.

"Hello, miss," he said, dropping his voice an octave lower than usual. "Might I interest you in a dance?"

"Hm." She eyed him, her hand to her cheek as if considering. "It would be an honor, but I seem to have forgotten my ball gown at home, and I only dance with my boyfriend."

"A damp t-shirt and jeans will suffice for this particular ball."

"I'm glad to hear it." She reached out and pulled the mask off his face. "And there's the boyfriend."

Cerise shook her head to focus. Why was it so much easier to do things spontaneously with Titus around? When they were together, she hardly ever worried about deadlines and whether she'd be safe or on time. Why couldn't she do that when he wasn't around? Why was she worrying about finishing the project for work *today*?

Her phone vibrated, and she glanced at it. It was a text from her client and friend, Marjorie, the one who had commissioned the project.

> *We need to talk shop. Call me ASAP.*

Wincing, she stuffed her phone back in her pocket. She needed to get home now to finish by tomorrow. But Marjorie liked to check in a few days ahead of schedule. Maybe that was all she wanted this time, too.

Cerise folded the paper into squares to tuck into her jacket, but something stopped her. Had this clue been too easy? It felt odd that he'd only written on the top of the page and left so much blank space below.

Flipping the page over, she ran her light across the backside. At the bottom ran a long number. She took her phone back out and typed as she read it.

9781402714597

Interesting. Well, she could try to puzzle that out as she rode to the bookstore. Surely this had to be the last stop. Titus had to be there, waiting for her.

After returning the key to Robin and thanking her for the help, Cerise set off for the market. It was a short ride. She knew she was close when the smell of fresh-caught fish assaulted her.

Breezing to a stop, she parked her bike and entered the bustling market center.

A cacophony of colors, sounds, and smells flooded her senses. On one side of the aisle, whole fish lay on ice, and on the other were artichokes, heads of broccoli, fresh tomatoes, and ears of corn still in the husk. Garlic hung from racks on the ceiling beside bunches of peppers, as if warding off any vampires who might be traversing the overcast city that day.

Cerise slipped between people, beelining toward her favorite bookstore. She soon crossed from yellowed tile onto a scuffed-up red concrete floor. The smell of fish faded, replaced with the grimy, comforting scent of old paper, dust, and the slightest hints of perfume and smoke.

Instead of going to her favorite section—the fantasy novels—she slipped through the aisles, peering around corners. Where was the face she longed to see more than anyone else in the world, a glimpse of scruffy orange hair, untamable no matter how often he combed it? His lean frame, or the light glinting off his glasses?

Her stomach fluttered in excitement at every turn, but soon, she'd searched the whole shop.

He was nowhere to be found. Disappointment crashed over her, but she pushed it down.

Cerise could feel eyes on her back. With a glance behind her, she found the bookstore workers staring at her. She moved behind a shelf and pretended to examine the books as if searching for one in particular.

To finish the charade, she picked up a book she'd never read before. The cover showed a rendition of what had to be Big Ben in London. The sun set behind it with two figures flying across the cityscape, a trail of glitter in their wake.

Flipping to the back cover, she glanced over the endorsements and down to the barcode. Cerise frowned. The ISBN... how long was it? She counted the digits. Thirteen in total.

She took the last note out of her pocket. Throughout the ride here, the number Titus gave her still didn't make sense.

Maybe...

She counted the digits.

Thirteen.

Grabbing her phone, she searched the number in her browser. Her Wi-Fi was too slow, so she approached the counter with a smile that she hoped said, *No, I wasn't traipsing about the shop like a fool earlier, looking for my boyfriend. Why do you ask?*

"Hi," she said instead. "Can you find out what book connects to this ISBN?"

"Of course." The woman poised her hands over her keyboard, and her fingers flew as Cerise recited the number. "It's to *The Secret Garden* by Frances Hodgson Burnett. We got that exact copy earlier today."

She gestured to the children's section, and Cerise thanked her and walked to the shelves. Of course it was *The Secret Garden*. How could it not be? She and Titus had read it together two years ago, not long after they started dating.

Cerise found the book quickly, sticking partway out of the shelf as if waiting for her. She flipped through the book, but nothing caught her attention. She reached the end, and a scrawled number on the inside of the back cover read *49*.

She flipped to page 49 and skimmed it. Apart from the words written by Miss Burnett herself, it was blank, and nothing about the scene popped out at her.

However, the last time there was a blank page...

Cerise pulled her blue light from her pocket and shone it across the paper. Near the bottom right of the page, he'd circled the word "waters." And on the margin, he'd written *106*.

She turned to that page and found the word "falling" marked near the top of the page and *233*.

Water falling? Water almost always fell from the sky in Seattle.

As she thumbed to 233, she caught sight of some non-invisible ink on a page between. She stopped and read over the passage. It was a lovely description of the garden in bloom, and next to it, in Titus's writing, were the words, *Cerise, you are my garden. You are the place I long to be, the most beautiful thing I've ever seen. I love you.*

She smiled and pressed the book to her heart.

If she still needed confirmation that this was his doing, she'd found it.

I love you too, Titus.

She skipped to page 233 and blinked. He'd circled "garden." Otherwise, the page was truly blank. There was no next number to turn to.

"Waters falling garden," she said aloud. The sound jolted her in the quiet building, but she repeated it. "Waters falling garden. What? Waters falling... water fall, maybe? Waterfall garden?"

Yes, it must be. The Waterfall Garden was Seattle's Secret Garden.

She flipped through the book again, breathing in the faint smell of his cologne lingering on the paper. Her gaze landed on more annotations she'd missed in her first scan. They were more of the same, telling her he loved her and she was beautiful inside and out. That even if he didn't like a single person in the world, he would've liked her.

As she tried to absorb all the notes, her heart swelled, tears pricking her eyes. He'd done this and planned this intricate quest for her.

Only an hour and fifteen minutes or so before, she'd agonized over getting her work done, almost refusing to embark on this spur-of-the-moment hunt.

But if Titus had been planning this for years, her deadlines felt silly.

Something whispered in the back of her mind that maybe there were some parallels with her and God's relationship, too. He planned everything out before the beginning of the world, right? So why did she worry about getting her work done ahead of schedule? Why did she hate being spontaneous and following His lead unless it was with Titus?

She'd have to mull that over later.

After asking the workers if Titus had donated the item and if she'd have to pay for it—he had, and she didn't—she headed back through the winding market, clutching the book to her side.

Her phone dinged in her back pocket. She stopped and pulled it out, glancing at the screen.

Her heart plummeted.

> *What's the ETA on the graphics? There's been a change of plans, and I need them by the end of the day. I'm sorry! Call me, please!*

Stupid, stupid, stupid. This was why Cerise did her work ahead of time. This was why she didn't take more time away from work than she had to, why she gave herself such strict schedules. She would've finished the graphics tonight if she'd just—

No.

A chill ran down her arms. Did that word come from her or the Holy Spirit? The sudden panic subsided, and her body relaxed.

Her mind cleared.

She had two options. She could call Titus and apologize for having to go home and finish the project, or she could continue this journey and see where he and the Lord were leading her.

If she didn't finish, she could lose Marjorie, her most consistent client, which would set her income back significantly. And without the money, she'd probably have to cancel her trip to Maine to see Titus this fall.

She risked disappointing her friend, too. If Marjorie said she needed the graphics sooner, Cerise would've typically moved heaven and earth to finish them. She didn't ask for things like this lightly. Her publisher was probably pressuring her to up her marketing game.

But if she went home now, she might never know what Titus had done. She might hurt him and lose this opportunity to trust him and to trust God.

She needed to choose who she prioritized.

She brought up the mental image of Titus, with soaking hair, a smile broadening his freckled face. Titus, eyes twinkling beneath plastic glasses at the toy store. Titus, hunched over a book, writing *You are my garden* in the margins.

Despite her love for Marjorie, Titus won every time. Even if he wasn't asking her to choose, the thought of hurting him made her chest ache.

Tomorrow, she could finish her work.

But today, she would choose spontaneity.

> *Hey Marjie. I'm sorry, but I can't complete them today. I will have them done by the original deadline. Titus is in town and I'm spending time with him.*

She sent the text despite her shaking hands and stuffed the phone back in her pocket.

The Waterfall Garden stood near the Glasshouse Studio, so she saw many familiar sights as she biked. Her heart throbbed, though less from the exercise and more from nerves.

He'd probably have more riddles waiting for her, but she didn't mind.

She slowed to a stop before the gated garden, but something about this felt more real than anything so far today. More real and yet, somehow, like she couldn't feel the concrete beneath her feet.

Cerise wheeled the bike through the entrance and leaned it against the wall. She took in the trees stretching to the sky, the flowers blooming all around her, the greenhouse-like shades over the patio area, and the man-made waterfall flowing across the rocks.

Her eyes caught on a figure standing before one of the foliage-filled planters. She froze, and her breath caught in her throat.

Titus.

Her legs started working again, and she ran down the ramp toward him, flying into his arms.

Titus caught her with a soft grunt, holding on tight as she clung to him. She savored his strong arms around her and the heat of his skin in the chilly air. One of them was trembling. She couldn't tell which.

Only when she looked up, meeting his brown eyes, did she notice the tears rolling down her cheeks. She sniffed and laughed, wiping them away with the palm of her hand. "Hi."

"Hi." His warm voice sent a shiver through her, his eyes roving her face like parched land soaking in a newly fallen rain. "I missed you."

A sob caught in her chest, and she swallowed against the lump in her throat. "I missed you, too. I thought you couldn't come down for another month."

"I know." He brushed a strand of her hair behind her ear, planting a kiss on her nose, then her forehead. "I'm sorry. But I couldn't tell you about this."

"I forgive you."

"Thank you." Titus released her and took a step back, then, slowly, he knelt on the damp stone. "Cerise Audrey Cartier—"

Though his voice broke on her last name, and his eyes grew red-rimmed and watery, he didn't look away from her. Cerise couldn't help bouncing a little on the balls of her feet—the only way to restrain herself from answering his still-unasked question.

Titus spoke again, his voice strained but still audible above the rush of the waterfall. "Cerise, your heart for Jesus shines through everything you do, and your smile lights up my soul. I want to love you for the rest of my life. I want to protect you, to hold you when you cry, to laugh with you, and to run through the rain with you. I never could've dreamed God would give me someone as amazing as you to love, and I will be thanking Him until my final breath for blessing me with you."

Reaching into his pocket, he removed a small box and opened it.

She kept her eyes on his face. If only she could memorize every detail of this moment.

Titus took a breath, searching her eyes as if seeking courage. Cerise couldn't have spoken even if she tried. Instead, she took his free hand in both of hers and squeezed.

"Will you do me the honor of marrying me? Please?"

At his "please," the dam burst. She dropped to her knees, pressing her lips to his.

When they broke apart, his cheeks were pink beneath his freckles. The corner of his mouth lifted in a smile. "I assume that's a yes?"

"Yes!" She wiped her eyes with her sleeve. "Yes, with all my heart."

He kissed her this time, and she barely noticed the way the knees of her jeans grew damp and cold.

Finally, Cerise sat back on her heels, her eyes still on his. "I love you."

"I love you, too." Titus removed the ring from its box and held his hand out for hers.

A bit of sunshine peeked through the clouds and caught on the simple gold band with two petite diamonds on either side of the center diamond. They scattered light across his face, highlighting a few freckles and giving his eyes an almost ethereal glow.

"It's beautiful." She placed her hand in his, and he slipped the ring onto her finger. It fit like it was made for her.

"We should take a picture together." She pulled out her phone and was about to open the camera app when she saw a text back from Marjorie. Cerise didn't want to read it, but her eyes skimmed over it anyway.

> *Aw, I'm so glad Titus is there! Say hi to him for me. Don't worry about the graphics. I can tweak one of the old ones and make something work for today's post.*

Cerise shook her head. "He had everything planned, didn't He?"

"What do you mean?" Titus asked.

She told him the story from the beginning.

"So," she finished, grinning at him, "God worked it all out, and I didn't have to worry for a minute."

"I didn't mean to make you choose."

"I know. But I'll always choose you."

"Ditto." Titus grinned, then stood, pulling her to her feet. He took a bouquet from the planter behind him. "This is for you. I thought they would look pretty in your new vase."

Cerise accepted the flowers and brought them to her face, breathing in the sweet aroma. "They're beautiful. Thank you. And I love the vase. It's perfect. I'm going to put it on my desk."

She set the flowers down, winding her arms around his neck. As she brought her lips to his, the scent of rain on concrete encircled her, mixing with the faint, woodsy fragrance of his cologne.

Wrinkles would form, and their backs would someday bend with age. Rain would soak them—this was Seattle, after all—and life would, at times, make them feel like laughter was impossible. Another world away.

That was reality.

And she wanted every second of it with him.

SAVANNA AMMONS

Savanna Ammons writes sweet Christian romances that deal sensitively and biblically with difficult topics. Her short story was inspired by memories of visiting her great-grandparents in Seattle. When she's not writing, you can find her working the front desk at her local library, snuggling her puppy, or pouring her next batch of epoxy resin for her small business. If you want to be her friend, prepare to endure dad jokes and puns as soon as she has the opportunity.

Achievements

- Has drafted eight novel-length projects and two short stories.

- Received and implemented a professional edit letter on a novel-length project.

- Semi-finaled in the ACFW Genesis Contest for romance.

- Received interest in her projects from multiple literary agents and editors.

- Started two small businesses and practiced in-person and online marketing skills, including reaching out to fellow authors as potential customers, building possible connections with them at the same time.

- Active member of the American Christian Fiction Writers and Faith, Hope, and Love Christian Writers.

- Attended multiple writing conferences in 2024 including Blue Ridge Christian Writers Conference, Write-to-Publish, and American Christian Fiction Writers.

- Launched her Instagram and grew her Instagram to over 900 followers.

Pitches

- A young woman works to save her bakery from foreclosure by entering a televised baking competition with the help of her food critic love interest—but her ex-fiance is doing everything he can to sabotage her.

- A retelling of *The Secret Garden* where Mary is a chronically ill woman at an experimental treatment facility and Dickon is the burnt-out heir of a flower farm, and they have to learn what it means to heal.

- A loose *Beauty and the Beast* retelling where a traumatized former ice dancer finds himself trapped with his ex-college sweetheart and dancing partner during a blizzard—and they have to work together to save the life of the son she never told him about.

THE POET WHO LIVED ON PICKPOCKET LANE

SARINA LOUISE

F or a moment, Elias swore he felt her fingers brush his cheek.

   Something deep within whispered that he'd open his eyes and find her next to him—her gentle smile, her soft caress. If only he could reach just a bit farther.

"Daddy, wake *up*!"

The shrill cry exploded against his eardrum. He jolted upright, back throbbing and a crick stabbing into his neck. *What the—?*

Rubbing at his bleary eyes, he glanced down at his desk, the blurred headline of *The Daily Herald* catching his attention. *"IRISH M.P. ARRESTED, Propaganda Minister and Talented Playwright."*

Saturday, February 12th, 1921. Yesterday's paper.

But what woke him tore his gaze away.

"Hi Daddy!" Deep chocolate curls bounced as Nina's eyes sparkled. His little girl beamed up at him, crawling into his lap, and placed her hands on his cheeks with a giggle. "Auntie Cassia's here!"

His gaze flicked up.

"My dear brother, what has *happened* to you?" Cassia leaned against the doorway of his study, dark ringlets swept back, an exasperated smile curving her lips.

Hollowness crawled through Elias's veins, as it did every morning when he woke to Rosa's absence. But being observed in his grief brought its own ache.

What a sight he must be, sprawled against the desk instead of a bed.

Elias groaned as Nina shifted, her knees digging into his thigh. He forced a soft laugh. "Nothing *happened*, Cass. I just lost track of time." His gaze fell to the blank sheet of paper, the dark mahogany beneath now decorated with drool. An obsidian pen sat next to it, begging to be used. Anything to shake the layer of dust disturbed by his fingerprints from when he'd taken it out of its box last night.

"Whatcha looking at, Daddy?" Nina craned her neck around, her eyes widening to the size of the moon.

Elias worked his jaw. He used to compare Nina to the moon, Rosa to the sun. When he was writing, that was. Since Rosa's death, though, her spirit saturated every word he wrote. Too much pain. For everyone.

A life without writing was better than reliving the memories.

Elias reached forward, fingers closing around the blank piece of paper. "Nothing, sweetheart, it's just—"

Nina gasped. "Is that my birthday poem?"

The joy, the *hope*, rippling through her tone sliced straight into the chinks of Elias's soul as his mouth opened and closed.

Cassia stiffened against the doorframe, her gaze meeting his for a split second. Just enough for him to notice the puffy, red skin around her eyes.

He shook his head, forcing his tone to stay level and light. "Nina, love, we aren't doing a birthday poem this year, remember?" He crumpled the blank page in his fist.

Even if he'd wanted to keep the tradition, last night had proved it was impossible.

Nina stuck out her bottom lip, staring up at him with puppy dog eyes. "But I want a birthday poem."

Elias reached behind her, wrapping a secure arm around her waist as he tugged open one of the secret compartments tucked into his desk. *This ought to distract her from that blasted poem.* "Daddy bought you something else—"

"But I don't *want* something else." Tears gathered in the corners of Nina's eyes as she slid both arms around his neck, burying her face in his chest. "I want a *poem*, Daddy."

Her muffled, shaky whisper tugged at him. He sighed, stroking her hair. "Sweetheart..."

The grandfather clock ticked in the corner as silence fell between them. Elias's own words strangled in his throat, just like every time he tried to put pen to paper. His gaze shifted from the picture of him and Rosa kissing at their wedding to her favorite vase. The pen she'd given him.

Too many memories swarmed him in this apartment.

He met Cassia's gaze. She opened her mouth, but he shook his head slightly, offering her a smile. Taking a deep breath, he squeezed Nina once. "All right, my little butterfly. All right."

He prayed his little girl couldn't feel his shaking hands.

Nina pulled back, beaming once more. "Yay! Thank you, thank you, thank *youuuu*!" She hugged him tight.

Don't thank me yet. He laughed softly, clutching her small body to him. "You're welcome."

"All right then." Cassia leaned down, brushing a stray hair out of Nina's face. "Why don't you go out into the kitchen and see the present Auntie Cassia brought, hm?" Her dark eyes shone as she grinned at Nina.

Nina squealed and scrambled off Elias's lap, knocking the wind out of him.

He groaned as he straightened, tugging himself out of the chair. A series of obnoxiously *old*-sounding cracks followed his movement—far too many for a twenty-seven year old—and he grimaced. With a sigh, he attempted to ruffle his curls back into submission using the murky reflection from the desk. But that was a futile task on the best of days. He collected his long coat from the back of the stiff-legged armchair, turning to his sister.

The sudden absence of a smile made her look far older than her mere twenty-three, though Elias supposed they all bore scars of the last year.

Just in different ways.

She searched his gaze, brow wrinkled. "Are you sure you can do this?"

"Yes. Could you watch Nina for me, just for a few hours, until our birthday lunch?" Elias turned away, snagging the newspaper and ripping out what he needed. No post on Sundays meant Saturday's newspaper held two days' worth.

Cassia blinked. "Watch her? Where are *you* going?"

"Cass." His whisper sliced through her words as he braced himself, palms splayed on the desk. "She wants a poem. I can't help Nina recover from losing her mother if I write here."

The blessing and the curse of a poet.

Writing made tangible, poems made *real*. He'd thought it magic until, a month after Nina lost her mother, he'd accidentally brought to life a memory that hurtled Nina into an even deeper spell of grief.

Elias shook himself, numb fingers fumbling with the buttons of his coat. "I'm going to find a new apartment. I know it sounds insane, but I have a plan. I just need new inspiration."

Cassia's brow furrowed. "I don't think Rosa would want that. She loved this apartment." She pursed her lips, playing with the chain around her neck. The cerulean butterfly charm had been Rosa's favorite. Cassia hadn't taken it off since they'd read the will. "I don't think Nina's going to be any happier if you move, Li."

Her words wrapped around him like a vice and squeezed.

He shoved aside the sensation and tugged her into a hug. Ruffling her hair with a gentle hand, he sighed, "Just watch her for me, please?"

Cassia squeezed hard. "Promise you'll be back for her lunch?"

Three hours to write a poem.

"Promise," he whispered and slipped into the kitchen. He swallowed hard, leaning down to kiss Nina's head. "Be good for Auntie Cassia, okay? Daddy will be back soon."

Nina blinked, scrambling up and clinging to his leg. "What? Where are you going? Can I come, pleeeeease?"

Elias laughed softly, extricating himself from her leech-like grip. "It's a birthday surprise, my little butterfly." He directed his next words to Nina, but glanced up at Cassia. "I'll be back soon."

As the front door clicked shut behind him, Elias took a deep breath.

He glanced down at the clippings in his hands as he took the stairs two at a time. Two same-day lease apartments—the only way he'd be able to move in today.

Two chances to escape the memories that dripped from his pen like poison.

Elias turned the corner, and the hair on the back of his neck prickled.

Cedar Street sprawled before him. Mist and drizzle lengthened the shadows across the cobblestones. A typical London morning.

But this was no time for cowardice.

Elias took a deep breath and strode forward, glancing at each glowering door's brass number. *14, 16, 18.*

20.

The rusted wrought iron gate creaked as he swung it open, sending shudders of revulsion through his body. Wilted lilies lined the cracked stone path, tugging at memories of a wedding bouquet.

He looked away.

Weeds crinkled beneath his shoes as he clambered up the three small steps to the door, its ebony paint peeling to reveal weathered wood beneath.

He grimaced. *Is this really where you want to bring a six-year-old?*

Even with all its memories and pictures, his and Nina's apartment on Pickpocket Lane was looking far more attractive than this glorified alleyway.

But the ever-present, pulsing grief raised his fist to the door, his knock echoing with a dull thud. He waited, half expecting a troll or a goblin to creak open the entrance, their beady eyes trained on him. If he were writing the story, perhaps that would happen.

"'Ello?" A reedy voice grated against Elias's eardrums.

He summoned his most winning smile. Rosa had always said it was one of his finest traits, the first thing she fell in love with. The thought nearly choked his expression before he could speak. But he shoved away the memories for Nina. For a chance to silence the aching call of poems trapped deep inside.

Words that, if he let them out, would cause more pain than just allowing them to lacerate his insides.

"Good day, sir. My name is Elias Thornbury."

The stout man before him raised an eyebrow, lips pulled back in a rather troll-like sneer. "Is that so? You sound like a right gentleman, Mr. Thornbury." The landlord's oily tone drenched Elias, matching the fellow's greasy, slicked-back hair. "'Ow can I 'elp ya?"

Elias cleared his throat, holding up the newspaper clipping, even as every instinct murmured a warning. "I'd like to inspect your listing, if you please."

"Of course, right this way." The landlord bowed low and stepped to the side. "*Sir.*"

Footsteps echoed from behind him. Elias hesitated, casting a casual glance over his shoulder.

Two men loitered in the alley, hats tugged low over their brows.

Elias's smile began to waver. He swallowed hard, taking a step inside to glance into the apartment. His gaze snagged on a pile of wallets on the counter. Conveniently out of sight of anyone standing in the doorway.

The landlord shifted, forcing Elias to back up once more.

"You, my good fellow, are much too trusting." The corners of Rosa's eyes crinkled as she handed him a lily. "I know it's not your wallet, but perhaps it will soothe your wounded pride."

She'd always told him to trust his gut.

Elias straightened. "On second thought, I believe I have the wrong address. Thank you for your time." Before the slimy landlord could respond, Elias turned on his heel, and hurried down the steps.

As he stepped through the gate, one of the burly men sauntered over. A gold tooth glittered in his leering grin. "Where do you think you're going, mate?"

Blast propriety and manners. Elias ducked under the brute's arm. His shoes slapped against the cobblestones, shouts echoing behind him.

He didn't dare look back.

How long he ran he couldn't guess, but the voices soon dwindled.

He slowed. His chest burned as he gasped for air, resting his hands on his knees. An incredulous laugh fell from his lips.

In that moment, memories of a day long past burst through.

"Stop! Thief!" Elias darted through the crowd, his wallet barely visible in his quarry's tight grip.

The mob of people in the street shifted, murmuring, but refused to move, like some large herd of mildly interested sheep.

He cursed, trying to shove through them. His foot caught on a loose cobblestone, and he let out a cry, wobbling, until a gentle hand wrapped around his upper arm.

"Careful! You're certainly not going to catch them if you fall flat on your face."

Laughter swirled around him like a warm summer breeze as he stared at the dark-haired girl before him. Curls framed her face.

"My name's Rosa. Want me to help you catch a pickpocket?"

The heady, unmistakable warmth of magic flowed through him. Words poured into his mind, begging to be written.

He stared at his trembling hands.

He'd promised he'd write something new. Something that wasn't inspired by the potion of love and agony Rosa's memory brewed. So he buried the words down as far as they would go, taking a deep breath.

The second tattered newspaper clipping fluttered in his hand.

One last chance to find somewhere with new inspiration.

Elias should've remembered this street.

But after the whirlwind of the near-mugging, along with the words still trying to hum in his mind, he'd simply glanced at the address and gone on his way. Cars trundled by, once something that would've sparked inspiration.

Now all he could see was Rosa's smile, the memories of the pickpocketing simultaneously so long ago and right before him.

For others, his poems created magic.

His works allowed the reader to step into whatever the poem sparked in their imagination. Only for a short time, while they read his piece, but long enough to experience the wonder of a poet's power.

But for him, as the poet, the act of writing or reading a poem allowed him to step into memories as though he were living in the moment once more.

He just hadn't known Nina was also a poet.

That she'd be able to see his pain, that it would hurt her, too.

The smooth cream facade of the building stared down at him, its large windows and sweeping buttresses so different from the shadows and weight of Cedar Street. Hawthorne Avenue—with snow settled upon groomed lawns, blanketing what would be blooming, golden forsythia bushes in a few months' time.

Elias took a slow step forward, but halted as soon as he felt it. The bubbling heat, starting in his fingertips, beginning to wind its way through to his mind.

The hint of a memory tinted the edges of his vision. He and Rosa, locked in an argument after he'd visited this very place a little more than a year ago. Looking for new inspiration—for something to unlock the words within.

A glint of deep blue caught his eye.

He watched the butterfly flit to a small pot beside the apartment building entrance. Church bells rang in his ears, marking 11:00 a.m. One hour left.

"*I want a* poem, *Daddy,*" Nina's voice whispered in his mind.

"I have to, Rosa," Elias whispered to the breeze as it brushed his cheek. "Please understand."

With a deep breath, he stepped forward, even as yet another poem stanza wrote itself across his mind. Sparked by lilies and butterflies and unwanted memories.

He couldn't let the poem have its way.

Not if he wanted to give Nina a gift instead of more pain.

"Can I help you?" The landlady cocked her head, looking him up and down.

This is your last chance. The only apartment in the whole city that will let you move in the same day you sign the lease.

Forcing himself to stand straight, he extended his hand. "Elias Thornbury, madam. It's a pleasure. I am in need of a new apartment, as soon as possible, and saw your advertisement."

She leaned against the doorframe, brushing a thick, dark braid over her shoulder, streaks of gray slicing through it like tinsel. "Please, call me Imelda. I'm no 'madam.'" With a dry laugh, she reached out, shaking his hand.

Electricity sparked up Elias's arm. *A poet's wife.*

Rosa used to joke that she'd be able to recognize a poet anywhere after marrying Elias, able to sense their magic.

Imelda sucked in a sharp breath, pulling her hand away, a grimace replacing her warm smile. "I see you failed to read the full advertisement."

Elias froze, hand still outstretched. "What?"

She held up a piece of paper, the first half identical to the one gripped in Elias's pale fingers. The bottom line, in bold, black type, read, "NO TEENAGERS, PETS, OR POETS."

"I'm afraid I can't help you, Mr. Thornbury." Imelda crossed her arms over her chest and took a step back, closing the door. "I wish you luck."

Under no circumstances would he, as a gentleman, enter a woman's home uninvited. But he couldn't let her go. He lurched forward, catching the door with his hand, careful to remain in the hall. "Wait, please. You don't understand—"

"I understand perfectly." The steel in her voice cut deep, yet her eyes glistened. "My husband was a poet himself. Always shut up in his study or out to find a muse of some kind. So, when he died, all I had left were his poems, and a handful of memories of the man himself. I am perfectly aware of the pain you poets cause, and I wish to have no part in it."

Silence fell between them as he searched for the right words, even as hers dug into his skin, her dark eyes reminding him of someone else.

"Imelda, I'm sorry you've been hurt, I truly am, but I need this apartment. For my daughter." His next words stuck on his tongue, but he forced them out.

"It's her birthday, and I can't write where we are now. I need a place to make new memories. Please."

Imelda tugged her shawl around her.

"Please," Elias whispered. "You're my last chance."

Tension stretched in the hall as Imelda considered his words.

Finally, she took a deep breath, eyeing him. "Very well, young man. For your daughter's sake, I propose a challenge. Write me a poem that does not make me cry, and the apartment will be yours. Fail, and you must leave. Do we have a deal?"

Elias swallowed hard. The last time he wrote a poem, Nina had cried for weeks. But this would have nothing to do with Rosa. This would be different.

"Deal."

Imelda nodded. "Then, if today really is your daughter's birthday, we should get this over with."

Less than an hour left.

With trembling fingers, Elias tugged the faded black notebook from his pocket. He took a deep breath. All he needed was a spark—something to tug up the magic.

"There's inspiration all around you, if you just look for it," Rosa's voice whispered, pulled to remembrance from long ago.

Elias glanced at Imelda, taking in her black shawl, the faded red of her skirt. His gaze caught on a glittering silver chain around her neck.

A rosemary bud lay against the hollow of her throat, preserved in a clear pendant.

The familiar humming rose as he uncapped his pen, pressing the dusty nib to the parchment, letting the stoppered words spill through the dark ink. Scratching filled the hallway. Pictures poured through Elias's mind, fluttering across his vision, blurring with the slanted handwriting upon the notebook.

A woman's voice murmured in his ear, a hint of Rosa. Longing filled Elias's chest as tears pricked his eyes.

The hum of creation faded.

He stared down at the parchment. The first poem he'd written in months.

Swallowing past the lump in his throat, he tore out the page with extra care.

Imelda reached out a wrinkled hand. The poem whispered against her skin as she took the paper, scanning the five short lines.

The only sound to break the thick silence was a clock ticking from within Imelda's apartment.

The paper began to tremble in her hand. And as he watched her eyes dip to the last line, he wondered what vision his magic had decided to create in her mind.

A crystalline tear splashed down the weathered lines of her cheek.

Yet, at the same time, a slow smile curved the edges of her mouth. She took a deep breath, carefully folding the poem.

Connection hummed between them—the experience of a creator and his audience, wrapped up together. Each seeing different things, but connected for the rest of time through a single moment.

Imelda's shoulders relaxed, the sharp lines of her skin softening, another tear joining its companion as they raced down her chin. He could nearly taste the pain in the air—the grief.

It had been all he could breathe for months.

Yet, as she turned to face him, new light shone from her dark eyes. She weighed the paper in her hand. "You are a master poet, Mr. Thornbury."

Elias let out the breath he'd been holding, knees wobbly. "Thank you, I—"

"But I'm afraid we had a deal." She brushed the tears from her cheeks. "The challenge was to write me a poem that did *not* make me cry. Clearly, this was not achieved."

You've failed. Elias forced himself to straighten, even as his shoulders threatened to give under the weight of her proclamation. He bowed his head stiffly. "I understand. Thank you for your time, Imelda. Good day."

Before she could answer, he turned, numb legs carrying him down the stairs. His notebook weighed down his pocket like a stone, Imelda's tears mixing with the memory of Nina's.

Just someone else he'd hurt.

"Come on, Elias. Come *on*."

The chill of the metal park bench soaked through his pants as he ripped yet another page from his notebook, the words flat, lifeless. Even the still image of Imelda in his mind refused to draw up the magic.

The whistling wind's icy fingers snuck beneath his collar, despite him turning it up to guard his neck.

Nothing came from his frantic whisper. The paper simply stared up at him, taunting.

"Blast it all." His words cut through the air, only to be snatched by the wind.

He set his small, leather-bound journal on the bench, resting his elbows on his thighs as he buried his face in his hands.

Even as he closed his eyes, Imelda's words still rang in his ears, twisting themselves deeper and deeper.

"The challenge was to write me a poem that did not *make me cry. Clearly, this was* not *achieved."*

How could he have thought he could write without causing someone pain?

It was as if a year had taught him nothing. He'd thought he was doing something *right* by writing that poem all those months ago—allowing himself to vent his grief without burdening Nina or Cassia or anyone else in the throes of their own sorrow.

He hadn't heard Nina come in the room. But now all he could hear was the sob that had cut through his concentration, leaving him with an unfinished poem and a heartbroken daughter.

Elias let out a shuddering gasp, shoulders hunched, as he stared down at his ink-spattered hands.

Cassia had said not to blame himself.

But how could he not when it was his magic—his *grief*—that had chosen that godforsaken memory, rather than any of the precious ones they'd shared?

The clock tower chimed, its booms echoing throughout the park.

One.

Two.

Three.

Four.

Elias pulled himself to his feet, gripping the back of the bench for support. He gritted his teeth, eyeing the newly-installed public phone booth only twenty feet away, various vines snaking their way up the concrete exterior of the box.

Five.

Six.

Seven.

Eight.

He forced himself to take a step toward the box. Toward admitting defeat. No matter where he went, Rosa's memory hounded his words. A muse that refused to be left behind, but also refused to let him write.

Nine.

Ten.

Eleven.

Twelve.

Time's up. His stiff, frigid fingers closed around the cool metal of the phone without his permission. He slipped a coin into the slot and pressed the receiver to his ear, mumbling directions to the operator.

"Nina, get *off* me for one second." Cassia's breathy laugh echoed in his ear and twisted his lips into a smile. Nina squealed with laughter in the background, and Elias's heart cracked.

I can't do this.

Just as he moved to hang up, Cassia's voice crackled through the receiver. "Hello? Thornbury residence, may I ask who's calling?"

Elias cleared his throat. "Cass, it's me."

"Oh, Elias! Nina, it's Daddy!"

He could picture the way the corner of Cassia's eyes crinkled with delight.

"Are you coming home soon? You promised we'd have lunch to celebrate and

I don't know how long I can keep her away from the cake."

Closing his eyes, he pressed his forehead to the payphone. "Cass... I... I couldn't do it. I don't—I can't...."

Silence.

"Where are you, Li?" Her voice softened. So gentle it made him want to break.

He swallowed hard. "Crestwall Park." Just saying the words aloud made it final. No more fighting, no more trying, no more pretending he could make something beautiful out of this wreckage.

"We'll be there in fifteen minutes."

She hung up with a click, and Elias listened to the soft beeping tone of the payphone until even that decided to stop.

Leaving him alone, just like Rosa had.

Elias wasn't sure how long it took him to extricate himself from the payphone and return to the bench.

Fifteen minutes had the ring of both an eternity and a millisecond, all at once.

Soon, Nina would arrive, glowing, awaiting the birthday present she'd been promised. Only for him to come up short. Just like he had with Imelda. Just like Nina a year before.

He picked up the journal, staring at the blank pages, raising his arm to toss it away.

A memory of Imelda's smile filled his vision. The way she'd folded the poem so carefully, as if she considered it precious. Her shoulders easing.

As though releasing a large burden.

Rosa had sparked the poem for Imelda. Not her memory, but the words she'd given him so long ago.

Elias had *felt* the grief in his poem for Imelda, and she *had* cried, but he'd also felt the unmistakable, tiny fire, flickering to life. It warmed his chest even now.

The stanzas he'd suppressed for hours finally arose.

Elias reached for the pen. Perhaps to heal was not to live without grief. Perhaps heal was to learn how to live alongside grief.

First stanza: Rosa and the pickpocket. The reason they'd chosen to live on Pickpocket Lane in the first place. The lilies scattering the path on Cedar Street.

Finally, Elias let the words pour out.

> *Where have you gone*
> *My love, my love?*

The release ached and soothed all at once.

> *Lily of the valley lies*
> *Soft against her hand*
> *'Til lily of the valley dies*
> *And finds a distant land*

The poem blurred before him as tears coursed down his cheeks, warm, wet. But he couldn't stop now.

Second stanza: the deep blue of the butterfly's wing. Rosa's necklace.

> *Where have you gone*
> *My love, my love?*

Nina's giggle.

> *Fly away, sweet butterfly*
> *To stars and dreams anew*
> *Though your past may cry*
> *My dear, it will follow you*

He paused, unable to keep a small smile from twitching his lips.

The words stopped. As soon as they were written, scrawled in dark ink across the brilliant white paper, the air erupted, tugging him back. Back to his study, back to that day.

"Amor, please. Will you just listen?"

Elias shook his head, pacing, raking his hands through his snarled curls. "Rosa, I've already explained this to you."

"And, clearly, I still don't understand." Rosa rested her hands on her hips,

brows creased, her crimson skirt swishing around her ankles. *"We've lived here for six years, and now you suddenly want to up and go? Already looking for apartments?"*

With a soft sigh, Elias turned away. Staring out the window as if it would reveal the answer.

A gentle hand took hold of his shoulder, tugging him back, Rosa's dark eyes staring up at him. *"Help me understand. Please."*

The necklace he'd given her a few days prior glittered around her neck. A white lily and a blue butterfly, each hanging on a separate golden chain.

"The inspiration is gone." The admission burned. *"I—we have to leave, go somewhere else and find inspiration so I can write."* He knew he could still provide for them, even without his poetry, but the itch to write something wouldn't stop wrapping its fingers around his throat and squeezing with all its might.

Rosa shook her head. *"Elias, there's no guaranteeing that, if we leave, you'll be able to find some new muse. There's inspiration all around you, if you just look for it. We have so many memories here; don't throw that away."*

Elias gritted his teeth. This wasn't *right*. This was the same memory Nina had seen his poem create. He could still see her now. The pain in her face as she fled. Her sobs echoing down the hallway...

Imelda's light purple rosemary necklace flashed before his eyes.

A spark.

Elias sucked in a breath. The pen scratched against the paper.

> *Where have you gone*
> *My love, my love?*

A tear of his own matched Imelda's from earlier, the words falling from his lips and his pen in unison.

> *Rosemary for remembrance*
> *An ash of what once was*
> *Find an echo of resemblance*
> *Write a letter just because*

The landlady's poem—the last piece of Nina's.

As though someone had added more film to the reel, the memory continued.

Elias's shoulders sagged and he leaned forward, crumpling into her embrace. "You're right, amor. I'm-I'm sorry. Will you please forgive me?"

Rosa's arms wrapped around him as tight as they could go. "Oh, Elias. You think with your head too much." Her whisper was the softest caress. "Your beautiful mind is so... loud."

He groaned softly, her touch bringing calm he hadn't felt in weeks. It loosened the knot in his chest, lulling him nearly to sleep. "Tell me about it."

She laughed softly, the sound warm and rich. "I forgive you, cariño." Pulling away just slightly, she rested both her hands on his cheeks and stared into his eyes. "Shall we stay, then?"

Elias leaned forward, pressing a soft kiss to her forehead, murmuring his next words against her skin.

"Yes. Let's stay."

He stared at the vision of his wife's face, mentally tracing every curve of her cheek, every wispy curl. But her gaze remained locked on a past version of him.

Behind the burning arc of grief followed a quieter, cooler companion. It nestled in the aching hollow deep within his chest, as though his magic had penetrated his walls, and relief could now find its way in.

He waited for the pain to ease, but it remained, pulsing beside the blossoming warmth. He reached out, brushing a finger against the memory version of Rosa. In suppressing all of his memories, he'd forgotten about this holy moment. Her frame tucked between his arms. His lips against her skin.

He'd forgotten that love was always tinged with a little bit of heartache.

"Daddy?"

He glanced up, gaze meeting Nina's. Tears poured down her cheeks as she clutched a single white lily in her tiny hand—Rosa's favorite.

He opened his mouth to apologize, to explain, but Nina ran up to him, through his memory of Rosa. The golden flakes of magic parted to allow her through, the scene dissipating as her thin arms wrapped around his neck.

She buried her face in the crook of his throat as she shook with sobs.

Elias clutched her close, brushing a gentle hand over her curls. "I'm sorry, sweetheart, you weren't supposed to see that."

"Thank you, Daddy. I love it," Nina whispered into his neck, sniffling. "Mommy is so pretty." She paused, tightening her grip, her voice hitching with tears. "I miss her."

A soft, choked noise was all Elias could manage in reply. He tugged Nina into his lap, burying his face in her hair, rocking her as they cried together. Finally, he managed to whisper, "I miss her, too, my little butterfly. I miss her, too."

Just admitting the words he'd kept buried for so long made his breathing come easier, if only slightly. A hand rested against his shoulder, and he looked up, blinking back tears.

Cassia's smile trembled as she crouched before them, ruffling his hair. "I'm proud of you, Li. It's beautiful."

He leaned into her touch, sending her a shaky smile. "You were right, you know."

"Was I?" Cassia let out a wet laugh, brushing stray tears off her cheeks. "I mean, I'm not shocked, but what exactly was I right about this time?"

Elias took a deep breath.

"Are we moving, Daddy?" Nina's small whisper cut through the silence as she pulled away, looking up into his eyes. "Auntie Cassia told me you were looking for ap-apartments."

He swallowed hard, searching for the right words, taking in her puffy, red eyes and her trembling bottom lip.

Cassia straightened, settling next to them on the bench.

Nina shifted, a glint around her throat catching his eye.

Elias smiled softly, brushing the lapis lazuli butterfly now hanging around Nina's neck, its lily companion resting with Rosa's body. "No, sweetheart."

Cassia's shoulder relaxed against his, and he rested his forehead on his daughter's. "Just like this necklace Auntie gave you," he reached over to squeeze his sister's hand, "Mommy loved our apartment. And we have so many memories of her there, hm?"

"Sometimes, I can see her, a little." Nina snuggled into the crook of his neck. "But not as much as when you make poems." She stared up at him imploringly. "Read it again, please?"

"Of course, sweetheart." He slid an arm around Cassia as she rested her head against his shoulder, Nina cuddled against his other side.

He smoothed open his notebook.

Magic swirled around the three of them as they laughed and cried, Cassia teasing him for his never-ending pig-headedness, Nina cooing over Rosa's dress, making Elias promise her she could take it out of storage when she was old enough.

As he finished reading the poem, Elias glanced up.

Across the park, Imelda stood in front of a gravestone. Rosemary in hand. She looked up as though sensing his gaze. After a pause, she offered him the slightest inclination of her head.

He returned it with a smile, lifting Nina as he stood.

Time for the poet to return to Pickpocket Lane.

SARINA LOUISE

As a teen, Sarina Louise was diagnosed with Chronic Lyme Disease, an illness that made her give up on her dream of being an author. Now, after walking a miraculous healing journey, she writes young adult stories that don't shy away from brokenness, but always promise that healing is coming. When not writing, she can be found at concerts all over the country, at home watching K-dramas like a hopeless romantic, or driving around visiting friends (or going to more concerts).

Achievements

- Finished three full-length novel projects and two novella projects.

- Received two manuscript assessments from professional editors through the Author Conservatory and one developmental edit from author Nadine Brandes.

- Prepared to submit my novel after receiving three full manuscript requests from publishers and editors.

- Started two businesses and practiced in-person/online marketing skills.

- Grew my email list from 0 to 170 subscribers in two months.

- Founded the Lion of Judah Learning Center in 2023 and taught Creative Writing to middle/high school students.

- Worked with The Author Conservatory as an Admissions Advisor and a Student Tutor.

Pitches

- *Darker by Four* meets *Belladonna* in a YA paranormal fantasy novel about a girl with cancer and the Grim Reaper who doesn't want to kill her.

- *Hades: The Video Game* meets *Hadestown* in a YA fantasy novel about the son of Hades and the girl who's supposed to be his Persephone—but hates his guts.

A NOTE FROM THE INSTRUCTORS

M erriam-Webster defines adventure as "an undertaking usually involving danger and unknown risks," and I can think of few more apt descriptions of doing creative work.

Whatever their craft or medium, an artist spends their days facing daunting challenges: the intimidation of the blank page or canvas, the inexorable march of the deadline clock, the unappeasable voices of critics. The artist pours from the deepest parts of their soul in an effort to connect with others, to embody beauty in a broken world, yet the artist never knows whether their work will resonate and inspire or fall flat and fade away.

Doing creative work involves risk. Shaping and sharing the images, characters, and worlds in our imaginations involves risk. Showing up to the desk every day, not knowing what the day will hold or where the work will lead, involves risk.

And it's a risk the writers in this anthology have tackled head-on with tenacity, courage, and grace.

As a Conservatory instructor, I am consistently inspired by the creativity and bravery of our students and their willingness to keep showing up to the work even when the road takes an unexpected turn. In writing as in life, sometimes the story doesn't come together the way we'd hoped. Sometimes we're thrown a curveball (or two or ten) and we scramble to keep our footing and our faith. Sometimes the discouragements keep piling up and we wonder if the work is worth it, if the risk is worth the reward.

The writers in this anthology would tell you that it is. They would tell you that the adventure is worth taking, that the dream is worth pursuing, and that the wisdom, beauty, and community that grow out of the challenges far outweigh the risks. And you don't have to take my word for it; the stories you hold in your hands are a testament to the journeys these writers have taken and the courageous paths they're walking into the future.

Over the years, my life has taken many unexpected twists and turns, but one of the greatest adventures I've ever known is coming alongside these young storytellers and watching them grow in both craft and compassion. Here's to their steadfast hope, servant hearts, and passionate spirits, and here's to many more bold adventures and unimaginable joys to come!

Katie S. Williams

Conservatory instructor, author, and speaker

On behalf of all the Author Conservatory instructors

A COLLEGE
ALTERNATIVE
FOR WRITERS

*Build the writing
career of your dreams*

the Author
Conservatory

CHARACTER. CRAFT. CAREER.

Made in the USA
Columbia, SC
26 November 2024

47106046R00214